RELIEF
OR
REFORM?

RELIEF OR REFORM?

Reagan's Regulatory Dilemma

George C. Eads
Michael Fix

The Changing Domestic Priorities Series

John L. Palmer and Isabel V. Sawhill, Editors

 THE URBAN INSTITUTE PRESS · WASHINGTON, D.C.

Copyright © 1984
THE URBAN INSTITUTE
2100 M Street, N.W.
Washington, D.C. 20037

Library of Congress Cataloging in Publication Data

Eads, George C., date
  Relief or reform?

  (The Changing domestic priorities series)
  Includes bibliographical references.
  1. Trade regulation—United States. 2. Administrative
agencies—United States. 3. Independent regulatory
commissions—United States. 4. United States—Politics
and government—1981–   . I. Fix, Michael. II. Title.
III. Series
HD3616.U47E23   1984   338.973   84-5283
ISBN 0-87766-343-2   (cloth)
    0-87766-333-5   (pbk.)

Printed in the United States of America

THE CHANGING DOMESTIC PRIORITIES SERIES

Listed below are the titles available, or soon to be available, in the Changing Domestic Priorities Series

NATURAL RESOURCES AND THE ENVIRONMENT
The Reagan Approach (1984), edited by Paul R. Portney

FEDERAL BUDGET POLICY IN THE 1980s (1984), edited by
Gregory B. Mills and John L. Palmer

THE REAGAN REGULATORY STRATEGY
An Assessment (1984), edited by George C. Eads and Michael Fix

THE LEGACY OF REAGANOMICS
Prospects for Long-term Growth (1984), edited by Charles R. Hulten and
Isabel V. Sawhill

THE REAGAN PRESIDENCY AND THE GOVERNING OF AMERICA
(1984), edited by Lester M. Salamon and Michael S. Lund

Advisory Board of the
Changing Domestic Priorities Project

Contents

Tables

Figures

Foreword

This book is part of The Urban Institute's Changing Domestic Priorities project. The project is examining changes that are occurring in the nation's economic and social policies under the Reagan administration and is analyzing the effects of those changes on people, places, and institutions.

Ronald Reagan gave regulatory policy a more prominent place in his economic program than any recent American president—assigning it a status rivaling that of tax, budgetary, and monetary policy in revitalizing the nation's economy. The status granted regulatory policy owed in large part to the president's belief that regulation had been a major contributor to the productivity slowdown of the 1970s and was too burdensome to individuals, businesses, and state and local governments in their day-to-day decision making.

In *Relief or Reform? Reagan's Regulatory Dilemma*, George Eads and Michael Fix identify the principal strategies relied on by the Reagan administration in delivering regulatory relief. They place the administration's campaign in historical context, noting where the Reagan policies represented a departure from, or a continuation of, efforts begun during the Nixon, Ford, and Carter administrations. They then proceed to assess the impact of the Reagan program from both economic and political perspectives.

The authors note that the president conspicuously titled his campaign regulatory relief, not regulatory reform. They conclude that the name was chosen to signal the administration's interest in moving more aggressively than its predecessors, and its apparent willingness to tackle head-on the politically complicated issue of altering existing regimes of both economic and social regulation. (Prior administrations had been far more involved in reshaping economic regulation.)

The authors state that by the time of Ronald Reagan's election in 1980 a wide consensus had developed that something had to be done about the mushrooming economic burden imposed by social regulation. They point out, however, that the strategies adopted by the Reagan team were primarily administrative by nature and that little political capital was spent in revising the basic statutes that underlie social regulation. Moreover, they contend that the regulatory relief efforts' implementation during the administration's first two years complicated the political task of obtaining legislative change and left the effort vulnerable to the kind of legal and political reversals it later suffered. The authors hold that the political difficulties the relief program encountered owed to a basic miscalculation of the extent to which social regulation—particularly environmental regulation—enjoyed popular support. The clear implication of this fact was that change in many areas of social regulation would have to proceed incrementally, be based on extensive factual and political groundwork, and be guided by trusted and competent administrators.

The authors note that changes initiated by the administration may have yielded some productivity gains for business. They contend, however, that the cost savings claimed by regulatory relief program spokesmen have been significantly overstated. Although fears of higher future regulatory burdens may have diminished somewhat within the business community, the program has not constituted the watershed the administration had promised.

Eads and Fix conclude by arguing that although the president inherited an ideal opportunity to substantially reform social regulation, the early political results of regulatory relief have only postponed the advent of a real, sustainable regulatory change and will in time be viewed as a detour on the road to regulatory reform.

The complete results of The Urban Institute's analysis of the Reagan administration regulatory policies will be found in this book and in a companion volume. That companion volume, entitled *The Reagan Regulatory Strategy: An Assessment,* contains papers presented at an Urban Institute conference in June 1983 and has been edited by George Eads and Michael Fix.

John L. Palmer
Isabel V. Sawhill
Editors
Changing Domestic Priorities Series

Acknowledgments

We have many people to thank as we complete this book. In particular, we thank Isabel Sawhill who proposed and guided the effort. We appreciate the assistance and insight of those whom we interviewed, both in and out of government. Their help was critical to the shaping of this book. Participants at a conference we held at The Urban Institute in June 1983 to assess the Reagan administration's regulatory relief efforts also made important contributions. We are especially grateful to the authors who produced the five papers upon which we have drawn so heavily: Gregory Christainsen and Robert Haveman, Christopher Foreman, Robert Leone, Jerry Mashaw and Susan Rose-Ackerman, and Murray Weidenbaum.

Marvin Kosters and Paul Portney made detailed, clear-eyed, and useful comments, which substantially improved the work. Our editor, Priscilla Taylor, did an excellent job of rewriting and helped us to rethink many areas of the manuscript. Rosalie Fonoroff, Bill Gellert, and Carolann Marino contributed greatly to the production of this volume.

The support of the Ford Foundation and the John D. and Catherine T. MacArthur Foundation is also gratefully acknowledged.

Finally, we wish to thank our wives, Maggie and Amy, for their sympathy and patience through the nights and weekends we often reluctantly devoted to this book.

About the Authors

GEORGE C. EADS is a professor in the School of Public Affairs at the University of Maryland, College Park, and a consultant to The Urban Institute. Between June 1979 and January 1981, he served as a member of President Carter's Council of Economic Advisers (CEA) where he was especially active in regulatory reform issues and, on behalf of CEA, chaired the Regulatory Analysis Review Group. He has written extensively on regulatory matters and is the author of *The Local Service Airline Experiment* and the coauthor of *Designing Safer Products: Corporate Responses to Products Liability and Product Safety Regulation*. He and Michael Fix wrote the chapter titled "Regulatory Reform" in *The Reagan Experiment*.

MICHAEL FIX is a senior research associate and attorney at The Urban Institute. His work at the Institute has concentrated on legal and institutional issues relating to regulation. His writings on regulatory issues have been published by, among others, the Joint Economic Committee of the Congress, the Urban Law Annual, and the American Enterprise Institute. He is currently completing a study of the impact of shifts in federal regulatory requirements on the provision of transportation to the disabled.

1

Introduction

When President Reagan announced his intention to revitalize the American economy at the beginning of his administration,[1] three elements of his plan were traditional: tax policy, expenditure policy, and monetary policy. But the president added a fourth element: regulatory relief. The idea of reducing the burden of federal regulation was not new; every president since Nixon had declared his support for eliminating "unnecessary and excessively burdensome" regulation. Presidents Ford and Carter made important contributions in this area, but neither viewed his regulatory initiatives as more than a sideshow to his administration's overall economic strategy. They viewed regulatory reform—which to them had meant the elimination of controls that had outlived their usefulness and the improvement in the functioning of those controls that needed to be retained—as having a significant, positive, but distinctly long-term impact on the economy. Regulatory reform was worth pursuing, but not for its short-term results.

President Reagan's view was different. He favored regulatory *relief*—a substantial scaling-back of the overall "regulatory burden" on businesses and consumers. His belief that regulatory relief could have a significant, immediate, favorable impact on the economy was perhaps best articulated by David Stockman, director of the Office of Management and Budget (OMB), in his now-famous "Dunkirk" memo (so-called because of its title "Avoiding a GOP Economic Dunkirk"):

A dramatic, substantial *rescission* of the regulatory burden is needed for the

1

short term cash flow it will provide to business firms and [for] the long term
signal it will provide to corporate investment planners. A major "regulatory
ventilation" will do as much to boost business confidence as tax and fiscal
measures.[2]

But Reagan had a second reason for wanting federal regulation to be
substantially scaled back. In his view, regulation—especially the "social
regulation"[3] enacted in the late 1960s—reflected, perhaps more than any
other federal activity, an unwarranted intrusion of the federal government into
private decision making. Such an intrusion was bad per se. As Reagan's first
chairman of his Council of Economic Advisers, Murray Weidenbaum, once
said in a speech to a group of businessmen:

> The basic framework in which economic policy in the Reagan Administration
> is made . . . starts with a fundamental view of the role of government. That
> view is based on the notion that the people who make up the economy—workers,
> managers, savers, investors, buyers, and sellers—do not need government to
> make their decisions for them on how to run their own lives. As we see it, the
> most appropriate role for government economic policy is to provide a stable
> framework in which private individuals and business firms can plan confidently
> and make their own decisions.[4]

Regulatory relief, thus, had a double virtue in the eyes of the president
and his advisers. It was good for the economy and good for the nation's
soul.

To produce the "major regulatory ventilation" called for by David Stockman, the president took several important steps immediately upon taking
office. On January 22, 1981, he announced the formation of a Task Force
on Regulatory Relief, a cabinet-level advocacy and appeals group headed by
Vice President George Bush. On January 28, he announced the suspension
of nearly 200 "midnight regulations"—proposed and final rules published
by the Carter administration that had not yet gone into effect. And on February
17, Reagan issued an executive order (E.O. 12291: "Federal Regulation")
in which he set forth the most significant features of his regulatory management program. Those features included a restructuring of regulatory oversight
responsibilities; a requirement that all proposed rules undergo cost-benefit
analysis; and a requirement that, to the extent permitted by law, these proposed
regulations demonstrate that they would generate more potential social benefits
than potential social cost.

Once this structure was in place, the White House began regularly announcing initiatives designed to show that the program was functioning and,
more important, that it was achieving significant results. On March 25, the
task force announced a list of twenty-seven existing regulations to be "reas-

sessed." According to information released by the vice president, this reassessment would result in annual savings to the economy of between $1.8 and $2.1 billion, and one-time investment savings of $6 billion.[5] On April 6, the administration announced its "auto package," a list of regulatory changes that, once fully implemented, would save consumers $9.3 billion over five years and free up $1.4 billion in auto industry capital.[6]

On April 16, Murray Weidenbaum devoted a major speech to praising the accomplishments of the regulatory relief program, which he characterized as "perhaps the most underestimated" of the "four interrelated, mutually supporting elements" of the administration's economic program. On June 13, the administration issued a report card on the program's first hundred days, which concluded:

> Implementation of the President's program of regulatory relief appears to be off to a good start. The Executive Order lays the foundation for a sound, continuing process to establish reasonable regulations and to eliminate those that are unnecessarily burdensome. Relationships between agencies and OMB have been established to ensure close communications in meeting the Executive Order's goals. And procedures for implementing the Order have been put in place at the agencies and at OMB. This is not to say that the program is working perfectly. . . . [b]ut given the magnitude of the problem being addressed and the reversal of historic trends envisioned, one should be reasonably optimistic based upon the first 100 days of the Executive Order.[7]

In fact, by the time this report card was issued, the regulatory relief program's most active days were behind it. James Miller III, the original director of OMB's Office of Information and Regulatory Affairs (OIRA) and the person whom the press referred to as the administration's "regulatory czar," soon left to become chairman of the Federal Trade Commission (FTC); Vice President Bush turned his attention to other matters; and David Stockman became increasingly preoccupied with the administration's tax and budget legislation.

Then criticism of the White House's regulatory relief efforts began to mount. Initially the administration was unconcerned. Indeed, early congressional hearings critical of the president's efforts simply provided still another forum from which to tout the program's successes and to stress its importance. For example, on June 18, just five days after the "report card" just mentioned was issued, Congressman John Dingell's Oversight and Investigations Subcommittee held the first of what would become a long-running series of hearings on the regulatory relief program. This particular hearing focused on the OMB's role in overseeing regulation, and the administration's principal witness was OIRA Administrator Miller. Correctly anticipating carping from

the Democratic-controlled subcommittee, Miller threw out the following challenge at the end of his prepared statement:

> We are engaged in an effort that is extraordinarily important and are approaching
> the task in a manner that is legal, equitable, and consistent with the best
> professional thinking on the issue. Regulatory relief just has to be accomplished
> if the American people are to realize the full potential of the president's program
> of economic recovery. . . .
>   Efforts to reform regulation are nothing new. But a commitment on this
> scale—by the president, by the agencies, and by the Congress—is unprece-
> dented. In my opinion, a successful effort will require bold and perhaps even
> controversial action. We stand ready to explain our program and defend it where
> necessary. We will alter our approach when this makes sense but we will not
> be deterred from the task at hand.[8]

In subsequent months, this picture of a confident administration, engaged
in a professionally directed, moral crusade to free the American economy
from the coils of strangling regulation, gave way to suspicions of political
favoritism and fears that basic regulatory protections were being dismantled.
Public opinion, which early in the administration had seemed generally supportive of the president's aims, shifted. For example, on the "litmus test"
issue of amending the Clean Air Act, a Harris poll taken early in 1983 showed
that, when compared with responses in 1981, the proportion of citizens who
supported stricter regulation had risen from 29 percent to 47 percent, while
the proportion supporting less regulation had dropped from 17 percent to 7
percent.[9]

As time passed and congressional and public attention shifted from activities at the White House to activities at the Environmental Protection Agency
(EPA) and the Interior Department, even the White House began to recognize
that the regulatory relief program was becoming a political liability. In the
early spring of 1983, President Reagan's controversial EPA administrator,
Anne Burford, was forced to resign, along with virtually her entire management team. Interior's similarly controversial James Watt managed to hang on
until October.

EPA and Interior were not the only places where important personnel
changes could be noted. The new secretary of transportation, Elizabeth Dole,
asked Raymond Peck, the controversial administrator of the National Highway
Traffic Safety Administration (NHTSA), to resign. Dole indicated a willingness to reexamine the issue of passive restraints much more sympathetically
than Peck had, especially in the wake of the Supreme Court's decision over-
turning NHTSA's rescission of the "air bag" rule, the centerpiece of the
administration's 1981 auto package.

The chief of the Occupational Safety and Health Administration (OSHA), Thorne Auchter, had displayed a willingness to challenge OMB's efforts to move his agency further and faster in the direction of deregulation. After Burford's fall, and apparently with some support from the business community, Auchter grew increasingly bold in his challenges to OMB.

There was an important change in personnel at OMB in June 1983. Jim Tozzi, one of the associate directors of the Office of Information and Regulatory Affairs, left the government. Tozzi's involvement in regulatory oversight dated from President Nixon's original Quality of Life Review, a process Tozzi had helped to set up. Over the years Tozzi had become a symbol of White House efforts to "rein in" environmental regulation. During the Carter years Tozzi was so controversial that environmentalists had been able to prevent his being named associate OMB director for management and regulatory policy. With Reagan's election, Tozzi moved up to associate director of the Office of Information and Regulatory Affairs, where he controlled the OMB desk officers who play a crucial role in deciding whether any particular proposed rule will be held up or passed. Tozzi was widely perceived to have influence within the agency second only to Miller's, and after Miller left, Tozzi became the de facto regulatory czar. He would talk informally with companies about proposed regulations that they were concerned about and then decide whether to permit the regulations to go forward. Few if any records were kept.[10] He is reported to have once bragged, "I leave no fingerprints." This operational style apparently was acceptable to the Reagan administration early in its lifetime, but not later.

When Tozzi retired, he was replaced by Robert Bedell, a career OMB attorney who had been deputy general counsel in both the Carter and Reagan administrations with an operating style quite different from Tozzi's. The replacement of Tozzi by Bedell was symbolic of the White House's altered attitude toward its regulatory relief program. Far from trying to attract attention to it, as had been the earlier objective, the White House was, by mid-1983, trying to play the program down.

Indeed, the words "regulatory relief" were heard less and less often, even from administration spokesmen. In testimony before the House Judiciary Committee in late July 1983, Christopher DeMuth, Jim Miller's successor as administrator of OIRA, several times pointedly referred to the administration's program as one of "regulatory *reform.*"[11]

The regulatory relief program enjoyed one last burst of publicity. On August 11, 1983, Vice President George Bush's office announced that the task force was going out of existence because it had succeeded so well in its job that it had nothing else to do. The vice president's statement took care to describe the administration's program as having been aimed at "regulatory reform" and to downplay the program's cost-saving aspects.[12] Simultaneously, however, the Task Force issued a report asserting that the administration's regulatory relief actions would save American business, state and local governments, and consumers more than $150 billion over the next ten years.

The vice president's announcement was presented not as an ending but as a natural evolution from an administrative to legislative emphasis, as many of the program's supporters had been urging. Murray Weidenbaum, for example, titled a publication written after he left the government *The Next Step in Regulatory Reform: Updating the Statutes.*[13]

The materials accompanying the vice president's statement contained a list of priority regulatory reform legislation. With a single exception, however, this list consisted of proposals for ending various elements of economic regulation, not for revising the Clean Air Act, Clean Water Act, Occupational Safety and Health Act, or other "landmark" pieces of social regulatory legislation. Indeed, when administration proposals *were* forthcoming in connection with such legislation, they did not touch upon the issues that had so distressed critics.[14]

In declining to take on these important symbolic pieces of social legislation, the administration was tacitly acknowledging that its first two and one-half years had not marked the watershed in social regulation that had once been hoped. Indeed, we believe that this period can best be seen as a long, expensive detour in an even longer journey to develop a politically acceptable and economically efficient system of social controls over an important category of business activities. Furthermore, at the end of this detour, the country was well behind the point in the journey where it had been when the Carter administration left office. Murray Weidenbaum's own assessment, made in a paper prepared for an Urban Institute conference held in June 1983, sums it up well: "We will be lucky if, in January 1985, we will be back to where we were in January 1981 in terms of the public's attitude toward statutory reform and social regulation."[15]

The Organization of This Book

This book is an account of the Reagan administration's detour—why it was taken and what its short- and long-term economic and political consequences are. In order to tell this story, we must first establish the context within which the Reagan administration made its decisions. For this reason, we devote considerable space to summarizing what was known before January

1981 about regulation's impact on the economy, to detailing the efforts of previous administrations to reform social and economic legislation, and to describing the competing diagnoses of what the problems associated with social regulation actually were and what ought to be done to solve them.

The main body of the book is organized into three parts. The first, consisting of chapters 2 through 5, sets the stage. Chapter 2 examines the economic underpinnings of the administration's claim that a substantial redirection of regulatory effort was needed if the economy was to recover its vitality. The conclusion of the chapter is that, based on the quantitatively verifiable evidence alone, the claim that regulation was to a large extent responsible for the economy's poor performance during the 1970s cannot be supported. The chapter does show, however, that by the late 1970s, regulation had become a major absorber of the nation's economic resources. This finding, plus the nonmeasurable (and, in our view, extremely important) economic consequences of having turned the entire business sector into regulated entities, did indeed make the achievement of genuine and lasting regulatory reform a matter of considerable importance to the economy.

Chapter 2 also includes a brief critique of the theory of rational expectations—the concept that significant and virtually instant improvements in the economy can be generated even though the specific actions leading to these improvements will occur only in the future. An understanding of this theory (or at least of its broad outlines) is necessary to appreciate the prominence given to regulatory relief early in the Reagan administration.

Chapter 3 traces the history of White House regulatory oversight during the Nixon, Ford, and Carter administrations. Chapter 4 surveys the history of legislated deregulation, principally during the Ford and Carter administrations. As we have already seen, Reagan acknowledged his debt to the efforts of his predecessors but intended his program to represent an important break with theirs. In the case of the White House oversight program, an understanding of how his program differed, both in philosophy and operation, is crucial to an appreciation of the controversy it generated. The history of legislated deregulation illustrates the importance of continuity and attention to extensive groundwork to obtaining statutory results. Such capital building was *not* a conspicuous feature of the first two years of the Reagan administration.

Chapter 5 summarizes the various critiques of regulation that were prominent by late 1980 and the range of remedies that were being advanced. The critiques centered on regulation's cost (both in absolute terms and in terms of what regulatory expenditures did to overall economic performance), its unreasonableness and arbitrariness, its limited effectiveness as a tool for

solving important social problems, and the impossibly large information requirements that regulation implied for its effective and efficient
administration.

The remedies being advanced varied with the perspective of the people
advancing them. Libertarians looked at the problems associated with regulation and concluded that it should be gotten rid of entirely—that the problems
it was trying to solve were better left to the market or to alternative methods
of social control. A larger group favored substantially paring back regulation,
but members of this group, unlike the libertarians, were not opposed to
regulation in principle. The remedies they favored ran from increased presidential oversight (possibly using tools like "regulatory budgets"), to the
introduction of formal cost-benefit requirements for regulation and substantive
changes in regulatory statutes aimed at reducing the imperative to regulate.
A third group (composed primarily of economists) attributed the problems
associated with regulation principally to the tools it employed—the detailed
specification of permissible and impermissible behavior. This group's remedy
was to substitute marketlike mechanisms, created and monitored by the government, for "command and control" regulation, wherever possible.

The breadth of the critiques and remedies explored in chapter 5 helps
explain (1) why candidate Reagan's strong commitment to regulatory relief
had such strong appeal—regulatory relief meant very different things to different people—and (2) why the program's results have proved so disappointing
to many of its most fervent supporters.

Chapters 6 through 10 constitute the core of the book, in which the major
elements of the Reagan regulatory relief strategy are detailed. We begin with
an account of the White House oversight effort (chapter 6), which is appropriate because for the first six months or so of the administration, the White
House effort *was*, for all practical purposes, the regulatory relief program. It
was from here that the major regulatory relief "events" emanated and were
controlled. Moreover, the contrast between early successes, such as the auto
package, and later defeats, such as the "lead phase-down" decision, helps
set the context for the discussion of the program's other elements.

Chapter 7 explores the efforts of the White House to harness regulation
through the appointment of people sympathetic to its regulatory relief philosophy, through substantial budget cuts designed to hamper the ability of
the agencies to regulate, and through threatened and actual agency reorganizations. The discussion of the regulatory appointments focuses on one of
the central dilemmas confronting the administration: to accomplish significant
and lasting changes in regulation, especially social regulation, the administration would have had to have been willing to appoint highly skilled, technically competent administrators to key posts. But appointing people committed

to making regulation work, even if this achievement eventually resulted in substantial regulatory relief, would have collided with the administration's objective of producing rapid, significant results. Moreover, it would have clashed with the view that much social regulation represented unwarranted government intrusion. A commitment to rationalizing social regulation rather than rolling it back might also have limited the number of high-visibility positions available to conservative advocates more adept at articulating and defending the administration's philosophy than at administering complex regulatory programs.

This same dilemma was apparent in the administration's budget decisions affecting the regulatory agencies. The oversight apparatus put in place by the administration implied a greater use of economic analysis in regulatory decision making and the use of new but untested regulatory techniques. However, either making greater use of economic analysis in regulation or experimenting with new regulatory techniques would have required more resources, both at the agencies where most of the work would be carried out and at OMB, where it would be overseen. The administration was committed to *cutting* agency budgets, on the theory that "If they don't have money, they can't regulate." And budgets were indeed cut. This cast doubt on the administration's claim that its advocacy of the use of these techniques was intended as something other than a cover for dismantling social regulatory programs.

In chapter 8 we review the administrative changes in rules and regulations and the legislative proposals made by the administration to alter agency regulatory objectives and procedures. We observe that the administration's strategy has been to rely overwhelmingly on administrative actions; legislative initiatives have been few, and very few of these have won support in Congress. The administration's legislative scorecard is not zero, but the major shifts in legislative mandates some people hoped for have not been achieved.

As even the program's designers foresaw, the decision to rely primarily on administrative actions has left the regulatory relief program open to legal challenge. And, indeed, a number of important legal setbacks have occurred, although some may be reversed on appeal. The unifying theme of these challenges concerns the degree of discretion available to a new administration with a philosophical commitment to change established rules and regulations without being able to show that the underlying situation that led to their establishment has changed.

Another problem in relying on administrative actions is that a large number of new regulatory proceedings must be initiated and completed. (Modifying a rule to make it less burdensome to business requires proposing a new

rule, holding hearings on it, and building a record to justify the change.)
Seeing to it that such actions are begun and that progress is made according
to some reasonable schedule is a major managerial job. We trace the administration's record here and find, as others have noted,[16] that after the early
months of the regulatory relief program (when the major effort was the auto
package), the administration became less successful in assuring that the cumbersome rule-making process worked on schedule.

Chapter 9 examines one of the most complex and politically charged
regulatory issues of all—enforcement. Most people see enforcement as basically a simple task: the law says for people to do something, and the agency's
job is to make sure that they do it. What constitutes *appropriate* enforcement,
however, is by no means simple. First, Congress sometimes deliberately writes
laws in such a way that they cannot be literally enforced. Congress can then
look as though it is being "tough" on some problem like pollution while
preventing the law from forcing the economy to grind to a halt. Thus *any*
administration is forced to play certain "enforcement games." Second, even
for an administration that is committed to tough enforcement, the choice of
whether to prosecute or negotiate (or even to look the other way in some
circumstances) is not always clear. The dilemma is basically the same as that
of a policeman who, in trying to maintain peace in the neighborhood, must
make hundreds of seemingly arbitrary decisions.

In this context, the administration's enforcement activities proved to be
a distinctly mixed bag, not the outright disaster some of its opponents have
claimed. Certain of the changes in enforcement strategy had a clear and
justifiable rationale, even if they might have been executed imperfectly. Other
changes were less easy to justify. And coloring the public perceptions of the
administration's entire enforcement effort were fears of abandoned protections
and suspicions of giveaways to industry. It is easy to see why enforcement
issues turned out to be the rock upon which the Reagan regulatory relief effort
foundered, but the administration's record may not have been worse in this
area than in other areas or even significantly worse than the enforcement
record of earlier administrations.[17]

Chapter 10 explores the final element of the Reagan strategy—the transfer
of regulatory responsibilities that previously had been primarily federal to
other levels of government. As in the case of enforcement, certain of these
changes could be justified intellectually, but the manner in which they were
carried out undermined the administration's claim that the transfers were being
made primarily to achieve a more appropriate balance of regulatory responsibility. In particular, the transfer of regulatory responsibility to states, coupled
with cuts in the funds necessary to carry out that responsibility, was viewed

by supporters of regulation and even by the states themselves with great suspicion.

The final section of the book consists of the last chapter, in which we attempt to assess the economic and political impacts of the regulatory relief program. We also attempt to trace the program's implications for the longer-term course of regulatory relief.

As far as economic impacts are concerned, we believe that the program can perhaps be considered a moderate success. Disentangling the program's contribution from the contribution made by the efforts of previous administrations and from the effects of the back-to-back recessions of 1980–81 and 1981–83 is difficult. Nevertheless, the program appears to have reduced the expenditures businesses have reported for regulatory compliance and boosted measured productivity (though as chapter 11 shows, the cost savings due to the program are not nearly as large as the administration has claimed). The program also initially generated a positive "expectations shock," though this may be dissipating. One thing is certain: the program did not mark the sharp watershed in social regulation's economic burden that the administration had hoped for.

On the negative side of the economic ledger, the program also clearly resulted in some loss of regulatory benefits, the claims of the administration to the contrary notwithstanding.[18] Precisely how great this loss was is difficult if not impossible to quantify. However, the assertions of some of the administration's critics that regulatory protections came close to being totally dismantled are vastly exaggerated. Most social regulatory programs managed to survive, if with somewhat reduced vigor.

The program's political impact was decidedly mixed. Early in the administration, the program was clearly a significant political plus. It helped generate and sustain the political momentum necessary to get the president's tax and budget legislation passed. It also helped create the impression that the president's economic "game plan" was working. The program later became a significant political liability—so much so that it was eventually terminated. The last chapter examines the reasons and discusses the miscalculations that led the administration in August 1983 to terminate the program.

The largest cost of the regulatory relief program may well be the setback it dealt to the longer-term efforts at regulatory reform. Serious discussion of proposals for modifying social regulation to make it less costly, less intrusive, and more effective has largely ceased. Reopening this discussion will take time. Furthermore, the capacity of social regulatory agencies to implement innovative ideas has been undercut. Time will also be required to repair this damage. In the interim, the grasp of regulation may tighten.

Some Important Terminology: The Distinction between "Social" and "Economic" Regulation

Throughout the book the terms *social regulation* and *economic regulation* will be repeatedly used. The distinctions between these terms are important to understanding the book's central theme: the tension between eliminating regulation and making it "work."

The term *social regulation* has over the past few years been applied to the set of federal programs that use regulatory techniques to achieve broad social goals—a cleaner environment, safer and more healthful workplaces, safer and more effective consumer products, and the assurance of equal employment opportunities. (The term *protective regulation* is also used to refer to these programs.) Most programs of social regulation originated in the 1960s and 1970s, although some—the programs of the Food and Drug Administration (FDA) and the Department of Agriculture—go back several decades.

Economic regulation refers to the programs that attempt to control prices, conditions of market entry and exit, and conditions of service, usually in specific industries considered to be "affected with the public interest." Many of the programs of economic regulation are not new; the oldest—control over the railroad industry by the Interstate Commerce Commission (ICC)—goes back nearly 100 years. Another "burst" of legislation occurred during the 1930s; federal regulation of trucking, telecommunications, securities trading, and the airlines dates from that period. But peacetime use of wage and price controls in this country, surely among the most important examples of economic regulation, originated in the early 1970s.

These categories may overlap. Certain programs that are usually considered to fall into the category of economic regulation clearly have specific social objectives in mind. For example, the particular scheme of telecommunications regulation that this nation relied on for the past half-century (which is now being dismantled) had as a basic objective the use of differential pricing to achieve "universal" access to telephone service—clearly a social objective. Similarly, some social regulation works directly on the sort of variables usually considered to be the province of economic regulation. Certain controls exercised by the FDA and EPA to regulate the access of new chemical entities in the marketplace operate very much like the requirement of ICC and the Civil Aeronautics Board (CAB) that anyone wishing to operate a truck or airline prove himself "fit, willing, and able." Nonetheless, these "fuzzy" areas do not detract from the general usefulness of the distinction in terms.

The two types of regulation may be distinguished further in this way: the jurisdiction of agencies charged with administering social regulation generally extends to broad classes of industry, whereas the jurisdiction of agencies charged with administering economic regulation generally is limited to specific industries. To illustrate, EPA must deal with discharges into air and water of *all* industries (and thus must be somewhat familiar with the production techniques of *all* industries), whereas CAB deals exclusively with the airline industry and FCC with radio and television broadcasters and various firms engaged in the interstate provision of telecommunications service. Again there are exceptions. The wage and price controls mentioned earlier applied to all industry, at least in theory. And although the jurisdiction of FDA is theoretically limited to the two industries identified in its name, in fact, it shares a broad product-safety regulatory function with a number of other agencies, including the National Highway Traffic Safety Administration (NHTSA), the Consumer Product Safety Commission (CPSC), and the National Transportation Safety Board (NTSB). Of these, CPSC has the broadest jurisdiction, extending to most industries producing consumer products other than food, drugs, automobiles, and aircraft.

A third generalization to distinguish social from economic regulation is this: the agencies engaging in social regulation are housed in the executive branch of the federal government, whereas most agencies engaged in economic regulation are statutorily independent of the executive. (Exceptions include CPSC, a social regulatory body which is an independent agency, and the Energy Regulatory Administration, an economic regulatory body which administered the domestic petroleum price and allocation controls and was located in the Department of Energy.) This difference in agency location largely reflects when the agencies were created. By the time the great wave of social regulation legislation came along, the concept of the independent commission had fallen into disfavor because it was widely believed to be prone to being "captured" by those it regulated.[19]

The difference in agency location is important for several reasons. First, location of the agencies engaged in social regulation within the executive branch means that they are under the direct control of the president. The president is free to appoint virtually anyone he wishes to head such agencies, and he may take whatever steps are necessary to assure that such appointees share his basic economic and social goals. Moreover, these officials serve at his pleasure; he can request their resignation at any time. (However, as becomes evident in later chapters, the actual degree of power the president has to control the details of executive branch rule making has been disputed.) In the case of independent agencies, the president can appoint members only for specific terms; once they have been appointed and confirmed by the Senate, they can be removed only "for cause" (specific acts of malfeasance, not merely because the president objects to their decisions). Although the president is free to designate the agency's head from among the sitting members,

generally the president cannot appoint more than a majority of the commissioners from his own party. Moreover, the terms of service are staggered
specifically to prevent a president from stacking a commission.

Another reason why location is important is that the presence of most
agencies engaged in social regulation within the executive branch creates the
impression that the president, as the head of this branch, can in fact "do
something" to control the general shape as well as the detailed operation of
social regulation. We have already mentioned the possible legal constraints
on the president's power in this area, but perhaps even more important is the
practical impossibility of any president's actually controlling the regulatory
activities of the agencies under his nominal supervision. If controlling regulation means being on top of every regulatory action—or only every important regulatory action—at all times, then every president has failed to
harness regulation. The task is to keep general track of events, intervening
only when absolutely necessary—and running this tracking and intervention
process in a way that it does not seem to be purely politically motivated.

A fourth important distinguishing feature of social regulation (important
especially to economists) is that even properly functioning markets cannot be
counted on to produce the goals that social regulation seeks. As far as economists are concerned, the problems of environmental pollution, excessive
levels of workplace hazards, or unsafe consumer products exist largely because
"commodities" like environmental quality, workplace safety, and product
safety do not trade in markets. Economists worked hard to devise ways to
simulate markets for such "commodities," arguing that if this could be done,
the goals of social regulation could be achieved at far less cost and with far
less government interference in the details of business decision making. But
even the most optimistic of the economists' schemes contemplate some continued federal regulatory presence.

In contrast, many of the areas traditionally subject to economic regulation
are believed to be perfectly capable of operating well without it. That is, not
only do markets exist in these areas, but the markets are as able as regulation
(if not more able) to produce socially efficient results. One branch of economic
scholarship holds that the various economic regulatory schemes serve no
purpose other than to protect producer interests. Another branch holds that
the social goals once sought by these regulatory schemes either are practically
unachievable or have ceased to justify the burdens that striving to attain them
imposes on society. Both favor the sharp curtailment of economic regulation.

The preceding description of the differences between social and economic
regulation and their significance suggests the tension that has already been
mentioned but bears exploring, since it is critical to what follows. It is perfectly
reasonable in many instances of economic regulation to aim to eliminate the

regulatory framework; although the market may not work perfectly, it will work tolerably well, and certainly better than the regulatory scheme it is intended to replace. The underlying problem that social regulation is devised to attack, however, cannot confidently be handed over to the market in the expectation of satisfactory results. Some government presence is almost certainly required if the results society seeks are to be achieved. (Society might opt for an imperfectly functioning market in the belief that it was better than an even more imperfect government program designed to ''correct'' the original market imperfection.) Therefore, the task in social regulation generally is to make a regulatory process *work*, not to eliminate it.

''Making the regulatory process work'' means structuring government intervention in a way that realizes society's goals (possibly even helping society to determine the degree to which these goals are worth achieving) with the least burden on individual decision-making freedom and with the least cost to society. As long as regulatory reform is the stated goal, this difference in the underlying objectives of social and economic regulation can be accommodated. It is reasonable to include under the term *reform* (1) the elimination (or the radical reformulation) of regulatory programs that do not work or have outlived their usefulness and (2) efforts to improve the functioning of clearly necessary regulatory programs that will benefit from attention.

When the goal is changed to regulatory *relief*, however, the distinction between the underlying objectives of economic and social regulation becomes much more troublesome. Both *reform* and *relief* when used with respect to economic regulation imply a restoration to the market of most important economic decisions and cause no particular problem. But applying these terms to social regulation is a different matter. By stating regulatory relief as its goal, the administration created a strong presumption that it was trying to eliminate social regulation. The tension between interpreting regulatory relief to imply a sharp pruning back of social regulation *regardless of the merits of the individual programs* and interpreting it as a mandate to make social regulatory programs work more effectively and in a less burdensome and less costly manner has been continual within the Reagan administration.

2

The Impact of Regulation on the Economy

The primary justification the Reagan administration gave for the unprecedented importance accorded regulatory relief in its original economic "game plan" was that regulation was one of the principal factors responsible for the nation's poor economic performance during the 1970s. According to the administration, regulation was diverting labor and capital resources to "unproductive" uses, hampering innovation, and absorbing scarce management time and attention. Superficially, at least, the claim of a relationship between the vast expansion in federal regulatory activity that began in the late 1960s and the slowdown in productivity growth and speedup in inflation that occurred at about the same time seemed plausible. But the administration went even further. Not only would a substantial scaling back of regulation help the economy; the beneficial effects could be expected to be felt almost immediately, even though the specific actions required to reduce resulting burdens might take time to bring about.

In this chapter we review the economic theories and evidence that underlie both of these assertions. We provide an analytical framework for understanding estimates of regulation's "cost" to the economy and review major published studies that have explored various aspects of the relationship between regulation and economic performance. These studies are of three kinds: those that attempt to build up regulatory "costs" from microeconomic (i.e., individual firm and industry) data; those that attempt to estimate directly the impact of regulation on measured productivity; and those that attempt to

17

measure regulation's impact on broad macroeconomic variables such as inflation and growth. We then explore the theory of "rational expectations"—the theory that actions taken only in the future could produce important economic benefits today provided the administration's promise of future relief was "credible." With regard to regulation's share in the responsibility for the initial poor economic performance of the 70s, we conclude that although regulation has indeed become something to which our country devotes considerable resources and although there is good reason to link the growth of regulation to the deterioration of several important economic indicators such as growth in the gross national product (GNP), productivity, and inflation, regulation appears to have had relatively slight measurable impact. In other words, regulation may have hurt economic growth, depressed the rate of growth of productivity, and caused the rate of inflation to be higher than it otherwise would have been, but regulation cannot be blamed—at least on the basis of the evidence examined here—for more than a small fraction of the economy's poor performance in any of these dimensions.

Lest the reader jump to conclusions, we hasten to qualify this statement. The most important qualification is that the studies reviewed here, as their authors candidly admit, omit many cost and benefit factors that are crucial to a proper assessment of regulation's impact on the nation's welfare. This problem is most obvious with regard to benefits. Because many elements in the intended "output" of regulation—a cleaner environment, safer workplaces, more satisfactory consumer products—are not capturable in conventional GNP measures, regulation may be unfairly blamed for poor performance of these indicators when it is working precisely as it should.

Of course, certain regulatory benefits *do* show up, at least eventually, in variables that can be measured. Improvement of air quality may reduce the number of days of illness, thereby reducing the number of worker-hours required to produce a certain level of GNP. The same is true of improvements in workplace safety. But not all benefits of regulation are of this type. Freeman has estimated that only about 10 percent of all environmental benefits generated in 1978 were "cost reducing" or "output increasing." The remaining 90 percent were "amenity increasing." That is, they improved our welfare, but not in ways that show up in the GNP.[1] Furthermore, many of the output-enhancing benefits are realized only over the long term—periods of as long as decades perhaps. Thus these regulatory benefits require the sacrifice of current output, with consequent implications for measures of current economic performance.

Although our inability to measure the benefits of regulation may cause us to overstate the adverse impact of regulation on the economy, measurement problems on the cost side may lead us to understate regulation's negative consequences for economic performance. Investments made in pollution control equipment and worker-hours spent filling out regulatory forms represent obvious alterations in resource use occasioned by regulation. But what about socially valuable innovations that might be blocked by inappropriately stringent requirements for premarketing approval? Or new plants that might not be built, or plants that are built in less than the best locations because of inappropriately long delays in obtaining the necessary construction permits? Or—an even more subtle issue—what about the change in the character of entrepreneurial talent entering business today because of the increased importance of being able to deal effectively with government regulations? We do not know how common these problems are; we suspect that they are important.[2] But when they do occur, the kinds of costs they impose do not show up in the conventional measures of regulation's impact on the economy.

The studies we review here either do not address these factors or address them only superficially. Yet, over the long term, these "indirect" costs of regulation may be far more significant for economic performance than all the costs we *can* measure.

Thus, our statement concerning regulation's impact on economic performance must be seen for what it is—a summary of studies that attempt to measure how the use of certain physical resources—such as land, labor, capital, and energy—has been altered by regulation and how this alteration has, in turn, influenced the contemporaneous (or nearly contemporaneous) values of several closely watched, but admittedly incomplete, measures of economic welfare—the growth in GNP or national income per capita, the level of unemployment, the rate of inflation, and so forth.

Even with these significant qualifications, it is important to realize that not all studies purporting to measure the impact of regulation on the economy are, in fact, measuring the same thing. Some studies attempt to measure the total expenditures of business on regulation. Some seek to approximate the economist's concept of "marginal cost." Some employ hybrid estimates. Nor have all the studies been based on comparable underlying models of how the economy functions. Finally, the studies vary greatly in the care with which they were constructed and in the assumptions that they used to "fill in the blanks" when readily available numbers were unobtainable. This chapter aims to give the reader a basis for understanding and comparing these differences.

As noted earlier, the Reagan administration asserted not only that regulatory changes could improve economic performance but that such changes made today could have an important, immediate, positive impact on the economy even though their promised cost savings might not actually be realized for some years to come. This assertion has some support among economists, specifically among those who hold a "rational expectations" view of policymaking and its effects. We describe the "rational expectations" viewpoint and assess its validity in the case of regulatory changes.

The administration was probably claiming too much for its regulatory relief program, but its use of the "rational expectations" argument in the regulatory area was consistent with its use of this argument elsewhere in describing the possible consequences of its economic program. Indeed, we argue that the importance accorded the regulatory relief element of the administration's economic "game plan" might well be explained by the crucial role that the "rational expectations" view was expected to play in the administration's overall economic strategy.

Estimates in the Microeconomic Tradition

The annual report of the President's Council of Economic Advisers (CEA) published in February 1975 contains the following statement:

> Precise estimates of the total costs of regulation are not available, but existing evidence suggests that this may range up to 1 percent of the gross national product, or approximately $66 per person per year.[3]

On April 18 of that same year, in speaking before the White House Conference on Domestic Inflation and Economic Affairs in Concord, New Hampshire, President Ford said:

> Although it is difficult to come up with an exact price tag on the cost of unnecessary and ineffective government regulations, some estimates I have seen place the combined cost to consumers of Government regulation and restrictive practices in the private sector at more than the Federal Government actually collects in personal income taxes each year—or something on the order of $2,000 per family—unbelievable.[4]

Both these estimates, different though they may be, are drawn from what we will term the "microeconomic tradition" of estimating regulation's impact on the macroeconomy. To understand why we refer to the estimates in this way and how to interpret such results, it is useful to introduce a bit of economic theory.

The Basic Theory

Economists have long been interested in measuring the impact of certain activities on the economy. Attempts to estimate the "burden" imposed on the economy by private monopoly and other private forms of restrictive business practices go back more than a century. Efforts to apply the same methodology to measuring the burden imposed on the economy by government-supported, private restrictive business practices (such as legal cartels and regulated industries to which entry is protected) are much more recent, but still have a relatively long history. The idea of adapting the methodology to measure the impact of "social regulation" is quite new, dating perhaps from the mid-1970s.

The application of the methodology to publicly supported restrictive practices is straightforward and uncontroversial, but the extension of the methodology to social regulation is more complicated. To illustrate the assumptions involved, and the controversies connected with them, we first present the model that was originally developed to measure the cost imposed by individual private monopolies and then show the extensions required to apply the model eventually to social regulation.

Let us first consider the market for a single good, good X, which we will assume for the sake of simplicity is produced under conditions of constant cost. Figure 1 illustrates the situation under discussion. The demand curve for good X is designated DD and the average and marginal cost curve as AC

FIGURE 1

THE "COST" OF MONOPOLY TO THE ECONOMY

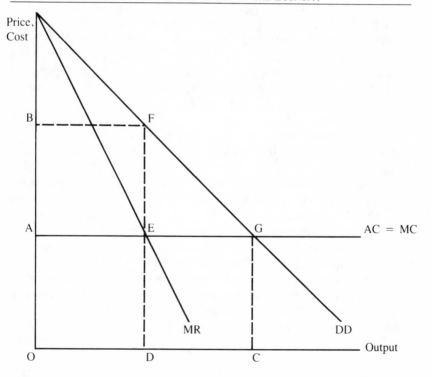

and MC. (Average and marginal cost are identical because of the constant-cost assumption, i.e., AC = MC). The AC = MC curve also is the supply curve for X in the competitive case.

Under conditions of perfect competition, all the many producers of X will be so small relative to the total market for the good that each producer will perceive that it has no influence over the price of X. That means that the demand curve the individual producer faces for X is a horizontal line, at whatever the current market price of X might be. Each of the small producers attempts to maximize its profits by adjusting the volume of X it will produce. Economic theory tells us that profits will be maximized if output for each producer is set at the point where marginal revenue equals marginal cost. In the competitive case, this will turn out to be the point at which the total supply of X and the total demand for X just balance. No producer makes "excess profits," but each covers its full cost of production and earns a normal return on the capital it has invested in the business. Market output in this case is OC, while price is OA.

Now suppose that a monopolist somehow gains control of the market for good X. The output decision rule for the monopolist is exactly the same as that for the competitive firm: set marginal revenue equal to marginal cost. But in the case of the monopolist, the choice of output will affect price, so the relevant demand curve is no longer a horizontal straight line at the current market price, but is the market demand curve. Marginal revenue to the monopolist is not identical with price but is less; in figure 1 marginal revenue to the monopolist is shown by the curve MR. The monopolist, applying the decision rule, sets output at OD, which is less than OC. This permits the monopolist to raise the price of X from OA to OB and to earn profits equal to ABFE.

To economists, these profits are not properly counted as a *cost* to the economy but as *transfers* from consumers to the monopolist. But the monopoly does impose a cost on the economy, measured by the area FGE. Why is FGE a cost and ABFE a transfer? Because the latter does not reflect a change in the way the economy allocates its productive resources. Each unit of X that is produced is produced in exactly the same way as it would have been had the industry not been monopolized. Payments to the individual factors of production are the same, too. In contrast, FGE represents a real change in resource allocation. This area represents the value of output DC to consumers; output that is no longer produced, less the resource costs of producing it, EGCD. The technical term for this area is *deadweight loss*, for it represents a loss to someone (namely, consumers) that is not offset by any income transfer. It measures the *cost* or *burden* imposed by the monopoly on the economy.

Applying the Theory: Monopoly's Cost to the Economy

As noted earlier, estimates such as these, which sought to measure the cost or burden to the economy of individual monopolies, have a long history. The first attempt apparently was made by the French economist Dupuit in the 1840s. But it was not until the early 1950s that an American economist named Arnold Harberger attempted to develop the first estimate of the cost of monopoly to the economy as a whole.[5]

Harberger used a model similar to that reflected in figure 1. That is, he used the methodology that had hitherto been employed to estimate the cost to the economy of individual monopolies. He developed numerical estimates of the parameters needed to calculate FGE for the economy as a whole—the average degree of markup above cost due to monopoly, and the elasticity of the economy's demand curve for all goods and services. Using these estimates and a bit of mathematical manipulation, he was able to develop his estimate. It was surprisingly small—about 0.1 percent of GNP.

Disputes over the accuracy of Harberger's calculations as well as adjustments by others eventually raised this number to between 0.5 and 2.0 percent of the GNP, although, as the author of one of these later estimates admitted, "Estimates nearer the lower bound (inspire) more confidence than estimates nearer the upper bound."[6]

To repeat, these estimates refer to the impact on the economy of private, restrictive business activities. Numbers of this kind were included in both the CEA and Ford estimates quoted earlier, although in the latter case, they obviously made up only a minor fraction of the total.

Extending the Theory: The Burden of Economic Regulation

It makes no particular difference to these calculations, however, how a producer obtains the market position that enables the monopoly profits to be earned. Economists have long recognized that the government itself is one of the most important sources of grants of monopoly power. (Indeed, some economists argue that *no* monopoly can be successfully maintained without some government support.) For this reason, it was no particular trick to extend Harberger's analysis to include cases in which the government itself was the source of the monopoly.

There is no need to modify the methodology to derive these expanded estimates. All one must do is compute the extent to which prices are raised by the sectors benefiting from the government grants of monopoly (generally the sectors of the economy subject to "economic regulation") and the share of the GNP they represent. Scherer, the source of the 0.5 to 2.0 percent estimate of the costs of private monopoly cited earlier, estimated in the same publication that the losses to the economy (measured as "deadweight loss") due to government-supported restrictive practices in these "regulated sectors" amounted to an additional 0.6 percent of GNP in the late 1960s. It is just such a combined estimate of "private" and "government-supported" "monopoly burden" that makes up the "up to 1 percent of GNP" figure in the 1975 CEA report.[7]

Is the Theory Applicable to Social Regulation?

Matters become substantially more complex when we try to use the above model to develop estimates of the cost or burden of social regulation. For one thing, social regulation operates in many ways—sometimes by directly raising the cost of producing (and hence the price) of certain items, sometimes by restricting the output of certain commodities, sometimes by altering the techniques of production permitted. Translating these diverse methods of operation into price increase equivalents, such as those used in the foregoing estimates, is difficult. To keep things simple, let us consider a type of social regulation that directly raises costs by a specific amount—say BA in figure 1. An example would be a requirement that an electric utility install pollution control devices that raised its generation costs by this amount. As a consequence, consumers would pay more for electricity, and the higher price would cause them to reduce their purchases of electricity by an amount equal to DC.

This result seems analogous to the two cases already presented, but it is not. For one thing, if the regulation is designed "properly," the increase in price, BA, merely reflects the fact that before the regulation was instituted, the production of electricity was inefficiently large. By failing to cause the price of electricity to incorporate the cost of its joint product—pollution—the market was subsidizing the production of electricity. The institution of the regulation merely offsets the previous distortion in the marketplace. This removal of an inefficient subsidy generates a deadweight gain equivalent to FEG.

But suppose the regulation is not "properly designed." Suppose instead that it is totally unnecessary—that the "market failure" it is supposed to correct does not exist. In this case, the regulation does generate a deadweight loss, just as did the private or government-generated monopoly. But in fact it imposes an even larger cost on the economy, and it is in estimating this larger cost of "ineffective regulation" that the figures cited by President Ford begin to diverge substantially from those cited by the Council of Economic Advisers.

To see why, it is necessary to recall the reason why economists refused to recognize the profits earned by private monopolists as costs but instead insisted on counting them as transfers and then see why regulatory costs fail to qualify as transfers. The key distinction was that the profits earned by private monopolists did not occasion a reallocation of real resources. In restricting output in order to be able to raise prices, the monopolist did indeed produce less of good X, and the value of that output, less the value of the resources freed up by not having to produce it, did count as cost. But the output of good X that *is* produced—the quantity OD—is produced in the same way as previously. No resource misallocation is involved in its production.

The possibility that something was being missed even in the case of the private monopolist was pointed out in a 1966 article by Harvey Leibenstein.[8] Leibenstein, like many other economists, was distressed by the small estimates Harberger obtained of the "cost of monopoly to the economy." Leibenstein pointed out the old adage that "the best of all monopoly profits is a quiet life." Although economic theory might suggest that monopolists should be as careful as competitive firms in minimizing the costs of the output they produce (in order to maximize their profits), monopolists might instead exploit their monopoly position, at least in part, by being less diligent in cost control than their competitive brethren. Or they might actively increase operating costs in ways that contribute to the satisfaction of managers (who in modern firms are not the same as the owners of firms). In some sense, behavior of this sort is perfectly rational. High profits might attract the notice of the antitrust authorities; high costs might be less conspicuous.

If private monopolists (or, for that matter, monopolists who owe their monopoly positions to the government) change the way they produce their output, as well as the level of output they produce,[9] then deadweight loss calculations of the sort that Harberger made no longer represent monopoly's total cost to the economy. To this deadweight loss must be added the costs occasioned by the resource misallocation (represented by the higher costs incurred by the monopolist). Resource misallocation occurs when a monopolist absorbs resources that are not actually necessary to produce the (reduced) level of output the monopolist chooses to produce—drawing those resources from other more productive employment elsewhere in the economy.

If the monopolist were to permit *all* the profits from the monopoly to be absorbed in the form of higher costs, then the "cost" the monopolist would impose on the economy would not be merely the "deadweight loss" triangle FEG, but that triangle *plus* the area ABFE. Both areas would reflect resource misallocation.[10]

What Expenditure Categories Do Legitimately Count as Costs?

The implications of Leibenstein's insight for the calculation of regulatory "costs" were pointed out most clearly by Marvin Kosters in an article published in the July/August 1979 issue of *Regulation*, "Counting the Costs."[11] Kosters was commenting on a detailed study performed by the accounting firm of Arthur Andersen and Company for the Business Roundtable, which sought to measure the "incremental costs" of regulation to fifty large companies. In his article, Kosters contrasted the "costs" the Andersen study included with the concepts of "cost" generally recognized by economists.

Kosters employed a framework similar to that illustrated in figure 1 to list the types of cost that regulation (principally social regulation) can generate. The first category of costs Kosters cited is *administrative costs*—the costs incurred by the government to write, manage, and police regulations. These costs show up in the federal budget, but they do not show up directly in calculations like those shown in figure 1 because they are financed from general taxes. They nevertheless qualify as costs in an economic sense because they reflect the use of real resources.

A second category of costs that Kosters mentioned is *transfers*—shifts in wealth analogous to the monopolist's profits created as a byproduct of regulation. According to Kosters, social regulation, unlike the more traditional economic regulation practiced by agencies like the Interstate Commerce Commission (ICC), Civil Aeronautics Board (CAB), and Federal Communications Commission (FCC), should not generate important transfers of wealth. Recent research, however, shows that conclusion was perhaps overly sanguine.[12] Such transfers would not properly count as costs.

A third category of costs discussed by Kosters is *compliance costs*—expenditures by private firms (and other units) occasioned by regulation. (It was this category of costs that the Arthur Andersen study focused on.) These costs include expenditures by business to analyze possible regulatory approaches, to shape proposed standards, to demonstrate compliance, and to defend compliance strategies against legal attack—in short, the private-sector analog of the administrative costs borne by government. Unlike the administrative costs, compliance costs *would* typically show up in calculations like those reflected in figure 1.

But this category also includes the important expenditures necessary to comply with the regulations—the wastewater treatment facilities, the flue gas scrubbers, the safer (and more expensive) punch presses in factories, and any additional labor and energy required to operate this equipment.

Are these expenditures legitimately counted as costs in an economic sense? Kosters noted that they (as well as the transfers mentioned above) generally show up as higher prices that consumers pay for the resulting products. But as we saw in the case of the private monopolist, that is not the relevant test. The test is whether these compliance expenditures reflect a reallocation of real resources. And, as Kosters pointed out, they do:

> It is extremely important to distinguish costs in the transfer category from the costs that arise through a process that in some respects may seem similar. For example, the costs of designing, building, operating, and maintaining a piece of pollution abatement or safety equipment show up as jobs, incomes, and profits generated by the firms that operate and maintain it. It is thus sometimes said that more jobs and income are gained as a result of regulatory programs than are lost as a result of failures or reduced production among the regulated firms. The basic error in regarding these designing, building, operating, and maintaining costs as a transfer—or even a net gain—is that, unlike transfers, they represent real resource use. That is, the jobs involved in the firms making the pollution abatement or safety equipment *are* the real resources represented by the cost estimates, so that diverting these resources to this use means a *net reduction* in resources available for other uses. The higher costs to consumers that result do not represent simply a transfer of income.[13]

The final category of costs Kosters mentioned is *inefficiency costs*, analogs to the *deadweight losses* mentioned earlier in connection with the private monopolist. He refers to these losses, which did not show up at all in the Arthur Andersen study, as "in a sense, the most serious because they represent a pure waste of resources."[14]

Assessing the legitimacy of including compliance costs as costs of regulation to the economy is crucial to evaluating the various regulatory cost estimates derived from the microeconomic tradition, since these costs, plus administrative costs, make up the vast bulk of such estimates. As Paul Portney, of Resources for the Future, has observed, in very few instances do estimates of "the cost of regulation to the economy" include estimates of the deadweight-loss component of these costs. But, as he also demonstrated, the omission of these particular costs may not constitute a serious problem because they are relatively small.[15]

Implications for Estimates to Be Discussed

The previous discussion of the validity of including compliance costs in measures of the cost of regulation to the economy was based on the assumption that regulation is *totally ineffective*—that is, regulation is imposed to correct a nonexistent market failure. What if the market failure is real?

The issue turns on the existence of an original market failure and on the efficacy of the regulation in correcting it. If a regulation corrects a market failure and does so efficiently, then it truly imposes no cost on the economy. Indeed, it produces a net gain in welfare. If it fails to correct a market failure, or if the correction takes place at a higher cost than is absolutely necessary, then the regulation does generate a cost to the economy. Whether the cost turns out to be a net cost depends on the size of the gains the regulation produces from its total or partial correction of the market failure. However, if a regulation is imposed to correct a nonexistent market failure, then all its costs, including a deadweight loss, are properly chargeable as costs to the economy.

This extremely rigorous definition of what properly counts as a cost of regulation has not been adhered to in preparing any of the estimates we report here. Instead, even the most conscientiously constructed of the estimates has settled for some measure of expenditure on regulatory compliance. This is not surprising, for to have done otherwise would have required the analyst preparing the estimate to have made judgments about the degree to which each regulatory program was correcting a genuine market failure and doing so efficiently. Nevertheless, as we consider the estimates in the sections that follow, it is important to remember that all of the analysts are making an assumption that overestimates (though to an unknown—an even unknowable—degree) the true burden that social regulation imposes upon the economy.

Weidenbaum's "$100 Billion" Estimate

There is, as we have seen, a defensible intellectual basis for estimates of the cost of regulation to the economy which include compliance cost figures. The person preparing these inclusions must be willing to assume that regulation is largely or totally ineffective. Given the magnitude of compliance costs, very large figures for the cost of regulation to the economy thus become plausible. But what about specific estimates that have been reported—estimates such as the $2,000 per family per year President Ford suggested in his April 1975 speech or the more widely publicized figure of $100 billion per year associated with Murray Weidenbaum? How much weight should be given numbers such as these?

The Ford number was based on information thrown together quickly and carelessly by the staff of the Office of Management and Budget (OMB). The entire estimate was compiled from inconsistent and overlapping sources and represented considerable double counting. A General Accounting Office study of this estimate has thoroughly discredited it.[16]

The estimate associated with Weidenbaum was far more carefully compiled. The documentation of the estimate, reported originally in a working paper by Robert DeFina[17] and later summarized in an American Enterprise

Institute study written by Weidenbaum and DeFina,[18] shows the effort to have been a serious one.

The Weidenbaum estimate was originally prepared using data for 1976. Six areas of regulation were covered: consumer safety and health, job safety and working conditions, energy and the environment, financial regulations, a category labeled "industry specific," and a final category labeled "paperwork." Expenditures in each area were broken down into two classes, *administrative costs* and *compliance costs*. Administrative costs were expenditures incurred by government agencies responsible for administering regulation in the indicated areas. (For example, those costs in the area of consumer safety and health included portions of the budgets of the Departments of Agriculture, Health, Education, and Welfare, Justice, and Treasury, and the entire budget of the Consumer Product Safety Commission.) Compliance cost estimates were derived from published studies prepared either by government agencies or by academics; care was taken to avoid double counting. When several estimates existed or when the original author reported estimates as a range, the lower bound was generally employed. In few cases did Weidenbaum attempt to convert the sums involved to dollars of comparable years (an important exception will be mentioned later), but most studies drawn upon seem to have been conducted at approximately the same time—the early to mid-1970s.

In the category labeled "industry specific," Weidenbaum and DeFina included the budgets of the agencies involved in "economic regulation," excluding those involved in the regulation of the financial industries. Thus, this category included the budgets of agencies like the CAB, FCC, ICC, and Nuclear Regulatory Commission, but *excluded* the budgets of the Federal Reserve Board, Cost Accounting Standards Board, Securities and Exchange Commission, and the Federal Trade Commission (which curiously found its way into the "financial regulation" category). Compliance costs in the industry-specific category included estimates (again, generally by academics) of the burden imposed on the economy by the regulation of industries like trucking, the airlines, and nuclear power. These estimates included, but were not necessarily limited to, the "deadweight losses" occasioned by this regulation. (This is the only area in which Weidenbaum and DeFina appear to have attempted to include deadweight-loss estimates in their calculation.)

Estimates in the paperwork category were based on a statement by Senator Thomas J. McIntyre, chairman of a Senate subcommittee that had examined the issue of paperwork costs in early 1972. The senator's estimate of $18 billion, contained in the statement with which he opened the hearings by his subcommittee, was adjusted to 1976 dollars (in contrast to Weidenbaum and DeFina's usual practice), yielding a figure of $25 billion.

The results are summarized in table 1. The total figure for *regulatory cost* is $66 billion, of which *paperwork costs* accounted for approximately 40 percent.[19]

But Murray Weidenbaum is not noted for claiming that regulation costs the economy $66 billion; the number most frequently associated with his name is $100 billion. How was this latter figure determined?

The figures in table 1 apply to the year 1976. By the time Weidenbaum wrote his article for *Regulation*, the fiscal 1979 budget had been submitted to the Congress. The budgets of the agencies included in the administrative cost components of the various rows of table 1 had grown from the approximately $3.2 billion shown to $4.8 billion. Noting that the ratio of total administrative costs to total compliance costs for 1976 was 19.5 to 1, Weidenbaum stated at the very end of the article:

> If the 1976 ratio . . . should hold for 1979—and there may be reasons why it would not—compliance costs would be $97.9 billion in that year. With administrative costs estimated at $4.8 billion, the estimated total costs of regulation would exceed $100 billion.[20]

Weidenbaum never intended that his estimate should be considered anything but rough. In fact, he emphasized that he considered the estimate conservative, because it omits several types of regulation and restrictive practices known to be quite costly. He also acknowledged that his estimates ignore the

TABLE 1

ANNUAL COST OF FEDERAL REGULATION, BY AREA, 1976
($ millions)

Area	Administrative Cost	Compliance Cost	Total
Consumer safety and health	$1,516	$ 5,094	$ 6,610
Job safety and working conditions	483	4,015	4,498
Energy and the environment	612	7,760	8,372
Financial regulation	104	1,118	1,222
Industry specific	484	19,919	20,403
Paperwork	a	25,000	25,000
Total	$3,199	$62,906	$66,105

SOURCE: Murray Weidenbaum and Robert DeFina, *The Cost of Federal Regulation of Economic Activity* (Washington, D.C.: The American Enterprise Institute, May 1978), Reprint No. 88, p. 2.

a. Included in other categories.

possible benefits of regulation. Indeed, near the end of his *Regulation* piece, he cautioned:

> To repeat my earlier caveat, note that our study examined only the costs of regulation and that it is impossible to determine from cost figures alone whether the amounts being spent are too large or too little. [21]

Therefore, the attacks on his methodology and conclusions that the publication of his study generated[22] did not especially concern him. He believed that he had proved his point, namely, that "the magnitude of the figures here outlines the need for increased attention to the problem from scholars, regulators, and policymakers."[23]

Other "Expenditure" Estimates

Weidenbaum's expressed desire was that the level and consequence of expenditures on regulation be given "increased attention" by "scholars, regulators, and policymakers." He certainly got his wish. During the mid-1970s, the government began to upgrade the figures it collected on private expenditures for regulatory compliance. Private surveys of planned and actual capital expenditures, such as those conducted by McGraw-Hill, began to request information on regulatory compliance costs. Studies like the one already mentioned by Arthur Andersen and Company were commissioned. And some larger firms began to compile and publicize estimates of their individual expenditures on regulation.[24]

Portney has recently reviewed the most prominent of the regulatory expenditure estimates explaining how, even if the broader conceptual issues mentioned earlier are ignored, the estimates can either overstate or understate the true costs of regulatory compliance.[25] Estimates understate true compliance costs because they generally fail to reflect "opportunity cost" concepts—such as the value of forgone opportunities for the resources employed. They overstate costs because they sometimes include transfers such as sales or payroll taxes. An even more serious overstatement is caused by the failure of most expenditure estimates to employ marginal cost concepts. (The Arthur Andersen study is a notable exception.) In short, most of these estimates, especially the private ones, represent compilations of actual cash outlays by firms for what the firms consider to be regulatory compliance activities.

Portney showed the discrepancies among several widely used series, each of which claims to measure "pollution control expenditures"—the series constructed by McGraw-Hill, the Department of Commerce's Bureau of Economic Analysis, and the Bureau of the Census. Table 2 shows Portney's comparison of three sources, all *ex post* estimates of actual 1978 pollution

TABLE 2

ESTIMATED CAPITAL EXPENDITURES FOR POLLUTION CONTROL
($ millions)

	1978 Actual		
	(1) McGraw-Hill[a]	(2) BEA[b]	(3) Census[c]
Iron and steel	425	441	
Nonferrous metals	293	247	793
Other primary metals	—	64	
Electric machinery	134	130	75
Machinery	243	111	82
Autos, trucks, parts	193	198	140
Aerospace	45	23	
Fabricated metals	137	—	
Instruments	58		
Stone	207	164	127
Other durables	190	181	186
Total durables	1,935	1,561	1,402
Chemicals	547	565	842
Paper/pulp	274	239	342
Rubber	100	58	28
Petroleum	834	1,294	420
Food/beverages	309	172	185
Textiles	81	29	60
Other nondurables	67	32	37
Total nondurables	2,212	2,389	1,914
Total manufacturing	4,147	3,950	3,316
Mining	511	206	
Railroads	54	36	
Airlines	20	15	
Electric utilities	2,791	2,472	
Gas utilities	60	35	
Commercial & other trans.	423	210	
	3,859	2,974	
All business	8,006	6,924	

SOURCE: Portney, "The Macroeconomic Impacts of Federal Environmental Regulation," in Peskin et al., *Environmental Regulation and the U.S. Economy*, p. 30.

a. *The 12th Annual McGraw-Hill Survey of Pollution Control Expenditures*, May 14, 1979.

b. Gary Rutledge and Betsy O'Connor, "Capital Expenditures by Business for Pollution Abatement, 1978, 1979, and Planned 1980," *Survey of Current Business*, June 1980.

c. *Pollution Abatement Costs and Expenditures, 1978*, U.S. Bureau of the Census, MA-200 (78)-2 (Washington, D.C.: U.S. Government Printing Office, 1980).

control expenditures by industry. Some of the differences are clearly attributable to differences in industrial definitions and differences in survey coverage. Still, differences of the magnitude shown for the total of what are *historical* numbers are troubling.[26]

Portney also suggested caution in using engineering estimates of environmental control expenditures, such as those employed by the Council on Environmental Quality and the Environmental Protection Agency in constructing their widely cited estimates of aggregate environmental compliance expenditures. In certain instances, these estimates are, unlike the expenditure surveys, estimates of *incremental* and not *total* expenditures. Moreover, these estimates are rapidly outdated and do not adequately reflect either subsequent technological improvements or "learning by doing," both of which may substantially cut regulatory compliance costs. Still, there seems to be no substitute for such estimates when seeking to understand the possible expenditure requirements of *future* regulations.

What are we to conclude from these estimates, whether based on surveys or engineering judgment? Portney's summary is instructive:

The following inferences seem warranted. First, the social cost of environmental regulation is probably greater, and perhaps significantly so, than actual direct expenditures for pollution control. This follows from the important costs of pollution control that are omitted from expenditure estimates. These omissions probably offset the occasional divergence between private and social cost that can cause expenditures to exceed resource costs.

Second, although costs probably exceed actual direct expenditures, both are likely to fall short of most estimates of expenditures, quite possibly by a considerable margin. Existing survey estimates are based on responses from those firms or plants likely to be the most severely affected by regulations. These respondents also have incentives to err on the high side when reporting their expenditures for pollution control. Engineering cost estimates can also be expected to frequently overstate pollution control expenditures because it is difficult to foresee the technological changes that will reduce compliance costs and expenditures over time. Neither can the possible regulatory innovations that will arise be foreseen.

Still, existing expenditure estimates are not without value. They do provide the information necessary to run the macroeconomic models [these models are discussed later]. They enable us, in this way, to determine roughly how the costs of regulation may manifest themselves in the economy. This does enable us to draw some inferences about the distributional effects of these regulations. Nevertheless, for the reasons outlined above, expenditure estimates are inevitably flawed and must be recognized as such. They can be viewed as no more than suggestive, and at times they may fall short of even this modest goal.[27]

Portney's final statement deserves emphasis. The expenditure estimates that are now available, even the best of them, are "inevitably flawed" and "no more than suggestive." Yet it is upon them that both aggregate compliance cost figures, such as those of Weidenbaum and the macroeconomic modeling estimates to be discussed in the next section, must be based. In view of the importance that analysts and policymakers have accorded these relatively frail numbers, it seems wise to suggest caution in basing major elements of economic or social policy upon precise estimates of regulation's impact on the economy.

Direct Estimates of Regulation's Macroeconomic Consequences

The preceding estimates of regulatory compliance expenditures leave the reader to make the link between them and macroeconomic performance. Their primary message is that "regulation costs money—lots of money." For example, Weidenbaum and DeFina provide the following benchmarks against which to compare the $66 billion figure they derived for 1976. According to them, this figure was equivalent to—

- 4 percent of the gross national product
- $307 per person living in the United States
- 18 percent of the federal budget
- twice the amount the federal government spends on health
- 74 percent of the amount directed to national defense
- more than one-third of all private investment in new plant and equipment.[28]

Other analysts have attempted to develop direct measures of the linkage. The best-known studies are the attempts by Denison and others to estimate regulation's impact on productivity, and the macroeconomic modeling performed by Chase Econometrics and Data Resources, Inc. for the Council on Environmental Quality estimating the impact of regulation on economic growth rates, employment, and inflation.

Regulation and Productivity. Scholars differ as to the precise date that productivity growth in the United States began to slow down, but there can be no doubt that productivity in the United States has recently fallen considerably below the performance throughout most of the post-World War II period. Many explanations for this slowdown have been advanced. None has proven completely satisfactory, and much of the decline in growth productivity remains unexplained. Because the slowdown in productivity growth seems to have coincided roughly with the rise in federal regulatory activity beginning in the late 1960s, it is natural for scholars to investigate whether the two phenomena are linked.

Denison has performed the pioneering work on this subject.[29] Using the "growth accounting" framework he developed, he sought to disentangle the various causes of the poor productivity performance and, of particular interest here, the role that regulation played in it.

Denison used a conventional neoclassical production function as the basis for his estimates. Changes in national income per person employed (NIPPE) are generated by changes in labor input, capital input, and autonomous factors. Denison's contribution is unique, however, in the detail with which he has sorted out the various factors that underlie these changes. For example, he disaggregated changes in labor input to distinguish between changes in number of hours worked and changes in the "quality" of those hours—the composition of the labor force by age and sex, differences in the amount and quality of training, and so on. Denison also developed measures of the contribution, either positive or negative, that each of these makes to the growth in NIPPE. His results for the period 1948–1973 and 1973–1976 are summarized in table 3.

This table shows changes in the "legal and human environment" as contributing a *negative* 0.4 percentage points to the growth in natural income per person employed during the 1973–1976 period. Because the total slow-down in the adjusted growth rate amounted to 3.2 percentage points (from a positive 2.6 percentage points per year average between 1948 and 1973 to a negative 0.6 percentage point per year average between 1973 and 1976), changes in the legal and human environment can be said to be "responsible for" 12.5 percent of the slowdown—not the whole story, but still significant.

What is included in the -0.4 percentage point figure, and what does it actually measure? There are three principal categories: expenditures on pollution abatement (which contributes -0.23), expenditures to improve employee safety and health (-0.12), and the effects of "employee dishonesty and crime" (-0.09).

Denison was careful to explain his figures and to indicate what they do and do *not* show. For example, in his calculations, expenditures by government on regulatory administration and compliance *increase* the gross national product because of the way the expenditures are treated in the national accounts. Therefore, these expenditures do not show up as "growth reducing." Similarly, when consumers purchase automobiles equipped with pollution control devices, government statisticians typically adjust their estimates of output to account for the "improved quality" of the product, so these improvements show up in the form of increased national income. Purchases by

TABLE 3

Sources of Growth of National Income Per Person Employed,
Nonresidential Business Sector, 1948–1973 and 1973–1976

Item	1948–1973	1973–1976
Growth rate	2.4	−0.5
Irregular factors	−0.2	0.1
Adjusted growth rate	2.6	−0.6
Changes in labor characteristics		
Hours at work	−0.2	−0.5
Age-sex composition	−0.2	−0.3
Education	0.5	0.9
Changes in capital and land per person employed		
Nonresidential structures and equipment	0.3	0.2
Inventories	0.1	0.0
Land	0.0	0.0
Improved allocation of resources	0.4	0.0
Legal and human environment	0.0	−0.4
Economies of scale from larger markets	0.4	0.2
Advances in knowledge and n.e.c.[a]	1.4	−0.7

Source: Edward F. Denison, *Accounting for Slower Economic Growth* (Washington, D.C.: The Brookings Institution), p. 2.

a. Not elsewhere classified.

business, however, are treated differently. Indeed, even labor and capital input by business must be treated in distinctly different ways:

> Costs of environmental protection that are incurred by business on current account, whether for purchases from other enterprises or for the direct hiring of labor, are not counted as purchases of final products in the NIPA [National Income and Product Accounts]. Because they absorb inputs that would otherwise be used to produce final products, they lower the output per unit of input below what it would have been in the absence of the diversion of inputs to environmental protection. The dollar cost of the environmental expenditures, when expressed as a percentage of measured output plus these expenditures themselves, measures both the percentage of input diverted to unmeasured production and the percentage reduction in measured output per unit of input that they cause.
>
> Capital goods acquired by business for pollution abatement are counted as final products when they are purchased, so their production in place of other final products does not immediately reduce measured output per unit of input. What does reduce measured output per unit of input is the use of part of the

stock of capital for pollution abatement, because the proportion of the stock of capital goods present at any date that business devotes to pollution abatement is not available to produce products that are counted as final. Given the total stock of capital, measured output is reduced by the value of the services that this capital would have provided if used to produce final products.

This value is measured as the sum of depreciation on pollution abatement capital and an imputed net return on this capital. It represents the opportunity cost of using capital for pollution abatement.[30]

This quotation illustrates the care Denison exercised in constructing his estimates. Although he was hampered by having to rely on the same expenditure data whose shortcomings were discussed in the previous section (he relied upon the BEA expenditure surveys), Denison was as careful as possible to convert these data into figures that closely reflect marginal cost and incorporate opportunity cost elements. Furthermore, he was careful to net out any salable byproduct resulting from the operation of the pollution control equipment.

The consequences of these adjustments can be seen by comparing Denison's 1975 figure for "incremental pollution abatement costs that reduce national income per unit of input in nonresidential business" with the BEA figures for "pollution abatement and control" for that year (both measured in 1972 dollars). Denison's total is $9.5 billion, an amount equivalent to 0.967 percent of nonresidential business factor inputs for that year.[31] The BEA expenditure figure for that same year is $22.9 billion.[32] It is also worth noting that $2.8 billion of Denison's $9.5 figure consists of "net opportunity cost of invested capital," a figure that does not show up at all in the BEA series.

Other scholars have developed their own estimates of the effect of regulation on productivity in the 1970s. Haveman and Christiansen, employing a somewhat more complex production function than Denison but not disaggregating causal factors nearly to the degree he did, concluded that "between, say, 12 and 25 percent of the [total] slowdown in productivity growth in the private sector between the early 1960s and the mid-1970s can be attributed to the entire bundle of regulations."[33] Nordhaus, after conducting a survey of various studies (including Denison's but not including Haveman and Christiansen's) provided a "best guess" consensus estimate of 10 percent (0.2 percentage points out of a total "cyclically adjusted" decline of 2.2 percentage points).[34]

Each of these authors stressed the incompleteness of his estimates, noting that at best they measure only what the national income accounts measure. Each observed that many of the intended benefits of regulation, not being captured in the national accounts, go unrecorded. Yet the striking thing that emerges from all of these estimates is the relatively small proportion of the productivity slowdown they explain. If these figures do fully capture regulation's adverse impact on productivity (and we argue in the next section that they probably do not), it is clear that even *total* regulatory relief would have made only a small dent in the core inflation rate of 7.5 to 9 percent that prevailed when President Reagan entered office in early 1981.

Are These Estimates Missing Something Important?   Most studies that attempt to explain the productivity decline end up with a large unexplained component. Table 3 shows that in Denison's case, this category, which he labeled "advances in knowledge and n.e.c. (not elsewhere classified)," accounts for 2.1 percentage points (from a positive contribution of 1.4 percentage points to a negative contribution of 0.7 percentage points), or 66 percent of the total. Might not a portion of this "unexplained" component reflect the influence of regulation?

In a separate chapter of his book, Denison reviewed seventeen factors that might account for the unexplained 66 percent of the productivity decline. Among these are regulation-related factors not already captured in his measures, including the diversion of input to comply with regulations other than environmental and safety, the burden of government-imposed paperwork, the diversion of executive attention, the delay of new projects, and, finally, the consequences of regulation-induced misallocation of resources.[35] Each of the seventeen factors is thoroughly discussed and evaluated in the light of whatever evidence Denison was able to discover.

In the end, Denison rejects some, expresses skepticism about some, has no opinion about others, and characterizes the rest as "probably correct but individually able to explain only a small part of the slowdown."[36] Most of the regulation-related variables fall into this last category. For example, with respect to the paperwork burden (which constituted 38 percent of Weidenbaum's "regulatory cost" estimate), Denison reviewed the estimates of the Commission on Federal Paperwork, the much lower estimates compiled by the Office of Management and Budget from individual agency submissions, and the estimates that exist of the distribution of this burden as between tax forms and other federal paperwork. He concluded as follows:

> The evidence indicates that paperwork can be eliminated as a significant source of productivity decline from 1973 to 1976, although it may have been a factor—but not a major one—if one goes back to 1966. The general impression of the burden of paperwork may be exaggerated because, in Herbert Kaufman's phrase, red tape is universally an "object of loathing."[37]

Denison was correct to be wary of "intangible" (i.e., unmeasurable) explanations for the productivity slowdown. The consequences on productivity of certain factors that have been advanced—the paperwork burden, the unwillingness of workers to work anymore, and the like—are probably highly exaggerated. But unmeasurable doesn't necessarily mean unimportant. Despite the difficulty in measuring the effects of regulation, while we despair at ever being able to obtain a precise measure of its influence, we nonetheless believe that one of the most important longer-term consequences of regulation on the nation's economic performance—including its productivity performance—may be the change that regulation represents in the way American business does business.

Before the late 1960s, only a relatively narrow segment of the business community was subject to detailed government control. Although we are aware of no systematic study of this issue, anecdotal information suggests that firms in these "regulated industries" were different from firms in the remainder of the economy in their staffing, organization, and behavior. Moreover, as many of the regulatory controls that have traditionally governed the behavior of firms in long-regulated industries are removed, their staffing, organization, and behavior are clearly changing. These changes are most startling in industries like airlines, telecommunications, and banking. The changes are also obvious when the new entrants to these industries—firms that are unencumbered by the industry's regulatory traditions—are compared with the incumbent firms.

The majority of American businesses first experienced significant federal regulation at the end of the 1960s as agencies like the Environmental Protection Agency, Occupational Safety and Health Administration, Equal Employment Opportunity Commission, and the Consumer Product Safety Commission were created. President Nixon's imposition of wage and price controls in August 1971—the largest single extension of economic regulation ever undertaken in this country in peacetime—exposed many business people to the sort of regulatory issues with which their counterparts in the "regulated industries" had become familiar decades before. The panoply of controls that surrounded the pricing, availability, and use of energy after 1973 also impressed upon businesses the importance of understanding and being able to influence government regulators.

As Alfred Chandler has reminded us, business is an adaptable institution.[38] When conditions are such that the rate of return businesses can earn on an asset is based primarily on the nature of that asset's regulatory status, it is only natural for the businesses to concentrate their attention on this issue. People skilled in dealing with regulation naturally rise within America's corporations. They displace people who were skilled in dealing with the older problems, such as production management and design. With issues such as regulation increasingly dominating the attention of business, it is not surprising that people skilled in law and finance have increasingly come to dominate top management.

The problem we are describing is *not* generated by the fact that our nation has chosen to impose certain significant social costs on itself through regulating the conduct of its businesses. Instead, the problem stems from the *manner* in which we have chosen to regulate the conduct of businesses. (Similarly, the encouragement for "paper entrepreneurship" provided by our tax code has little if anything to do with the level of revenues we have chosen to raise from the corporate sector; instead, the phenomenon stems from the way in which we have chosen to raise those revenues.) Because of our "command and control" system of regulation, managers today plan and work not so much against the actions of their competitors as against the actions of the government (which, in many cases, can have a far more profound effect on their fortunes than anything mere private competitors can do.) This "gaming against the government" may well have more significant and long-lasting effects on business behavior and on productivity than the actual costs of regulatory compliance.

The Measured Impact of Regulation on Major Macroeconomic Variables: Growth, Employment, and Inflation

The other category of direct studies of regulation's impact on the economy consists of simulations conducted on large-scale macroeconomic models. Studies of this sort have been sponsored for several years by the Environmental Protection Agency and the Council on Environmental Quality. Portney has described in some detail how these estimates are constructed.[39] Again, estimates of regulatory expenditures from one of the major surveys—BEA, Census, or McGraw-Hill—are used as a starting point. These models are not designed to simulate the same kinds of changes that regulation causes in various industries, but are built for macroeconomic forecasting. As a result, various ad hoc adjustments must be made to certain of the model's equations. The choice of which equations to adjust and how to adjust them is crucial to the simulation's outcome. Realistic scenarios must be developed to characterize the economy both with and without regulation. The models are then run, and the difference in the solutions in the "with" and "without" cases is deemed the impact of regulation.

What do these models show? The results of one such study reported by the Conservation Foundation in *The State of the Environment—1982* are typical:

The study concluded that the 1981 real Gross National Product was 0.2 percent lower, the Consumer Price Index was increasing 0.5 percentage points faster, business fixed investment was 0.8 percent higher, and the unemployment rate was 0.3 percentage points lower with the programs than would have been the case without them. Over the past 10 years, the real GNP has been slightly higher than it otherwise would have been because of the programs, but since 1976 it has been growing at a slower rate, and from 1981 onward will probably fall slightly below the level it would have attained without the programs. Business investment and various measures of inflation are higher because of pollution control programs throughout the entire period of analysis. Unemployment is lower by an average of 0.2 percentage points.[40]

Since the adjustments required to produce these simulations are very much ad hoc, it is not surprising that each produces slightly different results. Indeed, simulations in different years conducted by the *same* contractor yield different results. Yet the overall impact of these variations is minor. All the models show results roughly similar to the results described in the quotation from the Conservation Foundation volume.

In view of the fact that both business investment and employment are *higher* in the "with regulation" case, we feel compelled to remind the reader of Kosters' caution that it would be wrong to consider the investment and employment generated by regulatory compliance expenditures as necessarily either a transfer or even a net gain.[41] The fact that expenditures related to pollution control are more labor intensive than certain other business activities says nothing about whether our nation is making wise choices about the vigor with which we should pursue social regulation. These large-scale macroeconomic simulations tell us *either* that regulation has relatively little impact on the variables that most economists watch as indicators of the health of the economy *or* that large-scale macromodels are not sensitive enough to reliably indicate the impact of such complex phenomena as a mass of individual programs that, when lumped together, might be called "regulation."

The Theory of Rational Expectations and Regulatory Relief

Understanding the claim that regulatory relief, realized in the future, could produce immediate benefits for the economy requires a short explanation of the theory of "rational expectations," a major underpinning of the entire Reagan economic game plan. As economists sought to discover how a persistent inflation could be "unwound," a dispute developed over the importance of actual results versus anticipated outcomes in generating the unwinding. Both sides in this dispute agreed that expectations of true inflation were a key element in keeping the inflation going. For example, by late 1980 long-term interest rates, acknowledged as a key barometer of expected future inflation, were running about 13 percent.[42] The consensus was that nine to ten percentage points of this represented an "inflation premium."[43] The disagreement concerned *how* inflationary expectations could be changed.

The conventional view was that these expectations could be affected only by actual performance. A period—perhaps a long period—of tight money or tight budgets, or both, during which time the economy would operate considerably below its potential, would be necessary before workers would moderate their wage claims and producers would cease trying to mark up their prices to "beat inflation." The alternative view was that a tough program, if announced in a way that made it "credible," might cause inflationary expectations to drop almost instantly. This latter view was the "rational expectations" view. It held that people looked only forward, not backward, in their wage and price decisions, and that the mere announcement of a *credible* anti-inflation program was all that was necessary to change these decisions. To return to our example of long-term interest rates, a "tight money" policy might double the "real" element in long-term interest rates—from three or four to perhaps six or eight percentage points— but if the "inflation premium" was simultaneously reduced to zero, the nominal long-term rate could still fall substantially. And once that occurred, the tight monetary or fiscal policies could be eased (in a way consistent with noninflationary economic growth) and long-term interest rates would fall still further— back to their 3 to 4 percent average of earlier years.

The Reagan administration's original economic game plan relied heavily on producing such an immediate "expectations shock"—and on reaping its reward. Applying "rational expectations" to regulatory relief, it becomes immediately clear that the actual timing of any relief that might be forthcoming would have less impact on business decisions than the secure knowledge that relief would in fact occur. Thus it was consistent with the general Reagan administration view to claim that a major "regulatory ventilation" could, if seen as credible by business, begin to have an almost immediate effect on investment decisions.

How valid is the "rational expectations" view? In theory, it is plausible. Altering expectations is indeed the key to unwinding inflation, and it is rational to expect businesses and wage earners to be interested primarily in the future, not the past. But how do businesses and wage earners form their expectations about the future? Most economists assign a role to past performance for two reasons. First, as the 1981 *Economic Report of the President* stated:

Simply announcing a set of targets does not guarantee that they will be steadfastly pursued in the face of mounting losses in employment, profits, and sales. Indeed, the tougher the targets and greater the demand restraint they seem to require, the less likely they are to be credible, for their success will rely on an uncharacteristic willingness on the part of the Administration, the Congress, and the public to accept large reductions in employment and production rather than abandon the targets. The mere announcement of a set of government intentions is, therefore, unlikely to produce a significant change in wage and price behavior.[44]

Second, our economy employs certain formal and informal mechanisms (both explicit contracts and what Arthur Okun labeled "invisible hand-shakes") in price and wage setting that explicitly link future wage and price changes to past wage and price behavior. In many cases, these contracts are multiyear. Thus, even if expectations somehow could be shocked, these continuing formal and informal arrangements would influence the rate at which actual wage and price changes would be adjusted.

Once the initial euphoria of the Reagan administration's first months in office had passed and inflation had not been immediately and painlessly conquered, a similarly sober view of "rational expectations" emerged among the president's economic advisers. Acknowledging that, based upon past experience, a business or a wage earner employing "rational expectations" might indeed require that a government actually deliver on its promises (or at least a portion of them), Reagan's Council of Economic Advisers remarked in its first report:

The mere announcement of new policies is not sufficient to convince people that they will be carried out. Rather, public expectations regarding the future course of policy are adjusted only gradually as policy actions turn out to be consistent with policy announcements. The credibility of policy authorities, like the credibility of anyone else, is enhanced when they do what they say they are going to do.[45]

It seems unlikely that businesses—the principal target of the administration's economic game plan—would be any more convinced by regulatory pronouncements than they would be by pronouncements relating to other elements of the administration's anti-inflation program. But there were some important differences between regulation and other government policies—or so it seemed. Changing tax and spending policies required congressional authorization. The mere word of a president was not enough to create a "credible belief" that these policy elements would change. Monetary policy was already "tight" as the Reagan administration entered office. Interest rates were at or near historic highs; and the administration did not want to seem to be promising to raise them still further. But there might be considerable room in the regulatory area for immediate and dramatic administrative actions. This could help generate the necessary "expectations shock."

An intellectual basis, therefore, did exist for the claim that the regulatory relief program could produce major and rapid changes in corporate investment behavior (and possibly even pricing practices), if only it could be seen as "credible." Combined with the administration's stated belief that regulation bore a major share of the blame for the economy's poor performance (a belief *not* supported by the studies we have reviewed), the appeal of an immediate, highly visible, largely administrative program of regulatory relief becomes evident. It was just such a program that the President proceeded to launch as soon as he assumed office.

3

Precedents for Executive Branch Oversight

For as long as the federal government has been engaged in regulation, presidents and their aides have occasionally taken an interest in the outcome of regulatory proceedings. Because direct or indirect grants of valuable rights are often involved and politically well connected people sometimes stand to gain or lose from the outcome of such proceedings, sporadic White House attention is all but inevitable. However, *continuing* White House interest in the impact of federal regulatory activities either on the economy as a whole or on important industries and sectors dates only from the early 1970s.

As has been noted, Presidents Nixon, Ford, and Carter all experimented with institutional arrangements and procedural requirements designed to bring rule making by executive branch agencies more firmly under White House control. These experiments, beginning with Nixon's Quality of Life Review process in 1971, have been intensely controversial, provoking several lawsuits and numerous confrontations with congressional committees. But by the end of the Carter administration, the concept of presidential control over executive branch rule-making activity was firmly established, provided certain safeguards were maintained.

Some observers have attacked the efforts of recent presidents to bring regulation by executive branch agencies and departments more firmly under central control as unwarranted—and possibly illegal—attempts to inject political considerations into the activities of expert agencies. Other people have characterized the White House efforts as legitimate and necessary steps to assure that executive branch regulatory policies are consistent across agencies, give due weight to important national concerns that otherwise might be overlooked, and are integrated appropriately into the complementary federal activities.[1]

The controversy these activities has generated, reflecting the tensions mentioned in the first paragraph of this chapter, is inherent in the task of regulatory oversight. Only at the White House level can many important issues be identified and priorities set. But the White House cannot (and should not attempt to) become involved in every regulatory issue. This necessary selectivity inevitably raises the suspicion—sometimes with very good reason—that political considerations rather than a desire to achieve coordination have been the primary reason that a particular regulation has been singled out for attention.

Each president has faced the problem of asserting the necessary authority to oversee the operation of agencies staffed by his appointees in a way that the public, the Congress, and the courts find acceptable. No president has developed the perfect solution, but by the end of the Carter administration (and mainly as a result of Carter's willingness to heed the experience of his two predecessors), the outlines of a permissible presidential role were becoming substantially clearer.

The Quality of Life Review Process[2]

Many of the procedures and institutional arrangements that would later be employed by Presidents Ford, Carter, and Reagan trace their origins to decisions made in 1971 by the Nixon administration. Indeed, the Reagan program most closely resembles an arrangement that was first considered and then discarded by the Nixon administration. An account of what the Nixon administration did—and, almost as important, did not do—about regulatory oversight is important to understanding the oversight programs of his successors.

Two concerns apparently led to the establishment of the Quality of Life Review process, the first emanating from the senior White House staff, the second from the professional bureaucracy within the Office of Management and Budget (OMB). When the newly established Environmental Protection Agency (EPA) began to spew forth regulations in response to the various statutes it was charged with administering, the period of good feeling that had generated a broad national consensus that something ought to be done to protect the environment—a consensus that had led to events such as Earth Day—quickly began to come unraveled. Industry became alarmed about the potential costs of the regulations. This alarm was transmitted to the Commerce Department and especially to its secretary, Maurice Stans. Stans began to publicly urge EPA to go slow (the title of one of his more famous speeches was "Wait a Minute"). When Stans pressed his point with the White House, John Ehrlichman, President Nixon's chief domestic policy aide, established a task force to determine how to bring EPA's regulatory program under more central control.

At about this same time, officials within OMB were becoming uneasy about the budgetary and broader policy consequences of EPA's programs. EPA's rapid staff expansion required budgetary resources. More important, certain EPA programs, especially those attacking water pollution, had significant budgetary implications. Although the bulk of the costs imposed in controlling air pollution, pesticides, or noise (EPA's other principal initial areas of responsibility) fell on the private sector, the water pollution control program, which involved substantial federal grants for sewage and water treatment plants, had an important impact on the budget.

In December 1970, OMB received a multimillion-dollar supplemental budget request from EPA including significant funds to enforce new water-quality standards. According to Glenn Schleede, a former OMB official, this request was instrumental in causing OMB to conclude that no one was looking at the impact of EPA's growing number of regulations on the budget, presidential policy, other federal agencies, or the private sector—and that OMB should fill this void.[3]

Under the Budget Act of 1920, OMB had clear authority to oversee the budgeting decisions of the executive branch. It had also traditionally been given a role in coordinating executive branch legislative initiatives and congressional testimony delivered by administration officials. But for the case at hand, these authorities meant little. The size of the EPA budget would be determined largely by the price and scope of EPA rule making. If the budgetary and other implications of environmental programs were to be scrutinized and some coordination with the programs of other agencies and departments achieved, the regulations themselves would have to be reviewed before they were issued.

But reviewing proposed regulations posed a legal problem. The formal authority to issue environmental regulations lay with the EPA administrator. To be sure, he was a presidential appointee and could be removed from office whenever the president wished—that is, "without cause." But how could effective budgetary oversight and executive branch policy coordination be achieved short of taking this draconian step?

Events apparently moved along two parallel tracks. In a letter from OMB Director George Schultz to EPA Administrator William Ruckleshaus dated

May 21, 1971, OMB asserted authority to review *and clear* EPA's regulations.[4] Then in June, John Ehrlichman issued a memorandum establishing a Quality of Life committee composed of Domestic Council members, such as Council on Environmental Quality (CEQ) Chairman Train, EPA Administrator Ruckleshaus, and other members of the White House staff. The job of this committee was to explore the desirability of establishing a high-level, possibly permanent body to review important regulations affecting the "balance" between "consumer and environmental interests, industrial requirements, and safety aspects."[5]

This group originally proposed that OMB and the White House share regulatory review responsibilities. OMB would identify actions requiring review by other agencies through monitoring by budget examiners and advance notice from agencies issuing regulations. When agency positions conflicted, either OMB's assistant director for natural resources or a high-level staff member of the Domestic Council would review the specifics of the case and render a decision. If disagreement persisted at this level, the matter would be referred to Ehrlichman and the Domestic Council for a decision.

It soon became clear that this proposal, which explicitly shifted significant regulatory decision-making authority from the head of the agency in which it was lodged (e.g., the administrator of EPA) to the OMB and the White House, would encounter significant legal and political barriers. Therefore, the proposal was modified to downplay the decision-making role of the White House and OMB. In fact, in the memo from OMB Director Schultz establishing the Quality of Life Review process, the formal clearance requirement was not mentioned, and the role, if any, to be played by the Domestic Council in resolving interagency disputes was not addressed.

The review process that was established emphasized prior notice and opportunity for interagency comment. At least thirty days before the publication of any "significant" proposed rule,[6] an agency was to submit the rule to OMB, along with an analysis including the principal objectives of the regulation, alternatives to the proposed action that had been considered, a comparison of the expected benefits and costs of the proposal and its alternatives, and the reasons for selecting the proposed alternative. OMB would then solicit the views of the other agencies and departments on the proposal, review the comments, and forward them to the agency proposing the regulation.

A similar set of requirements was to apply to final rules. Twenty days before a final rule was to be published, the agency proposing to issue it was to provide OMB with a copy of the draft final rule, a summary of public comments, and a statement of any new issues that had been raised. The interagency review process would then be repeated if necessary.

The Quality of Life Review Process in Practice

The operation of the Quality of Life Review process did little to quiet the fears of people who had been concerned that it represented nothing more than an attempt to "rein in" EPA. Although Schultz's memo establishing the program had indicated that it was to apply to the proposed rules of a number of executive branch agencies, in practice only EPA's rules were singled out for review under the Quality of Life Review procedures. One observer provides the following explanation:

> The reason for the narrow focus stems from the program's creation: it was the Natural Resource budget shop within OMB which developed the procedure, stimulated by White House interest which in turn was influenced by Secretary Stans' abhorrence of environmental regulations.[7]

The budget examiners for agencies other than EPA apparently made no moves to implement the procedures; the budget examiner for the FDA reported that he "simply ignored" the Schultz memo.[8]

The reviews themselves reportedly consisted of heated arguments between EPA and the Department of Commerce, its principal antagonist, with OMB at times playing a mediating role and at times pressing its own institutional interests (which generally were opposed to EPA's).[9] At first, the main "analysis" presented during such reviews was industry-prepared information presented by the Commerce Department.[10] Later, however, and as much for defensive reasons as anything else, EPA established its own Office of Planning and Evaluation to prepare analyses.

Participation by other executive branch agencies and departments and by executive office bodies like CEQ, CEA, and the Office of Science and Technology Policy, was sporadic. Certainly these bodies did not as a rule supply independent analyses of the impact of the proposed regulations.

We noted earlier that the issue of who would ultimately resolve conflicts that existed after the interagency review process was completed was deliberately not specified in the Schultz memo. But the White House apparently did take a hand—though quietly—in this dispute resolution process. A memo written by a White House participant in January 1973 reveals this information:

> EPA receives, consolidates and synthesizes these comments, and gives reasons why they are not following any other advice. The Executive Office agencies look over their shoulder at this point and resolve remaining differences either by papers or meetings.[11]

And former EPA Administrator John Quarles noted in a book published in 1976 that Ruckleshaus required as a condition of his remaining EPA administrator after the 1972 election that Nixon clarify that final authority over the issuance of rules lay with the EPA administrator. He reports that Nixon agreed to this, but that written confirmation of this point was not received until the summer of 1973.[12]

Although controversial and sometimes acrimonious,[13] the Quality of Life Review process did have benefits: (1) As already noted, it persuaded EPA that the agency needed to have its own in-house analytical capability. (2) It led EPA to begin informal consultation with industry and with other affected agencies and departments earlier in the regulatory development process in order to head off controversy at the formal interagency review stage. (3) Finally, it prompted EPA to establish an elaborate internal clearance procedure whereby proposed regulations of one program area were reviewed in EPA working groups and, if necessary, by assistant administrators or other program areas. But the seemingly arbitrary operation of the review created ill will among environmentalists, their allies in Congress, many of the professional staff at EPA, and former EPA officials. This legacy would haunt all future White House oversight efforts and become especially virulent during the Reagan administration.[14]

Innovations during the Ford Administration

Concern about the possible relationship between regulation—not merely EPA regulation, but regulation of all sorts—and inflation surfaced during the economic summit President Ford held soon after taking office. As a result, Ford issued an executive order requiring that "major proposals for legislation and for the promulgation of rules by any executive branch agency must be accompanied by a statement which certifies that the inflationary impact of the proposal has been evaluated." The order also empowered the OMB director "to the extent permitted by law, to develop criteria for the identification of major legislative proposals, regulations, and rules emanating from the executive branch which may have a significant impact on inflation and to prescribe procedures of their evaluation."[15] Although this order maintained the impact on the federal budget as one criterion for determining whether a regulation was "significant," the order clearly focused on the private, not the public, costs of regulation.

The Quality of Life Review process was still operating (indeed, it would operate until acting Administrator John Quarles sent a memo to OMB in January 1977 stating that the agency would no longer comply), but this new authority to require inflation impact statements was *not* lodged in the "budget" side of OMB but in the "management" side. It appears, at least originally, not to have been viewed as a substantive regulatory oversight tool (and therefore as a complement or even competitor to the Quality of Life Review process), but merely as a way of manifesting presidential concern with the potential inflationary consequences of "excessive and unnecessary" regulation.

However, OMB did not turn out to be the only executive office agency concerned with the inflation impact statement requirement. Three months before President Ford issued the executive order, he had asked for and obtained legislation creating the Council on Wage and Price Stability (CWPS), a small agency in the executive office of the president, which was charged with "jawboning" industry and labor to moderate their wage demands and price increases. This was the president's response to the political need to "do something" about inflation (which at that time was proceeding at the then-incredible rate of 11 percent per year, fueled by energy price increases and commodity shortages) while still eliminating the formal wage and price control authority that Ford found distasteful.[16]

But the Council on Wage and Price Stability became involved in regulatory oversight as well. In the president's October message to the Congress on the economy, CWPS was assigned a role in monitoring the inflationary costs of government action. The CWPS staff soon insisted, against minor opposition from OMB, that the inflation impact statement requirement in the president's executive order be treated substantively—not merely as window dressing. Thus, OMB did not delegate authority to oversee compliance with the requirement to the individual agencies—something OMB at first had wanted to do. Instead, monitoring responsibility was divided between OMB and the CWPS staff. The CWPS staff intended to use this power to pressure the executive branch agencies into analyzing the likely economic consequences of regulations they were proposing.

The CWPS staff's involvement in regulation went further. The legislation creating CWPS directed it to "review and appraise the various programs, policies, and activities of the departments and agencies of the United States for the purpose of determining the extent to which these programs and activities are contributing to inflation."[17] The staff, unaware of the Quality of Life Review process, began to prepare analyses of the economic impact of proposed rules, regulations, and adjudications and to file these analyses on the public record.

This program of public filings began almost by accident. In fact, the initial filing arose out of a desire on the part of CWPS to avoid being seen as attempting to control prices. In late 1974, when CWPS was just beginning operations, it was approached by the American Telephone and Telegraph Company (AT&T) and asked to "preclear" a large proposed increase in interstate rates that the company was preparing to file with the FCC. Such a process of "preclearing" regulatory filings had been required under the price control rules administered by CWPS's predecessor, the Cost of Living Council.

As we have already noted, the Council on Wage and Price Stability had no price control authority, and both it and the White House were eager to dispel any sense among industry or the public that it sought and, if given, would exercise (even indirectly) such authority. Therefore, it refused to issue the requested preclearance. However, staff members were concerned about the rate request and wanted to comment on it. They therefore decided to file public comments on the proposed rate request with the FCC.

At about the same time, the head of the National Highway Traffic Safety Administration (NHTSA) asked CWPS staff to review a cost-benefit analysis his staff had conducted on Motor Vehicle Safety Standard 121, a proposed regulation concerning the performance of truck air-braking systems. The staff found that the benefit estimates prepared by NHTSA were faulty and, following the AT&T precedent, filed its comments in the public record.

Thus was born the CWPS filing—a formal analysis of the possible economic consequences of important proposed regulations prepared by staff of the executive office of the president and filed on the public record at the close of the public comment period. By the end of the Ford administration, the CWPS staff had issued approximately 125 statements and analyses covering regulations proposed by ten executive branch and eleven independent agencies.[18]

A number of these filings concerned proposed EPA rules. These were handled just the same as proposals from other agencies, although to the best of our knowledge, CWPS staff never participated in any Quality of Life Reviews.

Few organizations within the Ford White House escaped some involvement with regulatory issues. Roger Porter, in his book on the operation of the Economic Policy Board (EPB), the Ford administration's top economic policymaking body, reports that EPB's agenda routinely included regulatory issues, including "inflation impact statements, banking regulation, financial institutions reform, antitrust policy, transportation regulatory policy, and the work of special task forces to improve government regulation by examining the regulatory activities of various regulatory agencies."[19]

We know that the EPB occasionally discussed important executive branch regulatory actions—one of the authors of this book participated in one such discussion. On this occasion, the head of the cabinet department proposing to issue the final rule was asked to brief the EPB on the content of the rule and to indicate how he prepared to deal with issues the CWPS staff raised in their public filing. If this occasion was typical of EPB regulatory involvement, there was no impression that this body was in any sense acting as the ultimate decision maker concerning the shape of the final regulation.

One of the special task forces Porter mentions in his book was the Domestic Council Review Group (DCRG) on Regulatory Reform, established in June 1975. In a report at the end of the Ford administration, this group summarized and analyzed the Ford administration's regulatory oversight activities. The DCRG noted that although the Quality of Life Review process (by then largely moribund) had been "criticized by some environmentalists," DCRG judged it to have been "effective in helping EPA decision makers test the water before going public in the *Federal Register.*" The requirement for an inflation impact statement was termed a "partial answer" to the problem of assuring that all relevant information on which to base regulatory decisions was made available and used. Although some agencies, aided by the requirement, had "exhibited increased sensitivity to the economic consequences of their decisions," the DCRG report said, it was "not clear whether the analysis was being used, as intended, early enough in the decision-making process to serve as an aid to comparing alternatives." The report also called for the creation of "more effective interagency review procedures for new regulatory proposals."[20]

The Ford administration was a time of testing and experimentation, not all of it planned, during which the operation of regulatory oversight was broadened beyond EPA, and the executive office units engaged in the oversight process were broadened beyond OMB. In keeping with the spirit of an administration determined to heal the wounds and suspicions of Watergate, the Ford regulatory review processes were more open and evenhanded than the Nixon ones had been.

The concept of public filings by the CWPS proved to be popular—enough so that when questions were raised in 1975 about the CWPS's authority to make such filings, Congress responded by amending CWPS's enabling legislation to confirm its powers "to intervene and otherwise participate on its own behalf in rule-making, ratemaking, licensing, and other proceedings before any of the departments and agencies of the United States in order to present its views as to the inflationary impact that might result from the possible outcomes of such proceedings."[21]

The increased professionalism that characterized the process of regulatory review (and indeed the entire process of social regulation) during the Ford administration was another important legacy. Environmental protection, worker health and safety, and consumer product safety might still be politically controversial issues about which reasonable people could strongly disagree. But most members of the Ford administration accepted the underlying principle that such regulation was socially desirable. The objective of the administration thus was to achieve the goals of such regulation, but to achieve them as efficiently and as inexpensively as possible.

Regulatory Oversight in the Carter Administration

President Carter received considerable support during his election campaign from environmentalists and organized labor, and he entered office strongly committed to an active and effective program of social regulation. Many of his appointees to important positions had strong protectionist leanings. Others among his close advisers, however, especially those charged with shaping his economic programs, although sympathetic to social regulation, made no secret of their strong belief that it should (and could) be made more effective and considerably less costly.

Probably the most vocal of these advisers was Charles Schultze, the president's choice to head the Council of Economic Advisers (CEA). In November and December 1976, just prior to his assuming the post of CEA chairman, Schultze, then a senior fellow at the Brookings Institution, delivered the prestigious Godkin Lectures at Harvard University. In these lectures, which were later widely published,[22] Schultze argued that the system of "command and control" regulation that had become the norm during the 1970s not only was a less than fully effective method of achieving social regulation's laudable goals but also imposed unnecessarily large costs on the economy.

The stage was therefore set for conflict. Carter's appointees who favored both the goals and the techniques of social regulation and believed that the previous two administrations had not pushed nearly hard enough in these areas were bound to clash with appointees like Schultze who were concerned with minimizing regulation's adverse impact on the economy. This clash was not long in coming.

Carter inherited certain oversight institutions and procedures from the Ford administration. Ford's executive order requiring "inflation impact statements" was still in force. The Council on Wage and Price Stability still existed, and its staff continued to make public filings on the economic impact of proposed regulations. Between January 20 and June 30, 1977, CWPS made 20 filings on EPA's air emission trading policy, OSHA's proposed lead standard, OSHA's proposed sulfur dioxide standard, EPA's proposed emission standards for grain elevators, the Department of Transportation's (NHTSA's) proposal on passive restraints, and others.

The Quality of Life Review process per se, however, was no more. After the Ford administration left office, but before President Carter's appointee to head the Environmental Protection Agency—Douglas Costle—had taken his post, John Quarles, the holdover acting administrator of the agency, wrote to the director of the OMB informing him that EPA would no longer comply with the requirements of the Quality of Life Review process. According to one author, no reply from OMB was ever received,[23] and the matter was allowed to drop. Once Costle *did* arrive, EPA reaffirmed its intention to continue the formal internal review procedures and the informal interagency consultation that the Quality of Life Review process had stimulated. Costle also strengthened his Office of Planning and Management, the inside group of economists and program analysts that had been created earlier to improve the quality of EPA regulatory analysis.

Almost from their very first day on the job, officials in the Carter White House began to wrestle with the problem of devising something that would give them some control over the rule-making activities of executive branch agencies (not merely EPA) without the perceived disadvantages of the Quality of Life Review process. Early in 1977, the Economic Policy Group (EPG), the successor to Ford's EPB, assigned CEA Chairman Schultze the main responsibility for developing this new review process. By late March or early April, a proposal had been developed and was circulated within the White House and then to certain interested agencies (such as the Department of Labor within which OSHA was located). On August 1, the proposal, which in the interim had been further refined, was formally circulated for interagency comment.

The CEA proposal had two main elements: a broadened requirement for analyses and a mechanism for formal interagency review of these analyses.[24] Because the Carter staff thought that the analyses prepared during the Ford administration had been too narrowly focused on regulatory costs and benefits, the new requirement was to be focused on achieving cost-effective regulation, not in deciding, through a formal or informal comparison of benefits and costs, whether a regulation was justified. These analyses (or a selected subset of them) were to be reviewed by a formal interagency group, to be known as the Regulatory Analysis Review Group (RARG), consisting of the principal "economic agencies" of the Economic Policy Group (Treasury, Labor, and Commerce), OMB, CEA, and other executive branch agencies with significant regulatory responsibility (virtually all other significant executive branch agencies). The decision to subject a proposed regulation to review would be made by an executive committee of their review group, consisting of the five EPG economic agencies just mentioned. If the committee decided to review a proposed regulation, it would formally notify the agency, and CWPS staff would prepare a draft review. Before the scheduled public comment period closed, the draft review would be circulated to all members of the review group; comments would be received; a meeting held if necessary to resolve conflicts; and the completed review, reflecting any changes resulting from this process and perhaps including dissents, would be filed.

The CEA proposal encountered opposition from various parts of the executive branch. EPA in particular raised questions concerning whether *any* review process involving the White House or executive office agencies was appropriate. Costle clearly stated the basis for his objections:

> As you know, the "Quality of Life Review" as practiced by the last Administration did little to improve government regulation; instead it became a battleground that has left deep scars. Many in EPA and in Congress, for example, perceive that it was used more to frustrate EPA in the pursuit of its legal responsibilities than to ensure responsible economic analysis. We must take care not to reopen these old scars now. Justified or not, these historical memories leave a series of sensitivities with which any system legitimately designed to encourage good economic analysis must deal.[25]

Costle proposed as an alternative a process modeled closely on what EPA was then doing, without a formal interagency review.

Questions also were raised about the composition of the executive committee (which clearly favored the "economic" agencies) and about the wisdom of putting into place a new review process before the old executive order (which was viewed as flawed) had been modified.

Discussions and negotiations went on into the fall, with the issue finally being taken to the president himself. In one memo to the president, Costle argued against the proposal on the grounds that introducing a process analogous to the Quality of Life Review (which he characterized as having been "misused" to "control/ muzzle" EPA) only nine months after that process had been ended "will probably be misinterpreted and actually hinder reform."[26] Carter sided with Schultze, but ordered that the program be reviewed after six months.[27]

When the Carter review process was finally announced, certain of the concerns that EPA had voiced had been dealt with. The membership of the executive committee had been changed to provide less weight to the economic agencies. The number of reviews per year per agency was limited to four—to prevent any one agency's regulations from being singled out for excessive attention. Care had been taken to structure the process so that it could not be used to delay regulations; the review would have to fit into whatever public comment period the agency proposing the rule normally would use (typically sixty days, but sometimes shorter).

Even after what one participant characterized as "months of intense interagency negotiations," disagreements remained over the powers that the reviewing group ought to have. For example, as late as mid-January 1978, the Treasury Department tried to persuade the EPG to reopen this issue. Terming the Carter program as "the direct descendent of the Ford Administration's Inflation Impact Statement program, which was widely regarded as ineffectual," Treasury proposed raising the prestige of the new Carter program by appointing a "full-time, highly placed official with adequate staff" to run it; giving the official authority to review existing as well as proposed regulations and to group related regulations for review; and charging the official with holding public hearings around the country in order to serve as a "lightning rod for public complaints."

Treasury also sought to reopen the touchy area of the authority of the executive to resolve disputes. Acknowledging that "it is not clear whether, or to what extent, a Presidentially designated review authority would have the legal power to second guess an exercise of regulatory discretion by an Executive agency (e.g., EPA, OSHA) granted that discretion by statute," Treasury nevertheless recommended that this issue be "re-explored" with the Justice Department "keeping open the possibility of introducing legislation to strengthen Presidential review power over Executive Branch regulatory agencies."[28] Treasury's recommendations were not accepted, but the later appointment of Alfred Kahn, the chairman of the Civil Aeronautics Board and a noted advocate of regulatory reform, to the previously ceremonial post of chairman of the CWPS and, at the same time, to the post of the President's Special Adviser on Inflation, seems to fit Treasury's description of the kind of appointee to head the regulatory analysis program. (Ironically, Kahn never was able to devote much time to regulatory matters, because inflation heated up and the wage- and price-monitoring activities of CWPS significantly increased.)

As already noted, the Carter executive order requiring agencies to prepare economic impact statements (rather than inflation impact statements) was promulgated in late March 1978. Despite all the assertions about how the order would differ from Ford's, the two were remarkably similar. The Carter order did expand the requirements for the public to participate in the regulatory process and for agency decision makers to actually be familiar with the regulations they were issuing. The analytical requirements in the Carter order were little different from those in Ford's order. Power remained with the agencies to decide what rules were "major" and thus subject to the requirement. The scope of an analysis was somewhat broader, and stress was laid on cost-effectiveness and the use of least-cost alternatives, but not all that much had really changed.

The Carter Review Process in Practice.   As was the case in both the Nixon
and Ford regulatory oversight programs, the issue of who bore the ultimate
responsibility for regulatory decision making was not addressed either in the
Carter executive order or in the memorandums establishing the requirement
for regulatory analysis review. But the question was soon to be starkly posed.
In late 1976, the Occupational Safety and Health Administration had proposed
to issue new and costly regulations limiting the level of worker exposure to
cotton dust. In June 1977, the Council on Wage and Price Stability staff filed
comments on the proposal, charging that it cost too much for the benefits
obtained, but CWPS took no further action at the time. In early May 1978,
as OSHA was moving toward the issuance of its final rule, Schultze requested
the Regulatory Analysis Review Group (of which he was chairman) to informally review the final OSHA standard. Secretary of Labor Ray Marshall
later wrote President Carter that "this request came at the very end of the
decision process and outside of the agreed upon procedures for regulatory
review."[29] The review, which actually was undertaken by the CWPS staff,
raised numerous objections to the final rule that OSHA was proposing to
issue and recommended that the rule be held up until the objections could be
dealt with. A number of them apparently were resolved at the staff level, but
eventually Schultze asked President Carter to agree to have the rule softened.
Schultze came away from the meeting convinced that the president had agreed,
and wrote Marshall conveying what he took to be the president's instructions.
Marshall, however, requested his own meeting with Carter and persuaded the
president to permit the rule to go forward largely unchanged. The only significant weakening was that it permitted a four-year phase-in period to lessen
the economic burden on the industry.

    Almost certainly this was not the first time that a president had intervened
personally to alter a final rule issued by a social regulatory agency. But the
episode attracted an unusual amount of public attention. OSHA had been
under a court order to issue the regulation by a certain date, and the dispute
at the White House prevented it from doing so. When OSHA went to court
to explain to the judge why the date had been missed, the presidential involvement came to light. On June 7, the week after the Schultze memo
instructing Marshall to alter the standard, the *Washington Post* ran a front-
page story titled "White House Orders Cutback in Program Against Brown
Lung Disease."[30] The story referred to Schultze's June 5 memo as "the
strongest evidence thus far of White House efforts to examine regulations for
their effect on inflation and clamp down when opportunities for cost-cutting
are found." The *Post* story also noted that EPA was under increasing pressure
to relax some of its control requirements.

Marshall's meeting with the president was also reported in the *Post*. The story, titled "Carter Clears Way for Issuance of Cotton Dust Limit," termed the results of the meeting a "partial reversal" of the president's earlier decision and characterized Labor Department officials as "almost ecstatic in their reaction" to it.[31] Finally, on June 20, the *Post* carried an account of the news conference at which Marshall and Schultze jointly announced the final regulations.[32]

The *New York Times* also covered the story, though not as intensely as the *Post*. A long article in the business section on June 14 treated the issue as one manifestation of the struggle over regulation's costs and benefits.[33] And in its lead editorial on June 16 the newspaper noted that the upcoming final rule would have "great symbolic effect."[34] The editorial did not come out against presidential intervention in rule making or even the consideration of costs in framing such rules. It referred to the intervention by the president's inflation fighters as "right," but stated that "the fight against inflation should not require risking the health of the nation's most vulnerable workers." The editorial argued that the trade-off that was being made should be explicitly stated: "That would allow a fair political challenge of its value judgments."

The cotton dust case showed the potential political costs to presidents and their aides of getting involved in major regulatory issues. According to Christopher DeMuth, who was to become head of the Office of Information and Regulatory Affairs in Reagan's OMB, Carter never again showed much stomach for trying to control regulatory costs, and his advisers (especially Schultze) were hesitant to take such issues to him.[35]

The handling of the cotton dust case contrasts with the handling of EPA's proposed revision of the national ambient air quality standard for ozone. These latter extremely costly regulations, which were proposed in June 1978 (in fact, during the same week the final cotton dust regulation was issued), also became a matter of considerable dispute between the president's inflation fighters and the agency that issued them. In this instance, the normal review procedures were followed. The Regulatory Analysis Review Group prepared and filed its report during the public comment period. Schultze and his staff followed the development of the final rule thereafter. As the time drew close for EPA to issue the rule, Schultze and Costle became involved in heated discussion about its content. Although EPA eventually softened the rule somewhat, cutting its annual costs by more than a billion dollars, Schultze chose not to take the issue to the president, even though he clearly thought the rule should have been somewhat further relaxed.

As in the case of cotton dust, EPA's relaxation of the rule and the involvement of the White House came to light in the newspapers. At a subsequent press conference, when the president was asked whether he had intervened, he replied:

> The regulators, Doug Costle and the others, know that they have authority to consider . . . economic considerations and they're to make their judgments accordingly. I have not interfered in that process. I have a statutory responsibility and a right to do so, but I think it would be a very rare occasion whenever I would want to do so.[36]

DeMuth interprets that answer as:

> a clear signal that [Carter] wished to leave final regulatory judgments to his regulatory officials themselves—and that his staff regulatory reviewers were to function primarily as kibitzers rather than as super-regulators threatening presidential intercession to force compliance with their own policy ideas.[37]

DeMuth probably overstates the impact of the cotton dust case on regulatory oversight during the Carter administration, but the case may have brought about significant changes in administration oversight procedures. In late June or early July 1978, just as cotton dust was being wound up, CEA staff began the review of RARG that Carter had ordered as a condition of his initial approval. Suggestions were solicited from various executive branch agencies and departments concerning how RARG could be improved. Numerous suggestions for both strengthening and weakening RARG were received.[38] And in late October 1978, President Carter sent a memo to the heads of executive departments and agencies announcing creation of a new regulatory advisory group, the Regulatory Council, and changes in the RARG.

The Regulatory Council was to consist of representatives of all executive branch and independent federal agencies having significant regulatory responsibilities. (The independent agencies were to be "invited" to join.) The council was charged with the task of compiling and publishing at six-month intervals a comprehensive calendar of all forthcoming federal regulations—the first time this had been done. The president also directed the council to help develop and encourage the use of more cost-effective methods of regulation.

The changes in the RARG were essentially procedural. The criteria that would be used in selecting regulatory analyses for review were made explicit, and the procedures for conducting a review were spelled out.

At about this time, Alfred Kahn joined the White House staff with the twin titles mentioned earlier—chairman of the Council on Wage and Price Stability and special adviser to the president on inflation. Kahn was fresh from his triumph of presiding over the legislative and administrative deregulation of the airline industry. He was persuaded to take the new job with the promise that he would be heavily involved in regulatory reform issues.

Some people interpreted these moves as a slap at Schultze and a downgrading of RARG. Kahn's appointment was viewed as a shift in the locus of regulatory oversight responsibility away from Schultze, who had had the field virtually to himself. The Regulatory Council, which was to be under EPA Administrator Costle's direction (indeed, it was to be funded from EPA's budget) was seen as a counterweight to RARG and a regulator's lobby.

As things turned out, the Regulatory Council and the White House economists managed to work smoothly together. RARG found the regulatory calendar an invaluable tool for planning the review of upcoming regulations. And the work of the Regulatory Council in publicizing problems caused by regulation and ways of using innovative regulatory techniques encouraged regulators to think seriously about both issues. The fact that the Regulatory Council—a body nominally controlled by the regulators—began to urge the use of more flexible, less burdensome regulatory techniques and focused attention on some of regulation's perceived excesses through its study, *Regulation: The View From Janesville, Wisconsin*, helped assure such issues increased attention among the regulatory community.

Kahn's appointment did not entirely change the locus of responsibility for regulatory oversight in the White House. For a while, he held a series of informal meetings at which the president's chief domestic policy aides discussed forthcoming important regulatory activities and developed priorities and strategies for intervention. But as we have already noted, Kahn soon became absorbed with running the administration's substantially broadened program of wage and price jawboning. Most of the responsibility for following regulatory matters shifted back to the CEA and was carried out at the deputies' level.

At about the same time (that is, near the end of 1978), the procedures for White House intervention in rule making following the formal public comment period were standardized. Kahn's role in stimulating this action is not known; in the aftermath of the cotton dust case, the administration may have decided that such *ad hoc* interventions caused more trouble than they were worth. Consultations between the Justice Department and the White House produced procedures that permitted White House involvement after the close of the comment period. The procedures and the contacts they authorized appeared to be legally valid.

In December 1978, CEA staff used these procedures to head off a potentially explosive (both politically and legally) confrontation with the Department of the Interior over White House postcomment involvement in stripmining regulation.[39] The procedures helped secure dismissal of a suit brought

by the Natural Resources Defense Council (NRDC) against the Council of
Economic Advisers seeking to have the latter barred from participation in the
development of the strip-mining regulations on the grounds that this participation constituted illegal ex parte contact.[40] The court cited the Interior
Department's insertion into the administrative record of a "catalog" of all
oral and written comments between the CEA and outside parties, as well as
a list of all contacts between the Interior Department's Office of Surface
Mining and the CEA (in accordance with the procedures worked out by the
CEA and the Justice Department), as rendering unnecessary the injunction
that NRDC sought. The court noted that the existence of this record would
enable any reviewing court to determine if the final rule was indeed "tainted"
by the CEA's having served as a conduit for improper industry influence on
the proceedings and to determine the appropriate remedy.

The procedures were to be subjected to further legal and legislative
challenges. In early 1979, two important EPA final rules were issued. The
revision of national ambient air quality standards for ozone has already been
mentioned. The second was the issuance of the new source performance
standards for steam electric power plants. Both regulations involved annual
costs running into the billions of dollars. Both had been "RARGed" during
the proposal stage. Both were the subject of active White House postcomment
involvement carried out under the new guidelines developed in late 1978.

The ozone standard, which "went final" in February 1979, seems never
to have actually been seen by the president. Under pressure from Schultze
and other White House economic advisers, however, EPA weakened the
standard somewhat. As a result, Senator Muskie called hearings of his Subcommittee on Environmental Pollution to explore the role that the White
House had played in this rule making. On February 27, Costle, Schultze, and
Kahn appeared before Muskie's committee to discuss these issues. Muskie
argued that EPA was an independent agency and thus should be as free of
White House pressures as the ICC, FCC, or CAB were. Schultze reminded
Muskie that EPA had been located within the executive branch and thus was
subject to presidential oversight, provided this oversight did not impair its
ability to carry out its statutory responsibilities.

Costle acknowledged that he had been strongly pressured by Schultze,
Kahn, and Frank Press, the president's science adviser, to weaken the ozone
standard, but argued that none of this contact was improper. Final decision-
making responsibility always rested with him, and all contacts between EPA
and White House officials had been logged and made part of the public
record.[41] In response to written questions submitted by Muskie after the
hearing, Schultze stressed the procedures employed by the Carter White House
to assure that White House staff did not exercise improper influence over

agency rule-making activities and that all contacts were logged and made part of the record.[42]

The issuance of the new source performance standards for steam electric power plants in June 1979 produced a less immediate but more significant challenge to the Carter regulatory oversight process. This rule making, which also originated in the Ford administration, involved a revision of regulations that would substantially affect the emissions characteristics and operating costs of all new coal-burning electric power plants. EPA formally proposed the regulations in September 1978, and an RARG report was filed on January 15, 1979, at the end of the public comment period. As EPA moved during the spring of 1979 to complete the rule making, White House staffs followed the issue closely.[43]

Several meetings involving successively higher-level officials at EPA and the White House were held in an attempt to settle the differences over the final rule. Eventually the president met with Costle, Schultze, Kahn, and a few others; after this meeting, EPA issued its rule.

As is typical in such instances, the outcome pleased no one. The environmentalists and their allies in Congress were unhappy that the final rule was not tougher. The electric power and coal industries and their allies in Congress were convinced that the rule should have been weaker. Not surprisingly, both groups brought suits to have the rule overturned. The case, *Sierra Club* v. *Costle*, focused heavily on the White House postcomment activities.[44]

The Environmental Defense Fund (EDF) charged that an "ex parte blitz" by the coal industry, in which White House personnel (and Senator Byrd of West Virginia) served as conduits for information supplied by the industry, was instrumental in causing EPA to promulgate a standard that was weaker than the one EPA had originally been disposed to issue. EDF listed nine meetings (including six in which White House staff were present and one in which the president himself participated) that it considered crucial in shaping EPA's final decision. Summaries of all the meetings except the one the president attended were included in the rule-making record.

In her opinion in *Sierra Club*, Judge Patricia Wald of the District of Columbia Court of Appeals weighed at length the conflicting pressures involved in presidential regulatory oversight. She rejected the claim that agencies like EPA, although located within the executive branch, should be immune from presidential scrutiny:

> The court recognizes the basic need of the President and his White House staff to monitor the consistency of executive agency regulations with Administration policy. He and his White House advisers surely must be briefed fully and

frequently about rules in the making and their contributions to policymaking considered. The idea of a "plural executive," or a President with a council of state, was considered and rejected by the Constitutional Convention. Instead the Founders chose to risk the potential for tyranny inherent in placing power in one person, in order to gain the advantage of accountability fixed on a single source. To ensure the President's control and supervision over the Executive Branch, the Constitution—and its judicial gloss—vests him with the powers of appointment and removal, the power to demand written opinions from executive officers, and the right to invoke executive privilege to protect consultative privacy. In the particular case of EPA, Presidential authority is clear since it has never been considered an "independent agency," but always part of the Executive Branch.[45]

But Wald also recognized that the ability of the courts to review an agency decision to assure its consistency with applicable statutes required that information concerning how the decision was made be part of the public record:

We recognize, however, that there may be instances where the docketing of conversations between the President or his staff and other Executive Branch officers or rulemaking may be necessary to ensure due process. This may be true, for example, where such conversations directly concern the outcome of adjudications or quasi-adjudicatory proceedings; there is no inherent executive power to control the rights of individuals in such settings. Docketing may also be necessary in some circumstances where a statute like this one *specifically requires* that essential "information or data" upon which a rule is based be docketed. But in the absence of any further congressional requirements, we hold that it was not unlawful in this case for EPA not to docket a face-to-face policy session involving the President and EPA officials during the post-comment period, since EPA makes no effort to base the rule on any "data or information" arising from that meeting. . . . The purposes of full-record review which underlie the need for disclosing ex parte conversations in some settings do not require that courts know the details of every White House contact, including a Presidential one, in this informal rulemaking setting. After all, any rule issued here with or without White House assistance must have the requisite *factual support* in the rulemaking record, and under this particular statute the Administrator must not base the rule in whole or in part on any "*data or information*" which is not in the record, no matter what the source. The courts will monitor all this, but they need not be omniscient to perform their role effectively. Of course, it is always possible that undisclosed Presidential prodding may direct an outcome that *is* factually based on the record, but different from the outcome that would have obtained in the absence of Presidential involvement. In such a case, it would be true that the political process did affect the outcome in a way that the courts could not police. But we do not believe that Congress intended that the courts convert informal rulemaking into a rarified technocratic process, unaffected by political considerations or the presence of Presidential power.[46]

Wald's decision thus upheld the procedures worked out by the Carter White House staff members to guide their postcomment activities. It upheld the concept of presidential involvement in executive branch rule-making activity provided this involvement was not conducted in a way to prevent reviewing courts from carrying out their assigned functions and provided it did not lead agencies to reach conclusions that were unsupported by the rule-making record or that lay outside their statutory mandates.

In a second case, decided soon after *Sierra Club*, the propriety of White House postcomment activity was also an issue. This case, known as *American Petroleum Institute (API)* v. *Costle*,[47] concerned the revision of the national ambient air quality standard for ozone, a final rule that, as noted above, actually was issued five months before the one that figured in *Sierra Club*. In the ozone revision rule making, discussions between the White House and EPA apparently did not reach the presidential level. But there was an important twist in ozone. Just before the final rule was issued, and *after* a series of EPA-White House meetings, EPA placed in the rule-making record a staff paper, which the Environmental Defense Fund claimed served as the primary basis for the relaxation of the standard to which Costle ultimately agreed. The court termed this last-minute addition of apparently important information "disturbing," but dismissed the objection on the technical grounds that it had not been made in a timely manner, thereby sidestepping this difficult issue. Judge Wald dissented from this part of the court's opinion, arguing that the issue should have been heard by the court.

The Status and Perceived Effectiveness of White House Regulatory Oversight by January 1981

By the end of the Carter administration, the procedures for interagency review of important executive branch regulations and for White House involvement in postcomment rule-making activities had been established and upheld by the courts (to the extent that the courts had chosen to address the issue). A generally acceptable set of ground rules had been worked out, and the pros and cons of an active presidential role were understood. The president would not himself become frequently involved in such issues, but his senior aides and their staffs might well do so, keeping in mind important limitations on their activities. They could not, for example, introduce policy considerations clearly outside an agency's statutory bounds. If, during the postcomment period, they wished to raise an issue that *was* permissible for an agency to consider, they would have to be sure that the information on which their intervention was based was indeed part of the rule-making record. The device of the RARG filing helped to assure that the rule-making record did include all issues that the White House might eventually wish to see raised. White House staffs also had to avoid becoming a conduit for the introduction of impermissible information from outside parties. They had to be careful about whom they talked with during the postcomment activities and to see that summaries of all relevant conversations with the agency in question (and with affected industry or public interest groups, if such conversations inadvertently occurred) were placed in the rule-making record.

What difference did this complex process make in the way social regulation was conducted and in the impact it had on the economy? The answer varies with one's view of the function of presidential regulatory oversight.

If the model is an all-powerful executive, able to control decisions made by his subordinates, then the process clearly failed to bring regulation under control. Neither President Ford nor President Carter—nor their close aides, for that matter—ever became the executive branch's "regulatory czar." During both administrations, executive branch regulatory agencies issued some regulations to which White House officials strongly objected. Although both presidents complained about overregulation, neither considered that he had the authority or the capability to wrestle social regulation to the ground.

The view of the president as superregulator is reflected in Christopher DeMuth's assessment of the Ford and Carter regulatory oversight programs published in early 1980:

> One is struck . . . by a depressing irony in the Ford and Carter regulation-review programs. They have attempted to alleviate the problems of regulation by adding another layer of regulation that replicates the original problems. The review programs have made no attempt to alter the natural incentives of regulatory officials. They have established for the regulatory agencies an "engineering standard"—the preparation of cost analyses—rather than a "performance standard." They have embraced the hope that the adoption of a particular technology might improve matters, but they have been without the resources or authority to make the improvement, and they have paid little attention to whether matters have actually been improved. They have been long on rhetoric, purpose, and moral suasion, and short on specific results.[48]

A similar but more colorful evaluation appeared in a column by Tim Clark, a writer for the *National Journal*, published just as the Carter administration was leaving office: "Process, process, process. That was the Carter administration's answer. . . . For all this, it would be difficult to prove that life has become simpler for the regulated or that money has been saved."[49]

Of course, there are other standards by which to judge the Ford and Carter regulatory oversight programs. One we find congenial (we admit to a certain bias in this matter) considers the president to have extremely limited abilities to control such a complex process as social regulation. It views the White House and executive office primarily as institutions that can set the tone for an administration's regulatory efforts, help raise issues that otherwise might go unexplored, and encourage policy experimentation that individual agencies, given their natural constituencies, would find difficult to initiate on their own. We also believe that the potentially constructive (but limited) role of the White House or executive office can be undermined if that role is seen as being driven primarily by short-run political considerations or by a desire to confer favors. Judged against this much more limited standard, the Ford and Carter oversight programs may have been more successful than DeMuth and Clark contend.

But the views expressed by DeMuth and Clark generally reflected the business community's disappointment over the apparent results of the Ford and Carter regulatory oversight efforts. For all the sound and fury, social regulation remained intact. The budgets of social regulatory bodies (adjusted for inflation) might not have been rising as fast as they had been during the early and mid-1970s, but they were still rising. The volume of regulatory paperwork might have been cut a bit, as the Carter administration claimed in its first "Paperwork Budget,"[50] but the volume was still formidable. The size of the *Federal Register* was still increasing, as was the size of the *Code of Federal Regulations*. Judged by these indicators, the efforts of both Ford and Carter were failures. Certainly Reagan and his advisers would portray them as such in justifying their own much more ambitious program.

4

Precedents for Statutory Change

Among the most impressive legislative accomplishments of the past decade was the ability of the Ford and Carter administrations to secure the passage of a series of statutes substantially reducing—and in some cases totally eliminating—economic regulation in a number of important "infrastructure" industries. When referring to the successes of these two administrations in deregulating industries like the airlines, trucking, railroads, and banking, no one could argue (as Christopher DeMuth had done with regard to regulatory oversight) that their efforts had been "long on rhetoric . . . and short on specific results."[1]

One of the principal criticisms of President Reagan's regulatory relief program is that it has been unable to generate a similar record of legislative success, especially in the area of social regulation. As of the time this book was written, none of the major social regulatory statutes had been changed to make it less burdensome or costly. An omnibus regulatory reform bill that the administration supports has passed the Senate unanimously but languishes in the House, its future uncertain. One reason for examining the Ford and Carter legislative successes is to see what lessons they might hold for the Reagan administration.

The principal lesson, it turns out, is *not* what it might at first seem. Indeed, in the next chapter we argue that the Ford and Carter legislative successes in deregulation may have generated unrealistic expectations about what could be achieved legislatively in social regulation.

The difficulty of designing appropriate legislation to reform social reg-ulation (or even of deciding what the term "appropriate legislation" means) is evident from an examination of the legislative record of the Ford and Carter administrations. No important, substantive reforms were enacted during either administration—indeed, none was even proposed. Ford paid no attention to the legislative reform of social regulation. Carter's focus was entirely pro-cedural. An examination of the struggles of the Carter administration, both internally and with Congress, over its own version of an omnibus regulatory reform bill may help to put the Reagan administration's problems in obtaining legislated social regulatory reform into better perspective.

Rolling Back Economic Regulation

The Carter administration's record in persuading Congress to pass leg-islation deregulating important industries was truly impressive. The major pieces of deregulatory legislation were the Airline Deregulation Act of 1978, the Natural Gas Policy Act of 1978, the International Air Transportation Competition Act of 1979, the Depository Institutions Deregulation and Mon-etary Control Act of 1980, the Motor Carrier Reform Act of 1980, the Staggers Rail Act of 1980, and the Household Goods Transportation Act of 1980. Most of this legislation originated in the Ford administration, and it is clear that these laws would not have been passed without the efforts of that earlier administration. There is neither room in this chapter nor reason to review each of these pieces of legislation, but an examination of the background of several of the efforts is instructive.

Grounding the Civil Aeronautics Board.   The history of the legislation that scrapped the forty-year-old system of regulation that had governed the airlines in this country—the fares they could charge, the routes they could fly—is the best documented. We will describe it in the most detail, contenting ourselves with briefer histories of some of the other laws.

The Beginnings.   Academics began to question the value of CAB regulation as far back as the early 1960s. Among the early studies were those that compared fares in largely unregulated intrastate California markets and CAB-regulated interstate markets and found the CAB-regulated fares substantially higher. But supporters of the status quo treated these studies as little more than curiosities. The observed fare differentials were said to reflect the better flying weather in California and the allegedly greater number of unprofitable short-haul, low-density routes flown by the regulated interstate carriers. Subsequent academic studies examined the various explanations and dynamics of airline competition in more detail. But still the results were considered of relatively limited policy interest.

In the late 1960s and early 1970s, the CAB conducted a comprehensive examination of airline regulation and its impact on the public and the carriers: the Domestic Passenger Fare Investigation. This investigation—and the decision of the Department of Transportation (DOT) to participate in it actively—marked an important watershed in public policy towards the airline industry. The studies and data generated enabled scholars to pose in detail questions that would have to be answered if airline regulation were ever to change. However, it was not until a series of procedurally questionable and probably illegal decisions by two Nixon-era CAB chairmen, Secor Browne and Robert Timm, came to light that the public began to take the issue of airline deregulation seriously.

The CAB had never been known for its liberal entry policy; indeed, no new trunkline air carrier had been permitted to enter the industry since enactment of the Civil Aeronautics Act in 1938. But beginning in 1969, and with no notice to other members, Browne imposed a de facto route moritorium, directing the CAB staff not to bring forward for hearing route cases filed even by existing carriers.

In 1970, after private (and unannounced) meetings with air carriers, Browne granted carriers antitrust immunity to discuss agreements limiting capacity on a number of important routes. In 1972, without the opportunity for a hearing (on the grounds that the action was an "emergency"), a number of these agreements were permitted to go into effect. (Later when a hearing was held, a CAB administrative law judge declared these agreements to be contrary to the public interest and ordered them suspended.)

Both these actions were the result of the industry's financial difficulties during the late 1960s and early 1970s. Browne and Timm made it clear that they felt that these difficulties were due to excessive competition and that they were prepared to take actions of the kind just described to facilitate the restoration of industry profitability.

A final administrative outrage was the refusal of Chairman Timm to permit the CAB staff to investigate allegations that certain airlines had made illegal contributions to President Nixon's reelection campaign. Timm even ordered his personal assistant to seize and hold documents obtained by the CAB staff.

These actions were highlighted in a series of well-publicized hearings launched in 1974 by Senator Edward Kennedy's Subcommittee on Administrative Practices and Procedures of the Senate Judiciary Committee. The report that was issued following these hearings charged the CAB with being interested primarily in protecting airline profitability rather than in regulating in the public interest. The report ended with a call for a substantial relaxation of CAB regulatory authority.[2]

Although the subcommittee's hearing proved critical to the development of the issue, it could not produce legislation that substantially affected the CAB. The Judiciary Committee to which Kennedy's subcommittee was responsible had jurisdiction over the Administrative Procedures Act and the antitrust laws, and so Kennedy's hearings nominally addressed only these areas. But the legislation controlling the CAB's substantive regulatory authority over the airline industry was under the jurisdiction of the Senate Commerce Committee. Any effort to change this authority would have to come from that committee (or, more specifically, from its Aviation Subcommittee, headed by Senator Howard Cannon).

The Ford Administration's Contribution. The Kennedy subcommittee hearings were held not long after President Ford took office. The position that the Ford administration would take in these hearings was in doubt almost until they began. Eventually, after a certain amount of internal conflict, the administration decided to strongly support regulatory change in the airline industry. Indeed, in the first *Annual Report* of President Ford's Council of Economic Advisers the administration announced its intention:

> . . . during 1975 . . . to submit legislation to reform the regulation of airlines, railroads, trucking, and related areas . . . [to permit] more freedom for carriers to raise and lower rates without regulatory interference, greater freedom to enter markets and to exit from uneconomic services, and a narrowing of the regulator's power to grant antitrust immunity. . . .[3]

The Ford administration not only presented strong proreform testimony before the Kennedy hearings but also directed the Department of Transportation to begin studies that would prove essential to persuading an understandably skeptical Congress that it should consider substantially altering the CAB's regulatory mandate. These studies examined seemingly mundane issues such as which airline actually had what route authority; how much current authority was dormant (i.e., unused); to what extent air carriers were actually serving unprofitable routes; what the prospects were for substitute service if exit were liberalized; and what types of pricing responses might actually emerge under deregulation. The studies were conducted in substantially greater detail (and were much more expensive) than any academic studies and were done by consulting firms with recognized track records in gathering and analyzing airline data.[4]

The Ford administration's third important contribution was its appointment to the CAB of a chairman determined to try to get the CAB to use its existing authority to liberalize airline regulation and to examine whether its activities were really needed. It is an axiom that no bureaucracy will ever support a reduction in its own powers, but John Robson's special study group within the CAB did just that. Robson even persuaded a majority of the CAB to support significant regulatory reform. Furthermore, under Robson, the CAB permitted pricing innovations that previously would have been denied.

Ford did introduce his promised airline legislation, and the Department of Transportation produced important backup material making the case that airline deregulation would in fact work. Hearings were held in April 1976 before a clearly skeptical group of senators. CAB Chairman Robson announced that the CAB would support legislative changes in its mandate—not exactly the administration's bill, but something reasonably close—but the subcommittee took no action during that session of Congress. The Ford administration thus ended with the groundwork for airline deregulation having been laid, but the goal not having been reached.

Carter's Contribution.   When President Carter entered office, his position on airline regulatory reform was unclear. Some of his campaign statements suggested that he might not be sympathetic to legislation such as that which Ford had submitted to Congress, but certain of his close aides insisted that he did indeed support reform.

The issue was soon settled. Prodded by his economic advisers, the president authorized that strongly supportive testimony be prepared for a second set of hearings that Senator Cannon had scheduled for the spring of 1977. These hearings promised to attract much more attention than the ones in 1976, for in the interim Senators Cannon and Kennedy had agreed to introduce jointly an airline deregulation bill.

With the Carter administration on record as supporting legislated airline deregulation, the Department of Transportation sponsored additional studies aimed at answering the "nuts and bolts" questions that would have to be dealt with if the legislation were to pass. In June Carter appointed Alfred Kahn, the chairman of the New York State Public Service Commission, noted academic and advocate of regulatory reform, as CAB chairman. Kahn let it be known that he intended to use all his power to increase competition in the airline industry and that he was prepared to invite court challenges to CAB decisions expanding competition in order to test the limits of his power. In short, if Congress would not deregulate the airlines, he would do it, insofar as he could, administratively.

In April 1978, the CAB announced its intention to allow carriers to cut their fares up to 50 percent without CAB approval. Route realignments (which often had the effect of substantially increasing competition) were made easier. Through a "show cause" order, the CAB effectively placed the burden of proof on those airlines that *opposed* the entry of new competition to demonstrate why the entry should be denied. The mere fact that an incumbent's profits might be lessened by such entry would not be taken as evidence that the entry was contrary to the public interest. To prevail in opposition, the incumbent would have to show that the entry would threaten its solvency or impair its ability to provide essential air transportation—a very heavy burden of proof. Finally, the CAB adopted the policy of multiple permissive entry. If, as usually was the case, several firms sought to offer service between two given points, the CAB would permit *all* who were "fit, willing, and able" to offer the service, leaving it to the market to sort out whose service was preferred.[5]

The mood in the Senate hearings of early 1978 was therefore quite different from the mood in earlier years. Not only were two powerful senators, Cannon and Kennedy, and the Carter administration strongly backing legislation to deregulate the airlines; the agency charged with regulating the airlines seemed to be in a race with the Congress to see who would deregulate the industry first. Certain of the CAB's actions might well have been eventually overturned by the courts (although few were—Kahn had hired excellent lawyers to staff his Office of General Counsel), but there clearly would be no returning to the status quo ante. The only question was how much the scheme of regulation would change.

Faced with this situation, the solid opposition to legislative change that the airline industry had thus far maintained crumbled. United Air Lines, the nation's largest carrier, announced that it would support deregulation. Other airlines, but by no means all, followed. The Senate bill passed by a vote of 83 to 0 in April 1978. In September, the House passed a similar bill. (The House version called for abolition of the CAB in five years.) The differences between the two versions were resolved, generally in favor of more rather than less deregulation, and President Carter signed the bill on October 24, 1978.

It had taken nearly twenty years and the work of many people to finally effect airline deregulation. Critical to the outcome was the continuity of interest between the Ford and Carter administrations. Ford was in office too short a time to build the support necessary to pass such complex and controversial legislation, but his administration built the "intellectual capital" without which Carter's eventual success would have been impossible. Kahn's activities at the CAB were vital, but Kahn built on Robson's work, and Ford's naming of Robson was only slightly less important to attaining airline deregulation than Carter's naming of Kahn. The building on the work of previous administrations that was noted with respect to the evolution of presidential regulatory oversight was perhaps even more crucial to the attainment of the airline deregulation legislation.

Curbing the Powers of the Interstate Commerce Commission. Federal regulation of certain activities can probably be traced to the very beginnings of this nation, but the modern era of federal regulation began with the establishment of the Interstate Commerce Commission (ICC) in 1887. Scholars have long debated the reasons for the ICC's establishment. The "received wisdom," at least for a long time, was that the ICC had been founded to protect users of railroad transportation, principally agricultural interests, from the excessive market power of the railroads, the nation's first giant business. Recent research, however, suggests that perhaps from the very first, and certainly by the early 1900s, ICC's main objective was to prevent competition among the nation's railroads, permitting them to "perfect" their rate cartels that the Sherman Antitrust Act had undermined.

During the 1920s and early 1930s, the ICC struggled with the problem of how to prevent the young and growing motor freight industry from undermining the structure of rail rate regulation based on "value of service" pricing. This system of pricing encouraged large markups above railroad costs on manufactured goods and low markups on bulk commodities. It enabled rates for rail shipment of bulk agricultural commodities to be kept low, but it attracted trucking competition for shipment of other goods. Even without this pricing system, the trucking industry enjoyed some cost advantages over rail in the transportation of certain manufactured merchandise. The solution, which was only partially successful, was to extend the regulatory umbrella to cover as much of trucking as possible.

Attacks by economists on ICC rail and trucking regulation had preceded those on airline regulation, and by the mid-1960s, the "conventional wisdom" among most economists was that ICC regulation, whatever its original purpose, had largely outlived its usefulness.

In the case of railroads the damage was obvious even to the regulated entities. From a peak in about 1920, the nation's rail network had deteriorated alarmingly. To be sure, much of this system had become redundant with the development of the motor truck and the improvement of the nation's highway system. But the rail lines that had been abandoned were not always those that should have been abandoned, and much more trackage needed to be scrapped.

Opposition to changes in railroad regulation did not come principally from the railroads, therefore, but from shippers who thought they would be disadvantaged if railroads were given greater freedom to price their product, to merge free of conditions, and to abandon what they considered to be unprofitable services.

Action under the Ford Administration.   By the time the Ford administration entered office, the situation of the railroads had become so bad that Congress was persuaded to pass a modest railroad deregulation bill despite this opposition. This legislation, the so-called 4-R Act (Railroad Rehabilitation and Regulatory Reform Act), was actually *very* modest deregulation. Its philosophy, which was attacked by numerous transportation scholars, was that the ICC lacked the statutory flexibility to permit the railroads to engage in the degree of competition required in the 1970s. The act therefore broadened the ICC's authority.

Unfortunately, the ICC did not play along. Far from using its newly enlarged discretion to permit considerably more railroad competition, the ICC hobbled the railroads by defining the markets in which they exercised dominance (and, under the terms of the statute, were not permitted more pricing freedom) so broadly that little was changed. However, the ICC did begin to take a more lenient attitude toward abandonments and mergers.

The 4-R Act was a major disappointment, but Congress was not about to revise the legislation unless it absolutely had to. The resurgence of demand for coal in the aftermath of OPEC's oil price hikes, the vast expansion of western coal mining, and the advantage that certain railroads took of whatever opportunities they had to raise coal hauling rates created strong opposition among coal shippers and in Congress to any further weakening of ICC control over railroad rates.

But action was heating up in trucking, another area in which Ford had promised to introduce legislation. He kept his promise, but with a hostile ICC and opposition from the trucking industry and the Teamsters Union, the legislation got absolutely nowhere. As in the case of the airlines, the Department of Transportation sponsored research on the likely consequences of various forms of trucking deregulation.

The issue of small community service was central in the trucking debate. This issue was controversial enough in the case of airlines, but airlines served only a couple of hundred small communities, and it was clear that this service existed primarily because of substantial government subsidies. Virtually every small community in the nation might be affected by trucking deregulation. The trucking industry and its allies made the most of these communities' fears, spreading stories of communities' becoming totally isolated if the regulation of trucking ended.

Among the work begun by the Ford administration and continued under Carter were studies of where the trucking service for small communities actually came from. These communities were found, in fact, to rely very little on the common carrier trucks that the ICC regulated; instead these communities used unregulated private carriers. Generally, where ICC-certified truckers had permission to offer service to smaller and more isolated communities, these truckers ignored their service obligations. The services that *were* provided were provided not because the regulated common carriers were altruistic or because the ICC forced reluctant carriers to meet their service obligations (indeed, it was discovered that the ICC made absolutely no attempt to do this), but because the service was, in fact, profitable for some carriers. In short, the "small communities issue" turned out to be as bogus in the case of trucking as it had been in the case of the airlines. Without the research sponsored by the Department of Transportation, however, this fact never would have been known, and an important (and perhaps insurmountable) impediment to the passage of trucking reform legislation would have remained.

The Carter Administration Picks Up the Ball.   Trucking deregulation was not nearly so far along as airline deregulation when the Carter administration took office, and it took a back seat to airline deregulation until that legislation had passed. As already noted, DOT research on trucking issues continued throughout the Ford and Carter administrations, but little high-level attention was focused on trucking until 1979. Carter's original ICC Chairman, Dan O'Neal, was at best a reluctant deregulator.

Again, one of the important catalysts was Senator Kennedy. His 1979 subcommittee hearings on trucking deregulation raised a number of important issues but did not attract nearly the attention that the earlier airline hearings had. For one thing, the outrageous pattern of conduct engaged in by certain former CAB chairmen and their top staff, which had enabled the senator to generate so many stories in the press at the hearings involving the CAB, was not present in the case of the ICC. ICC officials had not abused their offices— they were just doing their jobs. The most important role of the Kennedy hearings was to cause the Carter administration, always concerned about Kennedy's popularity, to decide not to abandon the field of trucking reform to him, despite the warnings of Carter's legislative liaison staff that the chances of obtaining trucking legislation were close to nil.

But trucking reform refused to die. One thing that kept it alive was increasing pressure from the ICC. In 1979, Carter appointed one of Fred

Kahn's deputies at the CAB, Darius Gaskins, to a seat on the ICC and indicated that he would name Gaskins chairman to succeed O'Neal. Carter also began to stock the ICC with deregulators. Gaskins, his deregulation-minded colleagues, and, increasingly, even O'Neal began to try to duplicate at the ICC what Kahn had done at the CAB. That is, they began to use every bit of discretion they had and then some—they were willing to let the courts be the judge—to reduce the scope of ICC regulation over the trucking industry. The ICC's new deregulatory spirit so alarmed Senator Cannon and other senators (who at that time were lukewarm about trucking deregulation) that Cannon extracted a promise on November 1, 1979, from O'Neal (then still chairman) and Gaskins (vice chairman) that they would not make any irreversible decisions affecting trucking deregulation until after June 1, 1980, at which time a bill would be "on the president's desk."

The truce was tenuous, especially after Gaskins assumed the chairmanship in early 1980. The ICC kept up the pressure, and the legislation slowly advanced, reaching the president's desk close to the promised date. It was signed July 1.

The trucking legislation was far less sweeping than the airline legislation had been. ICC jurisdiction was not abolished, but the bill did provide for consideration to be given to abolition in the future. Market entry was liberalized; exemptions were expanded (prior to the passage of the 1980 act, more than half of all traffic carried by motor carriers—principally traffic carried by privately owned truck fleets and trucks transporting certain agricultural commodities—had already been exempt); inefficient and anticompetitive restrictions in carriers' operating certificates were targeted for elimination; and a rate flexibility zone was established. Antitrust immunity for motor carrier rate bureaus was maintained, but after January 1, 1984, this immunity was to be substantially weakened.

After trucking reform was out of the way, Congress managed to take up again the politically explosive issue of railroad pricing freedom. The compromise that was finally reached was, unlike the 4-R Act, prescriptive, not permissive. The ICC was forbidden from interfering in any individual commodity rate a rail carrier proposed as long as that rate was below a given threshold level designed to enable railroads to recover all their variable costs and at least a portion of their fixed costs. This act too created a rate flexibility zone, permitting carriers to increase rates an average of 5 percent annually until September 20, 1984, and 4 percent annually thereafter. The collective rate-setting activities of the railroads were also substantially curtailed.

Thus by the end of the Carter administration, federal regulation of transportation had been substantially relaxed. In addition to the deregulation already described, laws were enacted that relaxed ICC regulation of the interstate transportation of household goods and substantially eased CAB regulation of American air carriers' international operations. All this legislation can be credited to the efforts of both administrations and, in some cases, to groundwork laid by even earlier ones.

Other Legislative Achievements. Similar stories can be told about other parts of the general body of controls known as economic regulation. From the federal legislation that permitted states to grant antitrust exemptions to manufacturers (thereby enabling them to force distributors to charge minimum prices for their products, the so-called "fair trade" laws) to the elaborate structure of federal controls that sought to "manage" pricing and other dimensions of competition in industries like banking, stockbrokerage, telecommunications, and natural gas production—all came under scholarly attack.

As was true in the case of airlines, trucking, and railroads, attacks by scholars could not by themselves produce statutory or administrative change. Yet by the end of the Carter administration, change of such magnitude had occurred in each of these areas as to render unrecognizable the scheme of regulation that had earlier existed. In banking, moves to liberalize Depression-era restrictions went back to 1970, but they accelerated after about 1974.[6] Enactment of the Depository Institutions Deregulation and Monetary Control Act in March 1980 marked an important milestone in this effort. The fight to free natural gas pricing from federal control reached a watershed of sorts with the passage of the Natural Gas Policy Act of 1978. Unfortunately, as a result of subsequent energy price increases unforeseen by the law's authors and a mistaken belief that the transition to deregulation and its inevitable windfall gains and losses could be precisely managed, the natural gas pricing issue almost certainly will have to be reopened in the future.

In some cases, substantial deregulation was achieved without legislation. For example, the Securities and Exchange Commission ended the system of minimum stockbrokerage commissions as a result of years of pressure—and sometimes suits—by the Antitrust Division of the Justice Department. Minimum commissions on trades exceeding $300,000 in value were eliminated by April 1972; the entire system of fixed commissions was ended on May 1, 1975.

In other instances, although the primary activity was administrative, a credible threat of legislation served as an important prod. The most important case here is telecommunications. Liberalization began in the late 1950s with the end of AT&T's monopoly on long-distance communication. In the early 1960s the first "foreign attachments" (i.e., non-Bell equipment attached to Bell lines) were permitted. During the 1970s the structural change in telecommunications began in earnest. The active pursuit of a federal antitrust suit and legislative proposals, first by Congressman Lionel Van Deerlin and later by Congressman Tim Wirth, kept a reluctant Federal Communications Commission (FCC) moving toward competition.

In each case, the important change that was achieved transcended any single administration. Any president who signed an important piece of regulatory reform legislation had to acknowledge (although not all did) that, but for the foresight of his predecessors in building the necessary intellectual capital and political support, the signing ceremony would never have been held. Presidents interested in promoting regulatory reform had to give considerable thought to their appointees to the independent regulatory agencies, especially to the chairmanship of such bodies. This is not to say that *all* appointees to these agencies during the Ford and Carter administrations were of high caliber—that is a standard not met by *any* president. But the quality of the typical regulatory appointment during these two administrations clearly exceeded that of appointments presidents have often made, and some appointments were far above the usual standard.

Stalemate in the Legislative Reform of Social Regulation

In contrast to the impressive series of legislative successes that resulted in rolling back economic regulation virtually across the board, neither the Ford administration nor the Carter administration was able to formulate a coherent legislative program to reform social regulation. Indeed, the legislative trend during both administrations was toward increased social regulation. During the Ford years the Resource Conservation and Recovery Act, the Toxic Substances Control Act, and the Medical Device Amendments to the Food and Drug Act were enacted.[7] During Carter's term, the reach of the Clean Air Act was substantially broadened through amendment, and legislation was enacted that provided for cleaning up hazardous spills and toxic waste dumps. This is not to say that either administration supported all legislation expanding the scope of social regulation. But neither administration was notably hostile to such expansions.

During the second half of Carter's term, however, pressure began to grow within the administration for changes in some of the most important (and symbolic) pieces of social regulatory legislation. In particular, some of Carter's advisers believed that three pieces of legislation were both undesirable and unworkable: (1) the Delaney clause, which required that the Food and Drug Administration (FDA) ban *any* "artificial" substance found to cause cancer in laboratory animals—a prohibition that the agency, with the help of Congress, had found a way to avoid in the cases of nitrites and saccharine;

(2) the Clean Air Act's prohibition on the consideration of costs in setting national ambient air-quality standards; and (3) the Occupational Safety and Health Act's prohibition on considering costs in setting workplace health standards. Because of the fear of adverse political consequences, however, the Carter administration never proposed modifications to these regulatory sacred cows.

Substantive reform of the standards that FDA applied in approving new drugs was proposed, but Congress did not support the measure. A brief account of this experience is instructive.[8]

In 1962, the Congress had enacted legislation significantly expanding FDA's authority concerning new drugs. The expansion had been prompted by the thalidomide tragedy—an event that the U.S. escaped because FDA had not approved the drug for use in this country. These amendments substantially altered the regulatory procedures for approval of new drugs, requiring FDA to confirm both safety and effectiveness before a new drug could be marketed rather than, as previously, requiring proof only of safety and permitting a drug to go on the market if the FDA *did not* act.

This legislation clearly reduced the risk of the public's being exposed to dangerous drugs, but as time went on, it became increasingly clear that the legislation also was denying the public the timely benefits of new drugs. The rate of new drug approvals plummeted, and studies documented the fact that drugs were being introduced more rapidly overseas with little if any increase in risk.[9]

As a result of this growing evidence of excessive protection with its consequent loss in benefits, sentiment began to grow, even within FDA, for a modification of the agency's stringent standards for approval of new drugs. There was some support for making the necessary changes administratively, but Joseph Califano, Carter's secretary of health, education, and welfare, concluded that statutory change was needed. Lengthy negotiations were held with congressional leaders and others, and eventually the administration proposed the Drug Regulatory Reform Act of 1978. Extensive hearings on the bill were conducted, during which it was charged that, on balance, it increased rather than reduced the regulation of new drugs. The bill that the administration prepared was never reported out of committee in either house, although legislation resembling it in some ways did pass the Senate. The issue of the "drug lag" was left for subsequent administrations to deal with.

In this area there was widespread agreement about the nature of the problem caused by excessively stringent social regulation. Documentation of the trade-offs involved was unusually clear. Yet, if one investigator's characterization of the Carter legislation is correct,[10] concern about the risks of mistakenly approving unsafe drugs (a risk that, if taken incorrectly, produced identifiable "losers") outweighed concern about delaying the approval of safe and effective drugs (an action in which "losers" were much less readily identifiable). As Charles Schultze has noted, a cardinal principle of the American political system is "never be seen to do direct harm," and this principle prevailed in this case.

The choice was relatively easy compared with many in social regulation: It did not involve trading lives for dollars, only lives for lives. Yet it showed the difficulty of designing and achieving substantive statutory reform. Abolishing the agency in question was not at issue,[11] only deciding how it was to operate. Knowledge of the nature of the problem and even a reasonably broad consensus about how, in general, it ought to be remedied were not enough.

The episode should be sobering for anyone who believes that substantive reform of social regulation will be easy. It suggests why both Congress and the executive branch have been wary of it.

Legislating Procedures: A Substitute for Substantive Change

Although substantive changes in social regulatory statutes (other than ones increasing the scope of social regulation) were conspicuously absent during the Carter administration, several significant pieces of procedurally oriented legislation were enacted. Late in the administration, Congress passed the administration-backed Regulatory Flexibility Act and the Paperwork Reduction Act. The former was intended to provide for differentiation in regulatory approaches for small businesses, organizations, and governmental jurisdictions. The latter gave broad authority to the Office of Management and Budget (OMB) to control regulation-related paperwork, something the agency did by establishing a "paperwork budget."

But perhaps the most interesting legislative battle in the area of social regulation was over legislation that eventually failed to pass—various versions of the so-called omnibus regulatory reform bill. A brief history of this proposed legislation and the controversies surrounding it provides a useful glimpse of the politics of regulatory reform and of the difficulties of knowing exactly *how* to reform social regulation—problems that carried over into the Reagan effort.

The omnibus regulatory reform bills appeared to be efforts to write the various executive orders mandating regulatory analysis into law and to extend the requirement for analysis to the independent regulatory agencies. In fact, however, the legislation reflected the ongoing struggle referred to in the last chapter between the Congress and the executive branch over the roles of each in controlling social regulation.

Bills aimed at providing a statutory basis for regulatory analysis and imposing other procedural requirements on regulators proliferated in Congress during both the Ford and Carter administrations. For example, the American Enterprise Institute (AEI) has listed more than 100 regulation-related bills that were considered during the 95th Congress (the Congress that sat during the first two years of the Carter administration), the bulk of which were procedurally oriented.[12] Most died in committee. Listed in the order they appear on AEI's tally, the first nine items (1) provided a statutory basis for economic impact statements; (2) extended the executive order on regulatory reform to independent agencies; (3) established an Office of Regulatory Review in the General Accounting Office; (4) required a presidential ranking of regulatory programs; (5) required cost-benefit assessments of regulations; (6) required a 5 percent reduction in regulatory compliance costs; (7) established a regulatory budget; (8) allowed the president to delay implementation of a regulation; and (9) required flexibility in applying regulations to small business. The next nine items on AEI's list were all versions of the legislative veto, a procedure much favored by Congress but recently declared unconstitutional by the Supreme Court that allowed Congress to prevent the implementation of a regulation issued by an executive branch or independent agency. Bills pertaining to all but items (4) and (9) died in committee; in those two cases, legislation passed the Senate.[13]

One piece of legislation, S. 262, the Reform of Regulation Act, ultimately emerged as the principal legislative vehicle for procedural reform in the 96th Congress. It was the result of a three-year inquiry by the Senate Governmental Affairs Committee covering the entire range of federal regulation, economic as well as social. As described in an article by Senator Abraham Ribicoff, the committee chairman and the principal force behind S. 262, this inquiry had identified a number of general concerns with regulation, including (but not limited to) "questions on the costs and effectiveness of some 'social' regulation."[14] Rather than address this problem directly, however, the senator's bill proposed a procedural solution. In his words, S. 262 was intended "not to set up new political control on regulatory decision making, but to create mechanisms that would ensure more systematic considerations of proposed rules."[15]

Senator Ribicoff's legislation generally tracked the regulatory analysis requirements of Carter's Executive Order 12044 and extended these requirements to the independent regulatory agencies. It also indirectly addressed some of the issues that had concerned critics of presidential regulatory oversight like Senator Muskie. For example, according to Senator Ribicoff, S.

262 would have permitted regulatory analyses only when the statutory mandates of agencies permitted "costs and other external considerations" to be taken into account.[16] Carter's economic advisers had convinced the president that regulatory analyses should be conducted even when statutes prohibited their results from being given weight by administrators, arguing that, although decision makers probably could not, as a matter of law, take costs explicitly into consideration, the public had a right to know the costs that they were being asked to bear in the name of preserving health. If Senator Ribicoff's characterization of S. 262's requirements is correct, the bill would have ended the practice of conducting economic analyses in areas where they could not explicitly be considered during rule making.

Even more significant was a change that S. 262 proposed in regulatory oversight procedures. As we have noted, Carter had created the Regulatory Analysis Review Group to review and comment on regulatory analyses prepared by executive branch agencies. RARG analyses often formed the basis for subsequent interventions by the president or his advisers in the final phases of a rule-making proceeding—the so-called postcomment phase. Under S. 262, principal responsibility for monitoring the quality of regulatory analyses and for assuring compliance with the regulatory analysis requirement was to be lodged *not* in OMB but in the Congressional Budget Office. As a result, the president would have lost an important oversight tool that had been used during both the Ford and Carter administrations.

The Carter administration naturally objected to the portions of S. 262 that limited its ability to conduct regulatory oversight, but it did not want to oppose the bill outright because Senator Ribicoff was considered an important political ally. At the same time the administration could not ignore the legislation, because some procedurally oriented bill clearly stood a reasonable chance of passing Congress. Regulatory reform was becoming a congressional totem, and, for reasons already mentioned, procedural reform was much more popular—and therefore much more likely of passage—than substantive reform. S. 262 created problems enough for the administration, but even more troubling were the almost certain attachments to any piece of procedural reform legislation that appeared likely to pass both houses of Congress—specifically, some legislative veto and a fundamental change in the basic standard by which courts review regulations, known as the Bumpers Amendment.[17]

The administration was therefore forced to develop its own omnibus regulation reform bill. This painful process awakened many of the controversies discussed in chapter 3 relating to the structure and conduct of presidential regulatory oversight and social regulation itself. This bill, S. 755, paralleled S. 262 in many respects, but it omitted the offending shifts in the scope of and authority for overseeing regulatory analysis. It also gave the administration an opportunity to stress its opposition to the legislative veto and to the Bumpers Amendment.

Neither S. 262 nor S. 755 was enacted. A jurisdictional fight developed between Senator Ribicoff's Governmental Affairs Committee and Senator Kennedy's Subcommittee on Administrative Practices and Procedures. The proposed locus of regulatory oversight also became embroiled in this dispute. Eventually Senator Kennedy and his colleague, Senator John Culver, introduced their own omnibus regulatory reform bill, S. 2147, which, among other things, would have created a Regulatory Policy Board, which would have assumed the duties of both the Regulatory Council and RARG. Keeping track of just who was proposing what in the name of procedural reform became difficult.[18]

Process, Process, Process . . .

Why this passionate interest on the part of Congress in the normally dull issue of administrative procedure? For one thing, concentrating on procedural rather than substantive change of social regulation permitted Congress to appear to be responding to the increasing cries of protest—especially from the business community—against "overregulation" and against regulatory bureaucrats who were "running amuck," without having to address the much more difficult underlying issues—the authorizing statutes themselves. Being able to duck examining regulatory substance by concentrating on regulatory process was useful because, unlike the situation concerning economic regulation, there was no consensus at the time within either the country or Congress about just how social regulation ought to be reformed.

The problem was exacerbated by the fact that much of the social regulatory legislation was so new. Many of the original sponsors of the legislation—such as Senator Muskie—were still important powers within the Congress. It was impossible to deny the public concern about social regulation's various effects, but blaming the ills on "faceless bureaucrats" might prevent painful examination of the inherent workability of the programs themselves.

Focusing on procedure rather than substance had another important virtue—it permitted Congress and the president to spar over the proper division of power between the legislative and executive branches in controlling social regulation. These were the years when Watergate was still very much on people's minds. Despite the efforts of the Ford and Carter administrations to professionalize and depoliticize the regulatory oversight process, the actions of the Nixon administration still colored people's perceptions, especially with respect to specific regulatory programs. As we saw in the last chapter in connection with the hearings held by Senator Muskie's subcommittee in early 1979, occasionally the issue of unwarranted presidential interference burst forth directly. When it did, it immediately prompted an emotional response. Cloaking the question of the proper division of authority in the terminology of administrative procedure made it appear less contentious.

There were good reasons, therefore, why the debate over reform of social regulation during the Ford and Carter years centered on administrative procedure. For the same reasons, the Ford and Carter administrations could not record the same legislative accomplishment in this area that they had made in economic regulation. Timothy Clark's cry against the Carter administration's focus on "process, process, process" reflected a hope—indeed, a plea—that the Reagan administration would be different.

5

Social Regulation: Competing Diagnoses and Remedies

In the preceding chapters we traced three of the important intellectual and political developments that provided the setting for President Reagan's regulatory relief effort: (1) the growing recognition that government regulation was becoming a sufficiently significant activity to affect the performance of the economy; (2) the gradual development of a politically and legally acceptable role for the White House in overseeing regulation carried out by the executive branch of the federal government; and (3) the enactment of legislation, through efforts covering several years and several administrations, that significantly scaled back economic regulation, coupled with the beginnings of interest in the legislated reform of social regulation.

Despite these developments, by late 1980 few people thought that the country's regulatory "problem" had been solved. Federal agencies were still churning out social regulations at a furious pace, and the costs of complying with regulation, even by the calculations of its supporters, were clearly growing. Regulators seemed to lack the information they needed to regulate intelligently, yet regulatory paperwork seemed endless. Stories of conflicting regulations plus the apparent lack of improvement in many of the problems on which so much money was being spent raised questions about whether social regulation could *ever* be made to work.

More apparently needed to be done to bring social regulation under effective control, but what? There were many competing remedies. The libertarian-dominated group recommended dispensing with social regulation entirely; they opposed its paternalism on principle and favored letting the market and other social control instruments (such as civil liability) take over. Another group, probably including most businesses, objected less to the principle of social regulation than to its volume. They favored virtually any remedy that promised to reduce the burdens of regulation, including a stronger, more effective presidential oversight role; placing a cap on regulation's costs through a "regulatory budget"; mandatory cost-benefit standards for regulation; and changes in social regulatory statutes to eliminate what were considered to be some of their more unrealistic goals. A third group, composed primarily of economists, strongly supported social regulation as a cure for "market failure," but objected to the regulatory techniques that were being used—the detailed specification of permissible and impermissible behavior, otherwise known as "command and control" regulation. Their remedy was to replace command and control with marketlike systems established and maintained by the government.

This chapter summarizes the principal diagnoses and proposed remedies that were being widely discussed by late 1980. It is intended to help explain why, despite the efforts of previous administrations, candidate Reagan's promise that he was going to do something to bring social regulation under control had such wide appeal. It also illustrates why the strategies described in the chapters that follow seem such a strange mixture. Finally, it helps to show why President Reagan's regulatory relief program was so popular during its initial several months. Each of the various groups—the repealers, the tinkerers of various stripes, and the renovators—had reason to believe, at least for a while, that its favored solution was being implemented. Of course, when it became clear that this was not the case, President Reagan had to contend not only with natural opponents of regulatory relief—the environmentalists, the consumer activists, and the labor unions—but also with other people who originally had been among regulatory relief's most enthusiastic supporters.

Competing Diagnoses

This section concentrates on various diagnoses of the problems associated with social regulation—its costs, its seeming arbitrariness, its failure to produce promised benefits, and its impossibly large information requirements. These diagnoses are interrelated, but it is important to try to understand them separately. A person's basic diagnosis of the problem, together with the person's basic philosophical view of the proper role of government in society, often determined the particular solution he or she advocated.

Excessive Costs

In chapter 2 we reviewed at length the various estimates of regulation's impact on the economy. Although most of the studies reviewed included both social and economic regulation, it was the burden that social regulation imposed upon the economy that seemed to be of greatest policy interest. By late 1980, it was clear to much of the public and many policymakers that the burden was too large.

As our review stressed, studies of the impact of regulation on conventional indicators of economic performance—inflation, productivity, the rate of economic growth, employment—failed to attribute to regulation more than a fraction of that indicator's adverse performance. The growth of regulation was considered to be responsible for, at most, between 10 and 20 percent of the decline in measured productivity, for only a minuscule portion of the double-digit inflation that the nation was experiencing by late 1980, and for very little of the decline in the economic growth rate. Regulation actually seemed, on balance, to *increase* employment. But one did not have to accept Murray Weidenbaum's $100 billion estimate to conclude that regulation was becoming very expensive. During the Carter administration, the EPA estimated the cumulative cost of achieving clean air and water between 1977 and 1986 at $360 billion,[1] hardly small potatoes by anyone's calculation.

The rather esoteric point that not all these figures were "costs" in an economic sense, or that the figures ignored whatever benefits social regulation might be generating, seemed not to matter. For many people, the fact that the United States was spending anything approaching this amount on something as amorphous as social regulation and suffering a decline in conventionally measured living standards as a result was enough.

Specific studies, often conducted by government agencies, reinforced the impression that the costs of social regulation were excessive. Reports by the Council on Wage and Price Stability and the Regulatory Analysis Review Group charged that individual regulations threatened to impose billions of dollars' worth of additional costs in exchange for seemingly minor benefits. To be sure, the final regulations often did not go as far as the original proposals that had stimulated the analyses. But social regulation was clearly costly—too costly, according to many people.

Arbitrariness

Eugene Bardach and Robert Kagan have captured perhaps better than anyone else the set of issues referred to here as "regulatory arbitrariness."[2] Their Twentieth Century Fund study, *Going By the Book*, was an examination of how social regulation operated in practice and why its operation was guaranteed to generate resentment even among business people who might not be ideologically opposed to it or, for that matter, unduly concerned about its overall costs. In a related book they wrote:

> In a political system dedicated to the "rule of law," "due process," and "equal protection," regulators' powers of intrusion and coercion must be bounded by fixed legal rules, applicable uniformly and equally to entire classes of enterprises and operations. Even if scientific questions concerning risk and appropriate abatement methods are fairly well understood in general, in many programs the sheer diversity of enterprises to be regulated makes it almost impossible to devise a single regulatory rule that will "make sense" in scores of different copper smelters, nursing homes, and food processing plants, each of which employs a somewhat different technology or mode of worker supervision. . . .
>
> Laws also must focus on objective, measurable phenomena. The ultimate goal in many social regulatory programs, however, is to induce a general attitude of "social responsibility" whereby plant managers or nursing home administrators are continually alert and sensitive to all the diverse harmful acts that may result from their technologies and their employees' activities. A regulation that would instruct a plant manager, say, to "be alert to previously unrecognized sources of danger to employees and instill in employees a positive attitude toward safety" would clearly be unenforceable, and would probably violate due process norms as well. Instead, regulators are directed to things the enforcement official can measure or see on his intermittent visits to the site or whose absence can be easily proved. . . . These . . . are but proxies for the underlying attitudes . . . that we actually care about. And inevitably those correlations between the proxies and attitudes will be imperfect. . . .
>
> Similarly, the law usually is blind to the fact that regulated enterprises often differ in their attitudes toward regulation, and in their ability to afford specialized compliance staffs, and in the quality of their maintenance and supervisory staff. . . . The greater the diversity of regulated enterprises—in terms of technology, attitudes toward cooperation, and organizational or financial capacity to control the risks in question—the greater the probability that regulatory requirements and penalties will be overinclusive and hence excessive in a considerable proportion of cases.[3]

Bardach and Kagan's examples are drawn largely from the activities of the Occupational Safety and Health Administration (OSHA), particularly from its workplace inspection program, which inevitably generated tensions. Much as a taxpayer audit seems arbitrary, the workplace inspection appears arbitrary to businesses that are in fact complying with OSHA's rules—the "good apples" in Bardach and Kagan's terminology. Indeed, since the purpose of the program is to ferret out the noncompliers—the "bad apples"—the higher the proportion of businesses that comply, the less necessary the program must seem.

Yet *no* inspection program will uncover all noncompliers. A certain proportion of bad apples will inevitably exist, and these bad apples will generate horror stories that will attract the attention of politicians and newspapers. Publicizing such cases will lead to pressures to strengthen enforcement—to tighten up the "regulatory ratchet"—producing an even greater sense of arbitrariness among complying businesses.

The frustrations of such a system are not confined to businesses. Bardach and Kagan describe the dilemma in which conscientious OSHA inspectors find themselves. On one hand, there are strong pressures to enforce rules literally—to go by the book. But a conscientious inspector, like the good policeman on the corner, knows that literal enforcement of safety regulations almost certainly will be counterproductive. No set of regulations can be adequate to cover all contingencies. In a given situation, some, perhaps many, rules will appear absurd. Attempts to enforce clearly absurd regulations in clearly inappropriate circumstances will feed the sense of resentment felt by enterprises that are being inspected—especially if they are fundamentally in compliance. However, attempting to "be reasonable"—to tailor enforcement to the particular situation at hand—inevitably opens the inspector up to charges of favoritism and leads to opportunities for corruption.

Regulatory schemes like the current system of workplace inspection thus generate resentment among people whose workplaces are being inspected, people who do the inspecting, and, because of the impossibility of an inspector's always being around when a violation occurs, among the employees whom the program is designed to help. Little wonder that President Reagan could always get a round of applause during his campaign speeches when he promised to do something about OSHA. And although OSHA may have been an especially egregious example of regulatory arbitrariness, it was by no means unique. Many of the programs that attempted to guarantee equal opportunity through regulation, such as those of the Equal Employment Opportunity Commission (EEOC) and the Department of Education's Office of Civil Rights, generated similar resentment for similar reasons. Resentment of their operations was not confined to the bad apples. One could applaud a promise to do something about these programs and still totally support the programs' objectives.

Ineffectiveness

Although most economists—and most Americans, for that matter—accepted the underlying rationale for social regulation, studies were regularly appearing by late 1980, generally by economists, that seriously questioned whether social regulation was generating the benefits that had been hoped for. Several studies of the OSHA workplace inspection program failed to find that, for all the resentment it generated, it had actually reduced accident rates in workplaces.[4] Studies of the efforts of the National Highway Traffic Safety Administration (NHTSA) found that, although automobile accidents per vehicle mile traveled were clearly dropping, the trend predated the agency's founding; indeed, the creation of NHTSA seemed not to affect the trend.[5] Finally, although the historical data were extremely poor and the appropriate baseline was uncertain, some scholars who examined the record of environmental enforcement questioned whether it had actually significantly reduced pollution. Few series measuring ambient emissions went back much before the founding of EPA, but two that did (the series showing ambient levels of sulfur dioxide and particulate matter) showed a declining trend long before the establishment of the agency and the existence of a significant federal presence in controlling air pollution.[6] Lave and Omenn, for example, attributed the bulk of environmental improvements to the switch from coal to oil (which substantially reduced particulate and sulfur emissions) rather than to standards issued under the authority of the Clean Air Act.[7]

These studies were, of course, controversial. NHTSA and other researchers sharply refuted charges of ineffectiveness brought against the agency.[8] Environmentalists were particularly critical of assertions that the Clean Air Act had generated few benefits. They correctly contended that the proper baseline against which to measure emissions and ambient concentrations was the level they would have reached had no standards been put in place. They charged that the fact that pollution had not kept pace with the growing economy suggested that the standards had been effective. They countered with their own studies showing that the benefits of the regulations issued under the act exceeded the act's costs. [9]

Limitations on the Use of Standards to Control Behavior

But the issue went deeper than merely whether individual social regulatory programs were working. Increasingly, the wisdom of using regulation as a tool of social control came into question. One line of argument concerned the inherent inability of regulation to alter behavior. (That is our focus in this section.) Another concerned the impossibility of fulfilling the vast informational requirements of regulation. (That is the subject of the section that follows.)

During the 1960s and 1970s the country had turned to social regulation in the belief that it could provide effective protection against what increasingly were perceived to be important social abuses. Policymakers recognized—though perhaps not adequately—that other tools of social control existed. For example, in the consumer product safety area, consumers injured by improperly designed or manufactured products could sue and collect damages. The standards under which a suit could be brought were eased throughout the 1960s, and the damages (in constant dollar terms) that injured parties were typically collecting increased.[10] Still, it was possible in 1970 for the National Commission on Product Safety to recommend in its final report:

(1) That the Congress of the United States enact an omnibus Consumer Product Safety Act committing the authority and resources of the Federal Government to the elimination of unreasonable product hazards.

(2) That an independent Consumer Product Safety Commission be established as a Federal agency concerned exclusively with the safety of consumer products.

(3) That the Consumer Product Safety Commission be directed to secure voluntary cooperation of consumers and industry in advancing its programs and that, when necessary to protect consumers from unreasonable risks of death or injury, the Commission be empowered to—

- Develop and set mandatory consumer product safety standards;
- Enforce compliance with consumer product safety standards through a broad range of civil and criminal sanctions; and
- Enjoin distribution or sale of consumer products which violate federal safety standards or which are unreasonably hazardous.[11]

Congress agreed with the commission's recommendations, and the Consumer Product Safety Commission (CPSC) was born.

In practice, the CPSC has been able to set relatively few standards. The designers of the legislation establishing the agency never adequately recognized the difficulty—not to speak of the cost—of setting enough specific product standards to make much difference in the overall level of product safety. As time has passed, the agency has increasingly devoted its attention and resources to recalling products deemed defective, thereby operating in a way that is quite parallel to (and, substantially reinforces) the product liability system.

It was not only in the area of consumer product safety that policymakers began to recognize the difficulty of issuing a volume of standards large enough to make an appreciable difference. In 1977, the EPA's Office of Toxic Substances was established to regulate the use of chemical entities believed to pose a danger to the environment. But the agency was totally unable to keep up with the flood of new chemicals, let alone make a dent in the backlog of existing potentially hazardous chemicals. Environmentalists complained that the agency was not working hard enough; in fact, its task was impossible.

Once EPA began to flesh out the "cradle to grave" system of tracking hazardous wastes envisioned under the Resource Conservation and Recovery Act, the system quickly became recognized as a paperwork nightmare of dubious effectiveness. Hazardous wastes were a problem of growing concern to the country, as the outcry over Love Canal and other abandoned dump sites showed, but the systems of regulation being proposed to control this problem just did not seem adequate for the task.

Lester Lave portrayed the underlying problem well in his book *The Strategy of Social Regulation*:

> Billions of decisions concerning health and safety are made each day in the United States. Only a minute proportion of these decisions is subject to a specific regulatory standard; and of this minute proportion, only a tiny fraction can be monitored by regulatory agencies. . . . Far from being able to do the whole job, regulatory agencies can do so little that they must be used carefully if they are to have any effect.[12]

By the end of the 1970s, it was becoming clear that we had placed excessive faith in the ability of federal regulators to solve social problems through the promulgation and enforcement of detailed rules and regulations. Serious social problems might exist, but they were not going to be solved if we had to rely solely on the regulations that our regulatory agencies could turn out.

Impossibly Large Informational Requirements

Although, as Lave pointed out, it was impossible for the federal government to issue enough rules to substantially alter behavior in areas like consumer product design and manufacture or workplace safety, the rule-making and enforcement activities in which the social regulatory agencies *did* engage generated immense informational requirements. Businesses resented the paperwork and demanded a change; the Paperwork Reduction Act of 1980 was passed in response to their concerns.

But, as in the case of questions concerning the effectiveness of regulation, a deeper issue was involved. By its very nature, the system of command-and-control regulation that Congress had chosen in establishing most social regulatory programs generated demands for vast amounts of information. Charles Schultze described the situation this way in his Godkin lectures at Harvard University in 1976:

> The more complicated and extensive the social intervention, the more difficult it becomes to accumulate the necessary information at a central level. It is relatively easy to set up a system for payroll records from which to determine

social security benefits. Doing something about the delivery structure of medical care or controlling industrial accidents imposes informational requirements of a much higher order. . . . An efficient regulatory scheme to control the discharge of pollution into the nation's waterways requires that regulatory authorities know the production function, the range of technologies for pollution control, and the demand curves of every major polluter.[13]

The paperwork demands generated by social regulation were thus both a burden in themselves and a symptom of a much deeper problem, one going to the heart of the techniques that the nation had chosen to use to conduct social regulation. Statutes like the Paperwork Reduction Act might somewhat reduce the volume of regulatory related forms, but as long as command-and-control regulation was the principal chosen regulatory device, information requirements would remain immense. Indeed, cutting back on paperwork without changing regulatory mandates or techniques would only make regulation seem less effective and more arbitrary.

Prescriptions for "Doing Something" About Social Regulation

This section identifies some of the prominent prescriptions being discussed in the country by late 1980 to remedy the problems of social regulation described in the earlier sections. It will quickly become clear that the various solutions to the problems associated with social regulation stemmed from significantly different (and often quite inconsistent) views about what the problems actually were. But these differences actually proved to benefit the candidacy of Ronald Reagan: different people could listen to him promise to do something about social regulation and believe that he was endorsing their favored remedy. Only later, when general statements had to be translated into specific actions, did the inconsistencies become a problem.

Eliminate Many (If Not All) Social Regulatory Programs

Despite a widespread belief that social regulation was not working as well as it should, support for the underlying concept remained strong, even by late 1980. Yet the libertarians, who had long opposed social and economic regulation on principle, seized on studies of the cost, arbitrariness, and ineffectiveness of regulation to urge that the programs themselves be eliminated. Other groups who did not identify themselves as libertarians also argued that social regulatory programs were so flawed as to be beyond salvage.

The libertarian argument was based on the belief that most social regulation was an unwarranted intrusion by the federal government into private decision making. If *informed* consumers chose to purchase unsafe products, then the government had no business interfering in their choice. If unsafe products were chosen by *uninformed* consumers, the proper remedy was not regulation of the products to make them safe, but the generation, by the government or by private sources, of sufficient information to enable consumers, acting on their own, to reach informed decisions. Similar arguments were made with respect to many other social goals that regulation was used to advance—such as workplace safety and the promotion of equal opportunity.

A good statement of the libertarian critique of social regulation appeared in the February 1982 *Economic Report of the President*:

> Many government programs, such as detailed safety regulations or the provision of specific goods (rather than money) to the poor, are best described as paternalistic. Paternalism occurs when the government is reluctant to let individuals make decisions for themselves and seeks to protect them from the possible bad effects of their own decisions by outlawing certain actions. Paternalism has the effect of disallowing certain preferences or actions. . . . There is no reason to think that commands from government can do a better job of increasing an individual's economic welfare than the individual can by making choices himself. Moreover, the long-term costs of paternalism may be to destroy an individual's ability to make decisions for himself.[14]

The libertarian view that social regulation ought to be eliminated did not require acceptance of the proposition that the unaided market would necessarily produce optimal levels of consumer product safety, workplace health and safety, or environmental emissions. Two other additional arguments permitted people who might not consider themselves libertarians to support elimination of many social regulatory programs: (1) the recognition that governmentally imposed solutions, like markets, might be systematically flawed; and (2) the realization that alternative systems of social control in fact existed—that one need not choose between detailed regulation and something called the "free market."

To economists, the primary justification for social regulation was the failure of private markets. However, by late 1980, it was recognized that while market failure might be a necessary condition for regulation (though regulation might sometimes be imposed in its absence), it was certainly not a sufficient condition. Charles Wolf of the Rand Corporation, for example, developed a taxonomy of "nonmarket failure" that deliberately paralleled the well-known one that existed for market failure. Where private markets would "fail" in the presence of externalities (costs or benefits not taken into account by private decision makers; pollution is a classic "negative externality") or "public goods" (goods that cannot be provided to one person without simultaneously being provided to everybody; national defense is the classic example), government efforts to correct these market failures might suffer from "internalities" and "private goals" (systems of rewards and penalties that government agencies develop because their output is not priced in the market; sometimes these are antithetical to the broader public interest). As Wolf notes:

> The existence of externalities means that some *social* costs and benefits are not included in the calculus of *private* decision makers. The existence of internalities means that "private" or *organizational* costs and benefits *are* included in the calculus of *social* decision makers. . . .
>
> In the market context, externalities result in social demand curves higher or lower than market demand curves, depending on whether the externalities are, respectively, positive or negative. And the levels of market output that result will be, respectively, below or above the socially efficient ones; hence, there is market failure. In the nonmarket context, "internalities" boost agency *supply* curves above technically feasible ones, resulting in redundant total costs, higher unit costs, and lower levels of real nonmarket output than the socially efficient ones; hence there is nonmarket failure.[15]

Wolf makes it clear that, in general, one cannot tell whether market or nonmarket failures are quantitatively more significant. But his analysis is important because it showed that a basic argument that economists and others had used to justify the imposition of social regulation could be invalid. One could identify clear market failures and still not conclude that regulation was the proper solution.

The second argument permitting other than libertarians to argue for the elimination of certain forms of social regulation was based on the growing realization that there were both theoretical and actual alternatives to regulation. The existence of product liability in the area of consumer product safety has already been mentioned. Product safety decisions also were influenced by the private insurance system, by a system of voluntary private standards, and by concern about corporate reputation.[16] In the area of workplace health and safety there was, in addition to OSHA regulation, a "no fault" worker's compensation system, which, through its system of experience-rating premiums, provided employers with some incentive to take action to cut workplace accidents.[17] Also encouraging the reduction of workplace risks was the product liability system (injured workers could sue the manufacturers of the products that had injured them), efforts by private insurance firms to provide to manufacturers and other covered businesses information about how their safety practices might be improved, and the existence of risk-related wage differentials.

These alternatives, it was argued, often would be less intrusive and costly and possibly even more effective than social regulation. As the editor of one collection of studies examining such alternatives noted in his introduction:

> Each author concludes that true deregulation is a thinkable alternative. In the case of the traditional economic-regulatory agencies, the general lesson is that competitive forces in the market place can provide far better protection of consumers than can the formation of government-sponsored cartels . . . or the substitution of bureaucratic decision making for individual choice guided by independent information services.
>
> In the case of health and safety agencies, the alternatives are more varied. In general, the creation of regulatory agencies in such fields as aviation and drug safety has led to a major shift of responsibility from the insurance industry to the government. As a result, legal and market place mechanisms that exist in other fields have atrophied in these protected domains. Yet in consumer-product safety, for example, where government is a relative newcomer, liability-law and insurance mechanisms are far more advanced and, conclude our authors, fully capable of doing the job, and at less cost. In workplace safety and pollution problems, the costs and effectiveness of centralized, bureaucratic approaches are open to serious question, not in comparison with doing nothing but in comparison with more flexible, decentralized alternatives that protect people's rights while protecting their freedom of choice.
>
> Indeed, one of the most important aspects of our proposed alternatives to centralized regulation is the return to individuals of substantial decision-making power—the power to choose among transportation carriers that are newly freed to compete in price as well as service; to choose to watch television commercials that are free of a government nanny deciding what is misleading . . .; to choose between ingesting saccharin and risking cancer or not ingesting it and risking obesity-related health problems; or to choose to work in a more hazardous job in exchange for higher pay. True deregulation thus rests on an ethical foundation that recognizes the primacy of individual choice—albeit an informed and conscious choice—and full responsibility for one's actions. It removes prior restraints on the actions of both producers and consumers, substituting a more robust framework of information and insurance to protect both parties.[18]

The legislative accomplishments in the area of economic regulation heartened libertarians and others who thought that many social regulatory programs ought to be eliminated outright. (Indeed, the first chapter of the book just quoted describes how airline deregulation was brought about.) The deregulation of the airlines, trucking, railroads, telecommunications, banking, and stockbrokerage had once been declared impossible, but all had come to pass. The nation's experiments with wage and price controls and with the regulation of virtually every aspect of energy supply and use had been declared failures and had been ended. If programs of economic regulation could be disposed of, why not dispose of programs of social regulation—especially in view of the fact that alternative, possibly superior, instruments of social control clearly existed?

Keep the Programs but Pare Them Back Severely

The number of people who wanted to do away with the social regulatory policies on principle (or who considered them to be so fatally flawed that they were useless) was quite small. (However, they were prominent among Ronald Reagan's earliest supporters.) A much larger group was not necessarily opposed to social regulation per se, but believed that the nation had gone overboard in its use. This group, of which Murray Weidenbaum might well have considered himself a member, included people who wanted to right the gross imbalance they perceived between the costs of social regulation and its benefits.

Members of this group advanced two general prescriptions. One involved strengthening the presidential oversight role, equipping the president with tools adequate to impose control over what seemed the inevitable tendencies of agencies to overregulate. Either the president should be given the authority to intervene directly to modify important regulatory decisions or tools should be created to permit him to exercise a more decentralized (but possibly more effective) policy oversight. The "regulatory budget" (described below) became an important symbol of the latter solution.

The second prescription was to modify specific regulatory mandates that appeared to require the attainment of social goals without regard to the costs involved. Important symbols here included the Delaney Amendment (which required the FDA to ban *any* artificial substance that had been shown to cause cancer in laboratory animals), the portion of the Clean Air Act that appeared to require the setting of national ambient air quality standards without regard to cost, and the Occupational Safety and Health Act that dictated a similar setting of occupational health standards.

Improve the Effectiveness of Presidential Regulatory Oversight. This element of the prescription proposed augmenting the oversight efforts of the Nixon, Ford, and Carter administrations. Some critics who considered these efforts to have been failures saw the problem as a failure of will: the presidents themselves or their staffs had been too timid about exercising the authority they had over executive branch regulators.[19] For these people, a change in leadership was the proper prescription.

Other critics of this same general school believed that presidents lacked certain important oversight tools and supported procedural changes, such as

the omnibus regulation reform bills described in chapter 4. They saw enactment of such procedurally oriented legislation as the Regulatory Flexibility
Act and the Paperwork Reduction Act as giving the president significant
increased management authority.

Still other critics called for more radical procedural changes. Lloyd
Cutler, later to be President Carter's White House counsel, and David Johnson, a colleague in his law firm, proposed in a 1975 article in the *Yale Law
Journal* that the president be given clearer authority to overrule his appointees
on important regulatory matters.[20] Cutler and Johnson proposed that, subject
to a one-house congressional veto[21] and expedited judicial review, the president be authorized to direct *any* regulatory agency (independent or otherwise)
to take up and decide a regulatory issue within a specified period of time, or
to modify or reverse an agency policy rule, regulation, or decision (except
for grants, revocations, or renewals of a license or privilege).

In his two-part critique of the Carter administration regulatory oversight
efforts, Christopher DeMuth criticized those who saw the solution in either
changed leadership or procedural tinkering:

> In the case of the Ford and Carter regulation-review programs, the evidence to
> date is that a modest degree of further centralization from the regulatory agencies
> to the White House has failed to bring about much constraint on the private
> costs of regulatory decisions. Certainly the programs have failed to duplicate
> the panoply of institutional constraints that affect the government's expenditure
> programs, so as to eliminate the inappropriate (and increasing) incentives of
> government officials to pursue public goals through regulation rather than out-
> right taxing and spending. While it is conceivable that further increases in White
> House control over individual regulatory decisions would constrain regulatory
> costs more effectively, the most forthright proposal for doing so—the Cutler-
> Johnson ABA proposal—raises such serious institutional problems of its own
> as to give pause about the entire approach.[22]

DeMuth's preferred solution was the "regulatory budget." Although
candid about its "acute problems concerning the nature and measurement of
regulatory costs, problems that the more casual regulatory review programs
have never had to face directly,"[23] DeMuth nevertheless clearly found the
concept appealing, at least in theory:

> The President and Congress [would] establish prior aggregate limits on the costs
> that individual regulatory agencies may impose upon the economy, in a manner
> similar to the current process of fiscal budgeting; the agencies would then be
> obliged to live within their regulatory budgets just as they now must live within
> their fiscal budgets. In contrast to the regulation-review program and its variants,
> the regulatory budget would be a decentralized method of constraining regu-
> latory costs. The President and the Congress would be assigned their appropriate

role[s] (in the sense of setting boundaries on the share of the nation's economy to be devoted to particular endeavors), and the regulatory agencies would be left to make individual regulatory decisions within a budgetary framework that encouraged cost-effectiveness in particular cases. The institutional constraints upon regulatory costs would approximate those upon spending programs.[24]

Each of the proposals mentioned in this section reflected a growing willingness to explore giving the White House increased executive powers as memories of Watergate faded. But how far to go and how best to institutionalize the White House role remained to be determined.

Change the Regulatory Mandates and Decision-making Standards. An important group among the critics seeking to pare back social regulation saw basic flaws in the mandates that many of the agencies were required to administer. Although some of the mandates (for example, those of the National Highway Traffic Safety Administration or the Consumer Product Safety Commission) were relatively broad and embodied requirements for a balancing of regulatory benefits with the costs of regulating, others (such as portions of those governing the actions of FDA, EPA, and OSHA) prohibited agencies from considering anything other than health effects in reaching their regulatory decisions. Furthermore, many statutes had "action-forcing" and "technology-forcing" deadlines.

Increasingly, agencies were having to find ways around these totally health-based statutory mandates, and the action-forcing and technology-forcing deadlines often ended up being relaxed—although not without causing considerable tension between the firms, regulatory agencies, courts, and sometimes even Congress. As a result, some policymakers who were basically sympathetic to the social regulatory programs advocated modifications. (We have already noted the sympathy among some of President Carter's advisers for change.) Some of the proposed modifications would have continued to provide for a strong health-based mandate, but would have merely removed the absolute primacy that the present statutes appeared to give to health. Other proposed statutory modifications would have gone much further, raising cost and other economic considerations to a level equal with that of health. The most far-reaching would have required all social regulations to demonstrate that their likely benefits exceeded their likely costs. All such proposals were resisted by the supporters of regulation, and as of late 1980, Congress had shown little willingness to give them serious consideration.

Change the Way We Regulate

A small third group of critics viewed the principal defect of social regulation as the particular regulatory techniques it employed, the system of detailed command-and-control regulation. This group, composed almost exclusively of economists, proposed to replace these techniques with a system of marketlike incentives created and policed by the government.

From the earliest days of the "modern era" of social regulation, economists had advocated pollution charges and other marketlike incentives. In a classic article in *Science* in 1971 titled "The Economist's Approach to Pollution and Its Control," MIT Professor Robert Solow laid out both the problem and the solution as seen by economists:

> In the situation we have now, the assimilative capacity of air and water has become a scarce resource, but it is provided free of charge as common property to anyone with some waste to dispose of. It is easy to see that, in these circumstances, the scarce resource will be overused. The normal system of incentives is biased. A costly (that is, scarce) resource does not carry a price to reflect its scarcity. If high-sulfur fuel is cheaper to produce than low-sulfur fuel, it will be burned and sulfur dioxide wastes will be dumped into the air. Society pays a price in terms of damage to paint, to metal surfaces, to plants, and to human health. But that cost is normally not attached to the burning of high-sulfur fuel; only a part of the full social costs become private costs and influence private decisions.[25]

The natural solution (for an economist, at least) was to levy a charge equal to this unrecognized cost. Such an approach was considered to have several virtues:

> If two factories producing different commodities both contaminate the same stream to the same extent, it might seem natural to require each of them to reduce its contamination by, say, 50 percent. If that were done, it would be almost certain that the incremental cost of a small further reduction would be different for the two factories; after all, they use different production techniques. But then it would be better if one of the factories—the one with the smaller incremental cost—were required to pollute still a little less, and the other permitted to pollute a little more. The total amount of pollution would be the same, but the cost of accomplishing the 50 percent reduction would be smaller. . . . This would be accomplished if, instead of a direct imposition of standards, the two factories were charged an amount proportional to their emission of pollution. The height of tax could be varied until the desired total reduction in pollution occurred; the factories themselves would see to it that it occurred in the cheapest possible way. It is perfectly true that this way of doing things affects the distribution of income; the cost of preserving the environment is borne in a certain way. But that is true of any method, including simple prohibitions. The redistribution is only more visible in the case of a tax or effluent charge.[26]

Economists had originally advocated marketlike mechanisms as a substitute for regulation primarily on efficiency grounds. Use of these mechanisms would permit the attainment of any level of social goal (such as the reduction of pollution) at minimum cost. As both Solow and Schultze made clear, however, the replacement of command-and-control regulation with charges would also eliminate the need for government to be concerned with the details of business decision making and hence would cut regulatory paperwork. In addition, the detailed specification of permissible behavior and the enforcement effort that accompanied it would also no longer be necessary. To be sure, there would be a need to monitor behavior, but not (it was assumed) in the detail currently required. Therefore the regulatory system would be less arbitrary and intrusive. In short, economists considered all the various diagnoses of the problems associated with social regulation as supporting their prescription. In addition, the new system could be made consistent with any level of benefits that society might choose.

Lower cost, less intrusiveness and paperwork, greater transparency: the economists' solution seemed like a natural—to them. But outside the dismal profession, proposals for pollution fees, injury taxes, and the like were greeted with indifference or outright hostility. In 1971, when Senator William Proxmire introduced an amendment to the Clean Water Act permitting the use of discharge fees, it attracted no support. Environmentalists denounced economists' proposals as "licenses to pollute." Critics concerned with the ethics of pollution control claimed that the introduction of marketlike mechanisms would destroy the moral basis for society's fight against pollution.[27]

The opposition to charges and other marketlike mechanisms did not stem solely from environmentalists and philosophers. As Carter's EPA began to explore the issues, it became clear that economists had inadequately thought through how such mechanisms might be practically implemented. Markets were not simple to create or maintain. Information requirements, although perhaps fewer than those of command-and-control regulation, were by no means trivial. What economists had viewed as one of the virtues of their schemes—their ability to make the income distribution aspects of regulation transparent—proved to be extremely unpalatable politically. Finally, as businesses gained more experience in the "regulatory game," many of them began to discover how it could be used—just as economic regulation had been—to create or preserve market niches and to put competitors at a disadvantage. Few businesses saw much virtue in launching into a new type of control, just when they were becoming used to the old one.

Nonetheless, some hesitant steps in the direction of adopting marketlike approaches to controlling pollution were being taken. During the Ford administration, EPA had adopted a policy of permitting "offsets" in areas of the country not attaining national ambient air quality standards as a way of avoiding the draconian step of imposing bans on new construction in these areas. One highly publicized example of this policy was the "trade" developed by the State of Pennsylvania to permit Volkswagen to locate a new auto assembly plant in that state. To offset the new plant's projected emissions of hydrocarbons, the state shifted from a water-based to a petroleum-based asphalt for road paving in sixteen nearby counties. In other cases, the trades were privately negotiated. But the principle of creating and trading a "property right" in pollution was established. Indeed, the offset policy was confirmed legislatively in the 1977 Clean Air Act Amendments.

The next step was the development of what became known as the "bubble policy," a technique for allowing closely situated pollution sources in areas already meeting national ambient air quality standards to trade airborne emission reductions in ways that substantially reduced compliance costs.[28] Emissions "banks" had been established. These permitted firms with emission reductions above the levels required by existing regulations to store and possibly sell them. More elaborate trading systems known as "marketable permits" were under serious examination. EPA had sponsored a study of their possible use if it were to become necessary to control the emissions of chlorofluorocarbons from nonaerosol sources.[29] The California Air Resources Board had sponsored an elaborate investigation of the possibility of establishing a marketable permit scheme for sulfur oxides in the Los Angeles air shed.[30]

Each step in the process of introducing marketlike incentives into social regulation was laborious and controversial. Nevertheless, economists hoped that Reagan would embrace the concept as the principal vehicle for the regulatory relief he was pledging.

The Appeal of Regulatory Relief

Even this incomplete survey of prescriptions for "doing something" about the problems associated with social regulation is sufficient to illustrate the breadth of feeling that Reagan was able to tap as he campaigned against overregulation. Libertarians hearing his message believed that an all-out attack on the structure of social regulation was in prospect. Businesses hoped that a major strengthening of White House oversight, including the imposition of formal cost-benefit requirements and the striking down of some of the more extreme statutory mandates, might be on the agenda. Economists dreamed that someone was at last prepared to implement their proposals for pollution charges and marketable permits.

The very fact that previous presidents had made some progress in removing the burdens of regulation from the economy (although principally in the area of economic regulation) also fed this feeling that something significant might be about to be accomplished. After all, Ford in only two years had managed to lay an important foundation for future progress. Carter had managed to persuade Congress to enact major economic regulatory legislation, but the fact that he was a Democrat and was believed to be a "closet regulator" was seen to have limited his effectiveness. Reagan would be a president who could build on the work of these two, who saw control of social regulation as an issue worthy of his personal attention, and who owed nothing to the proregulation constituencies to boot! It is little wonder that his promise to get social regulation under control had a broad appeal.

6

Regulatory Oversight in the Reagan White House

As chapter 3 indicated, each of Ronald Reagan's three immediate predecessors sensed a need to bring about improved coordination and oversight of regulations issued by agencies under their direct control—the executive branch agencies—and created institutions and procedures designed for this purpose. No president succeeded in totally centralizing control over the regulatory process; it is doubtful that any could have even if he wanted to. But as a result of these previous efforts and court rulings concerning them, the principle of presidential control, as well as its general boundaries, had been pretty well established.

President Reagan chose not to be constrained by these precedents. He viewed the regulatory process as out of control and the oversight programs of his predecessors, especially President Carter's program, as failures. He intended immediately upon taking office to launch a bold initiative aimed not at regulatory *reform*, but at regulatory *relief*. A much more powerful and active White House regulatory oversight apparatus was to have a major role in this initiative. In this chapter we describe how this apparatus differed from Carter's and what the consequences of these differences were.

At the outset, however, we want to recap some of the conventionally acknowledged goals that prior oversight efforts had endorsed and the constraints that they came to acknowledge. Perhaps the most broadly accepted goal was coordination of regulatory policies across agencies and of complementary federal activities (tax and regulatory policy, for example). Clearly, the White House and the Office of Management and Budget (OMB) are well placed to ensure that federal regulatory policies do not conflict and that federal policymakers pull in the same direction.

A second goal has been to ensure that executive authority tracks accountability—that is, that the president, who is ultimately accountable for regulatory actions taken during his administration, has the information and authority needed to shape agency regulatory policies. To this end, enhanced oversight ensures that the political fallout of agency decisions made on technical grounds is anticipated and mitigated where possible. This goal is theoretically achieved by infusing an often technocratic agency decision-making process with a healthy dose of political reality. Under the model, the parochial and often self-serving outcomes of agency rule makings are routinely screened by the politically attuned generalists who advise the president.

Advocates of strong central oversight in the post-Nixon era have generally conceded that if the process is to work, it must be perceived as relatively open, decisions should appear to be driven by neutrally applied principles (such as cost-effectiveness), and the process should be invoked in an ostensibly uniform, nonarbitrary manner. These goals correspond to rather commonly acknowledged political and legal constraints—among them, that executive branch officers not serve as conduits for otherwise undisclosed information provided by interested parties; that the process of rule making on the basis of a public record be respected; and that the dictates of underlying statutory mandates be obeyed.

The Formal Structure of the Reagan Oversight Program

The administration's enhanced regulatory oversight program consisted of three major elements: (1) the creation of a highly visible regulatory relief advocacy group—the President's Task Force on Regulatory Relief; (2) the formal centralization of regulatory oversight authority for all executive branch agencies within a single office, the newly established Office of Information and Regulatory Affairs (OIRA) within the White House-controlled OMB; and (3) the promulgation of a uniform cost-benefit standard that all regulations would be required to meet "to the extent permitted by law."

The first of these elements—the task force—was announced on January 22, 1981, the president's first full working day in office. According to a White House "fact sheet," the task force's responsibilities were to include the following:

> Reviewing major regulatory proposals by executive branch agencies, especially those proposals that would appear to have major policy significance.

Assessing executive branch regulations currently on the books, especially those that are burdensome to the national economy or to key industrial sectors.

Overseeing the development of legislative proposals in response to congressional timetables (e.g., the Clean Air Act) and codifying the president's views on the appropriate role and objectives of regulatory agencies.

On February 17, 1981, the president issued a detailed executive order that formally established the other two major elements of his regulatory management plan. Certain sections of the order resembled or only modestly extended the executive orders issued by Presidents Gerald Ford and Jimmy Carter. The prime example was the requirement that agencies subject proposed "major" rules to formal economic analysis and make these analyses (now to be called regulatory impact analyses) available for public comment at the time the rules were proposed.

In many important respects, however, the order moved far beyond the orders of Carter and Ford. The Carter administration in particular had always taken pains to stress that its regulatory analysis requirement was not to be interpreted as subjecting rules to a cost-benefit test. Agencies were to identify costs and benefits, quantify them insofar as possible, and either choose cost-effective solutions or explain why they had not. The burden of making the case that proposed rules were *not* cost-effective lay not with the agencies but with senior White House aides.

Reagan's executive order went much further in each of these areas. Except where expressly prohibited by law, the order required that a cost-benefit test be applied and met. An agency was not even to propose a regulatory action unless it could demonstrate that the potential benefits to society were likely to outweigh the potential costs. (The order did not explain just how this demonstration was to be made, especially when many regulatory benefits and costs clearly would be nonquantifiable.) If the agency did choose to proceed to regulate, it was required to choose (1) the objectives that maximized net benefits to society and (2) the specific regulatory approach that minimized net costs to society. Finally, each agency was to set its regulatory priorities to maximize aggregate net social benefits, taking into account three factors—the condition of the national economy, the condition of the industries affected by its regulations, and the impact on those industries of regulatory actions contemplated by other agencies. This last requirement was especially puzzling. When asked how agencies could meet it, OIRA Administrator James Miller replied: "Relatively easily . . . by consulting the regulatory calendars that each agency is required to publish twice a year."[1] But that did not explain how an agency was, in practice, to calculate the cumulative impact of such regulations (no methodologies to do this are known to exist) or how it was to coordinate its actions with those of other agencies.

The oversight mechanism was also drastically changed. As we have already noted, under Carter the various oversight functions were deliberately parceled out among many offices. OMB monitored compliance with the regulatory analysis requirement and, beginning in late 1979, became increasingly active in monitoring regulatory paperwork as well. The Council on Wage and Price Stability (CWPS)—and, in the case of particularly important regulations, the interagency Regulatory Analysis Review Group (RARG)—maintained quality control of agency analyses and ensured that certain issues got onto the public record through their own public filings. The Regulatory Council compiled calendars of future proposed regulations, spotted and resolved regulatory conflicts, and encouraged the adoption of innovative regulatory techniques. Finally, several of the president's senior advisers followed important regulations from the close of the public comment period until the issuance of the final rule.

The Reagan executive order consolidated these functions into the newly established OIRA within OMB. The CWPS, the Regulatory Council, and the RARG were abolished.

The Reagan order thus brought the issue of the proper location of regulatory oversight authority full circle. The Nixon Quality of Life Review had, after all, granted that authority to OMB. Later, under Presidents Ford and Carter, responsibility for oversight had been dispersed to other actors within the executive branch. Now the Reagan initiative reestablished OMB as the preeminent authority for oversight.

By so doing the order raised an issue which had complicated prior efforts to vest regulatory oversight authority in OMB. OMB was, after all, a part of the Executive Office of the President. As its historical mission had been to fashion the president's budget from submissions by the Cabinet departments and independent agencies, it had developed through time a modus operandi of working in a relatively secretive, behind-the-scenes manner to sort out and balance competing funding requests. The method could be justified as the president's budget would be submitted to Congress and have to survive debate within that political marketplace.

The approach was more problematic when applied to regulatory oversight as OMB actions would not be subject to the same sort of subsequent congressional review. OMB's actions were thus vulnerable to being perceived as politicizing the technocratic process of translating legislative intent into implementing regulations.

The executive order gave OIRA extremely broad powers. In effect, it became the gate through which all important regulations had to pass—not just once, but twice—on their way to becoming law. OIRA could overrule agency determinations on whether a proposed rule was to be considered "major" and thus deserving of the full review "treatment." (In both the Ford and Carter administrations, this authority had remained with the agencies proposing the rules.) In the case of a "major" rule,[2] OIRA was to receive the draft regulatory impact analysis at least sixty days before the agency published the notice of proposed rule making (NPRM). If it found the analysis weak or believed that important alternatives had been neglected, it could delay publication of the NPRM until the agency had adequately responded to its concerns. There was no requirement (at least initially) that a record be kept of these requests from OIRA or of the agency's response. The agency might appeal OIRA's rulings, but only to the Task Force on Regulatory Relief (which was to be staffed by OIRA) or to the president himself.

The Carter and Reagan systems also differed in the use to be made of the formal public comment period. Under Carter, it was during this period that RARG or CWPS prepared and filed comments on agency proposals, but under the Reagan plan no such public filings by the White House or OMB were required. Presumably the communication of OIRA's or other agency views on proposed rules would occur prior to the formal comment period and be reflected in a published NPRM. In short, the procedure established by the Reagan executive order did not provide the public with an opportunity to learn what the White House's views were and how they differed from the views of the agency proposing a regulation.[3]

After formal public comment, when the agency was drafting its final rule, the Carter procedures had provided for monitoring by top presidential advisers—the chairman of the Council of Economic Advisers (CEA), the OMB director, and the president's assistant for domestic policy, as well as his inflation adviser and science adviser. They (or more typically, their aides) met regularly to track important rule makings, assign responsibility for White House agency liaison, and decide whether to involve the president. Under the Reagan system, OIRA was also to get one more chance to review the agency's proposal. Thirty days before the final rule was due to be issued, the agency was to transmit the final regulatory analysis to OIRA. If OIRA objected, it (OIRA) could hold up the rule until its objections were resolved or until those objections were overruled by the task force or by the president himself.

The process just described was to apply to new rules. Reagan, like other presidents before him, recognized that the vast body of regulations already in place needed attention. The Carter system required that agencies periodically review existing rules and eliminate or revise those that were outmoded, but it never created a formal "sunset" procedure to give this requirement force. Reagan's executive order did. It allowed OIRA to designate existing rules for analysis and to establish schedules for such reviews. Revising rules would require, of course, that new rules be proposed, at which point the procedural requirements and analytical standards of Reagan's executive order would apply.

OIRA was given still more powers. When President Reagan abolished the Regulatory Council, he transferred to OIRA the job of publishing the *Regulatory Calendar* (publication of the calendar ceased after the January 1982 issue) and of eliminating duplicative and conflicting rules. OIRA was also given the job of implementing the Federal Regulatory Flexibility Act of 1980, which addresses the regulatory problems of small business, and the Paperwork Reduction Act of 1980, which seeks to limit the paperwork that agencies impose along with their regulations. Finally, OIRA was specifically charged with developing procedures for estimating the annual benefits and costs of agency regulations, in the aggregate and by industrial sector—"for purposes of compiling a regulatory budget."[4]

Challenges to the Legality of the Reagan Regulatory Oversight Program

Given the scope of the Reagan executive order, it is little wonder that questions were raised about its legality. Debate over this issue was brought into focus by a report issued by the Congressional Research Service in June 1981 and written by Morton Rosenberg, a specialist in American law at the Library of Congress.

Rosenberg raised three major objections to the order: First, he suggested that administrative rule making should be viewed as a direct extension of congressional law making. Thus, when presidential intervention was not expressly authorized by a statute, the Constitution, or congressional practice, it displaced authority reserved to the administrative agency, thwarted congressional will, and violated the separation of powers. Rosenberg wrote:

> Rulemaking remains lawmaking even when it is performed by an administrative agency; and lawmaking remains a task committed by the Constitution to the Congress.
>
> Accordingly, rulemaking is to be considered . . . as a category of administrative activity which is presumptively subject to Congressional control. Thus it is clear there is neither express or implied Constitutional authority in the President to establish the scheme of control of administrative rulemaking envisioned by Executive Order 12291.[5]

The order, Rosenberg claimed, effectively converted the president to an administrative manager and institutional competitor to Congress, taking him beyond the limits of his constitutional power.

Rosenberg also charged that the president's order ran afoul of the Administrative Procedures Act (APA). This statute sets minimum procedural safeguards for the administrative process. According to Rosenberg, the order violated this act in four ways:

1. By permitting the director of OMB, rather than the head of an executive agency, to determine when an agency can promulgate a regulation;
2. By prescribing procedures to be uniformly applied across all agencies, violating the flexibility that the APA sought to engender in the informal rule-making process;
3. By requiring the use of substantive cost-benefit analysis, which is not consistent with the act's intent to require only "neutral, value-free" procedures; and
4. By superimposing a central coordinating authority over all agency rule making in direct contravention of the APA's legislative history.

A third legal problem Rosenberg attributed to the order was its failure to provide safeguards against undisclosed contacts by interested parties and the Executive Office staff—either within the White House itself or at OMB. Rosenberg claimed that this failure constituted a violation of the constitutional due-process rights of participants in the regulatory process. His report raised two distinct issues pertaining to such undisclosed, ex parte contacts. The first was the likelihood that White House officials would be employed as "conduits" for influencing agency rule makings. The second was the fear that the president and his aides, acting on their own initiative, would attempt to control agency rule making by making direct contacts with agency officials during the postcomment phase of informal rule making.

Of course, many of these criticisms were not unique to the Reagan executive order or to the oversight program it established. Indeed, major sections of Rosenberg's report are best viewed as a summary of the "executive branch regulatory agency as an extension of the legislature" point of view— a point of view traditionally favored by Congress. As we have seen in chapter 3, this view was considered—and specifically rejected—by Judge Wald in her *Sierra Club* opinion. She also rejected Rosenberg's claim that all contacts between the White House and an executive office agency during the postcomment period were illegal.

Sierra Club did not, however, resolve all issues concerning the legality of White House oversight of executive branch regulation. For one thing, it specifically did not address the conduit issue. And, since it applied to Carter administration oversight procedures, it clearly could not automatically be applied to those aspects of the Reagan procedures that went beyond Carter's.

The question of how much protection Judge Wald's decision *did* give the Reagan oversight program was addressed by Michael Sohn and Robert Litan, two Washington attorneys, in an article in *Regulation* commenting on the case soon after the decision.[6] Sohn and Litan acknowledged that the *Sierra Club* ruling generally supported presidential regulatory oversight (indeed, their article was titled "Presidential Oversight Wins In Court"), but they identified three principal areas where important legal questions remained.

The first was in the scope of the powers permitted White House regulatory overseers to control the pace of the regulatory process. Officials who had conducted regulatory oversight during both the Ford and Carter administrations had operated largely within the timetables the agency involved had set for rule making. This is not to say that the White House and the agencies never negotiated the date for issuing proposed or final rules, but the initiative lay largely with the agencies.

In contrast, OMB during the Reagan administration had specific powers to hold up a rule making until its concerns were dealt with to its satisfaction or until it was overruled by the task force or the president. (Exceptions were made for "emergency" regulations—agencies still had to demonstrate why an emergency existed—and for regulations whose schedule was controlled by statutory or court-ordered deadlines.) Did this additional conferral of powers create special legal difficulties? Sohn and Litan believed that it did not. They stated:

> When [the D.C. Court of Appeals] approved "the presence of a Presidential power," surely it was not so naive as to imply that this presence was to be felt only when the agency itself so desired. Similarly, when it decried the "isolation" of "single-mission agencies" that a nonconsultation rule would produce, it could not have meant to imply that self-imposed isolation would be satisfactory. In short, it seems most likely that the court would view the executive order's requirement of extra-agency consultation, and its adoption of procedures to ensure it, to be within the President's powers of managing the administration of the government.[7]

Sohn and Litan ducked the more difficult issue that would be raised by the president or an OMB director, acting pursuant to the executive order, instructing an executive branch agency to reach a decision that it would not otherwise have taken. Concluding that "such a case would test the outer reaches of the President's powers under Article II to 'see that the laws are faithfully executed,' " they despaired at ever seeing a direct test:

> As a practical matter, such cases may never arise. An agency head is unlikely to risk presidential displeasure by openly bucking a "strongly expressed presidential preference"—or even one from OMB, provided it is supported by the

President. Moreover, the judicial reticence to explore the contents of intra-executive branch deliberations exhibited in *Sierra Club* makes it highly unlikely that the "hard cases" will ever see the light of day.[8]

The second unresolved issue Sohn and Litan mentioned was the conduit question. *Sierra Club* did not address this issue because it did not need to. Carter administration procedures in place at the time of EPA Administrator Costle's decision helped to assure that the issue did not arise.

But, at least initially, the Reagan administration oversight process had no announced procedures on how OMB's contacts with industry and the agencies would be handled. The only part of the executive order that came close to dealing with the issue was the requirement, set forth in section 3(f)(2), that if OMB and an agency were unable to resolve their differences over a final rule, the agency was to suspend publication of the rule "until the agency has responded to the Director's views, *and incorporated those views and the agency's response in the Rulemaking file.*" (Emphasis added.)

Perhaps the designers of the Reagan oversight program thought that their appointees would know instinctively what to do, or perhaps such concerns seemed inconsistent with the "relief" emphasis of the president's program. On June 13, 1981, however, a month and a half after the *Sierra Club* decision and immediately before a set of hearings called by the Subcommittee on Oversight and Investigations of the House Committee on Energy and Commerce—hearings called specifically to review the legal issues raised by Executive Order 12291 and to examine OMB's performance under the executive order—OMB Director Stockman sent a memorandum to executive branch agency heads. This memo stated that OMB procedures in dealing with agencies would be "consistent with the holding and policies discussed in *Sierra Club.*" It informed agency heads that "where OMB receive[d] or develop[ed] *factual material* that [it] believe[d] should be considered by an agency during a particular informal rule making" it would identify such material as appropriate for inclusion in the rule-making record. Concerning the conduit issue, Stockman's memo stated:

> Under the Executive Order, both the Task Force and OMB will be reviewing factual materials related to regulatory proposals. Both the public and the agencies should understand that the *primary* forum for receiving factual communications regarding proposed rules is the agency issuing the proposal, not the Task Force or OMB. Factual materials that are sent to the Task Force or OMB regarding proposed regulations should indicate that they have also been sent to the relevant agency. Pursuant to this policy, the Task Force and OMB will regularly advise those members of the public with whom they communicate that relevant factual materials submitted to them should also be sent to the agency for inclusion in the rulemaking record. Accordingly, agencies receiving such materials from

the public should take care to see that they are placed in the record.[9] (Emphasis added.)

Sohn and Litan, among others[10] have noted the calculated ambiguity of this memo. For example, it was never made clear how OMB proposed to distinguish factual material from policy advice, and why only the former was included. Also left ambiguous was whether the requirement applied to oral as well as written communications, a point that had been much at issue in *Sierra Club*. Concerning this matter, Judge Wald had stated:

> If oral communications are to be freely permitted after the close of the comment period, then at least some adequate summary of them must be made in order to preserve the integrity of the rulemaking docket, which under the statute must be the sole repository of material upon which EPA intends to rely. . . .This is so because unless *oral* communications of central relevance to the rule making are also docketed in some fashion or other, information central to the justification of the rule could be obtained without ever appearing on the docket, simply by communicating it by voice rather than by pen, thereby frustrating [the statute].[11]

Sohn and Litan recommended that Reagan administration officials take note of Judge Wald's reference to the logging requirements that the Carter administration had imposed on itself in the wake of the cotton dust controversy. As will be recalled, these requirements covered *all* communications, policy and factual, written and oral, that were deemed relevant to regulatory proceedings in which the White House became involved. As becomes evident later, this advice was not taken.

The third issue that Sohn and Litan considered unresolved by *Sierra Club* was the weight that could be given to costs and benefits in regulatory decision making. Their conclusion was that when the underlying statute did not expressly forbid the use of cost-benefit analysis (as courts have interpreted the OSHA statute and the Clean Air Act—when setting national ambient air quality standards—to be doing), the requirements of the executive order could apply.

There are indications, however, that the administration may have found itself somewhat uncomfortable with respect to its legal position on this point. In the "Dunkirk" memo quoted in chapter 1, David Stockman raised a warning flag about how far the administration could expect to proceed in imposing cost-benefit requirements on regulations without fundamental statutory change. After stressing the cost-saving potential of his proposed "regulatory ventilation," Stockman declared:

> Finally, a fundamental legislative policy reform package to be considered after the administration's initial 100 days in office will have to be developed. This would primarily involve the insertion of mandatory cost-benefit, cost-effec-

tiveness, and comparative risk analyses into the basic enabling acts—Clean Air and Water, Safe Drinking Water, TOSCA [The Toxic Substances Control Act], OSHA, etc. *Without these statutory changes, administrative rule-making revisions in many cases will be subject to successful court challenge.*[12] (Emphasis added.)

As chapter 8 reports, this legislative package was never developed. Despite the concerns described here, no direct court challenge to the Reagan executive order was ever mounted. Why? Public-interest lawyers claim that no favorable set of facts had yet presented itself for a frontal attack on the order. Further, they worried that a premature challenge could end up strengthening the order. As a result, debate over the order's legality remained, somewhat surprisingly, in congressional hearing rooms.[13]

The Regulatory Oversight Program in Action

The establishment of the President's Task Force on Regulatory Relief, the formal centralization of responsibility for regulatory oversight in OMB, and the expansion of powers exercised by White House regulatory overseers created the potential for the president and his principal aides to exercise a much greater degree of influence over executive branch regulation than had existed previously. But how was this influence used? The location provided the opportunity to impose a greater degree of coherence and cost-consciousness on regulation as practiced by executive branch agencies. But it also created the opportunity to subvert the oversight process into serving primarily as a "political filter."

We use two approaches to describe and assess the operation of the Reagan oversight process during roughly its first two and one-half years. The first concentrates on the official accounts of its activities—the number of regulations reviewed, accepted, rejected—and uses official evaluations of the process. This approach has the virtue of relying primarily upon objective indicators. To capture the flavor of the Reagan oversight process's unrecorded influence on agency activities, however, we examine individual cases that, for one reason or another, attracted the attention of the press. Clearly these cases are not a random sample, and because the information has been provided by interested (and therefore nonobjective) parties, the resulting picture should be treated with caution. But it is a perspective that cannot be ignored.

In the next section, we review the official indicators of the task force's and OMB's activities and summarize the results of a published broad review of the oversight program's operation and influence conducted in mid-1982 by the General Accounting Office (GAO). Then we examine two specific cases that appear to constitute favorable and relatively unfavorable examples of the strengths and weaknesses of the Reagan oversight program: the administration's "auto package" and the "lead phasedown" decision. Finally, we discuss the perception that, at least during its early days, the program's primary purpose was to serve as a "political filter."

Broad Measures of the Activities and Influence of the Regulatory Oversight Process

In hearings held in the House of Representatives during the summer of 1983 which focused on OMB's regulatory oversight activities, OIRA Administrator Christopher DeMuth claimed that the Reagan White House oversight process had been "more open and public than any that has come before."[14] To support his statement, DeMuth referred to the periodic reports issued by both OMB and the task force detailing their operations.

In a sense, DeMuth is correct. The Reagan oversight process *has* generated a more voluminous official record of its activities and claimed accomplishments than have the oversight efforts of any previous administration. And this record *does* provide an important—though somewhat skeletal— account of the program's operation and influence. Consider, for example, the materials issued by the task force, which, during 1981 and 1982, published five lists of existing regulations slated for "expedited agency review." Under the provisions of the executive order, this designation, following its confirmation by OMB, was sufficient to initiate such a review.

We have already mentioned two of these lists—the first task force agenda announced by Vice President Bush in March 1981 (which included twenty-seven regulations) and the industry-specific auto package announced by the president himself in April of that same year (which included thirty-four regulations).[15] The regulations on the first list had been issued by a variety of agencies and consisted, in general, of regulations that certain of Carter's advisers had unsuccessfully objected to on grounds that they were not cost-effective. Analyses supporting their contentions were already a matter of public record. (The auto package will be discussed in greater detail later in this chapter.)

A third list, announced by Vice President Bush on August 12, 1981, consisted of thirty regulations culled from more than 1,800 suggestions submitted by "business, labor, consumer [*sic*], local government and other interests"[16] plus nine areas in which the task force believed that reporting and paperwork burdens could be reduced. A fourth list, also announced by

the vice president, was published in February 1982; it included eleven regulations deemed to be of special interest to small business.[17] Finally, in August
1982, the task force published a list of eight regulations designed to give state
and local governments greater flexibility in setting clean air standards, developing land in floodplains, and having a greater say in the saving or de-
struction of historic buildings.[18]

DeMuth's July 1983 testimony made it seem that such lists were intended
as formal announcements to give interested parties notice of the administration's intent to conduct reviews of the indicated regulations. In fact, they
were news "events," designed to build political support for the regulatory
relief program by demonstrating that it was alive and well.

The truth of this is shown by what happened to the lists after August
1982—they stopped. The 119 regulation total that existed at that time remained
constant until the task force went out of existence in August 1983. The
publication of the final list and the eventual disbanding of the task force did
not mean that OMB would no longer require agencies to review existing
regulations, only that the political value of issuing regulatory "hit lists" had
ceased.

Table 4, taken from the task force's final report, shows the distribution
of these "targeted" regulations by agency and their status as of August 1983.
As can be seen, the bulk of the regulations had been issued by three entities:
the Labor Department (which includes the Occupational Safety and Health
Administration—OSHA), the Environmental Protection Agency (EPA), and
the Transportation Department (which includes the National Highway Traffic
Safety Administration—NHTSA).

OMB itself published annual reports of its review activities listing the
number of regulations reviewed, the time required to review each, and the
disposition of the regulations. Table 5 is reproduced from OMB's report
covering 1981. It indicates that between February 17 (the date Executive
Order 12291 was issued) and December 31, OMB completed the review of
2,679 rules, 62 of which were "major." It also reviewed 172 "frozen"
rules—the Carter "midnight regulations."

Most of these rules—91 percent of all newly submitted rules and even
65 percent of the "midnight regulations"—were approved as submitted. That
is, OMB certified that they met the criteria of Executive Order 12291 and
the Paperwork Reduction Act. Another 5 percent were approved after "minor" changes (clarifications in the preamble to the rule, not substantive changes),
2 percent were returned unapproved, and 2 percent were subsequently withdrawn. Since OMB's data referred to reviews completed, information was
not generally provided concerning the number of rules that might have been

TABLE 4

STATUS REPORT ON 119 REGULATIONS UNDER REVIEW

	Total	Revisions Completed	Revisions Proposed	Review Under way
Advisory Council on Historic Preservation	1	0	0	1
Department of Commerce	2	1	0	1
Federal Emergency Management Agency	2	1	0	1
Department of Labor	10	0	6	4
Department of Health and Human Services	8	2	3	3
Department of Education	4	2	1	1
Environmental Protection Agency	25	17	5	3
Department of Transportation	27	24	1	2
Federal Energy Regulatory Commission	1	0	1	0
Federal Reserve Board	1	0	1	0
Department of Housing and Urban Development	7	3	4	0
Department of Interior	4	2	2	0
Department of Treasury	2	1	1	0
Department of Agriculture	7	5	2	0
Consumer Product Safety Commission	1	1	0	0
U.S. Army Corps of Engineers	2	2	0	0
Department of Energy	2	2	0	0
Equal Employment Opportunity Commission	2	2	0	0
Federal Trade Commission	1	1	0	0
General Services Administration	1	1	0	0
Department of Justice	2	2	0	0
Nuclear Regulatory Commission	1	1	0	0
Office of Management and Budget	5	5	0	0
Office of Personnel Management	1	1	0	0
TOTAL	119	76	27	16
Percentage	100	64	23	13

SOURCE: Presidential Task Force on Regulatory Relief, "Reagan Administration Regulatory Achievements," August 11, 1983, p. 68.

TABLE 5

DISPOSITION OF REGULATIONS REVIEWED BY OMB UNDER
EXECUTIVE ORDER 12291, 1981

Disposition	All New Rules		Major New Rules	Frozen Rules[a]	
Approved as submitted	2,446	(91%)		112	(65%)
Approved after minor changes[b]	138	(5%)	60[c]		
Approved after substantial amendment	—			12	(7%)
Returned unapproved	45	(2%)	1		
Withdrawn[d]	50	(2%)	1	18	(10%)
Still pending[e]	—		—	30[f]	(17%)
TOTAL	2,679[g]	(100%)	62[h]	172	(100%)[i]

SOURCE: GAO Report, pp. 48–49.

NOTE: All these data are for rules issued between the effective date of the executive order on February 17, 1981, and December 31, 1981.

    a. Pursuant to president's memorandum of January 29, 1981, "Postponement of Pending Regulations," 46 F.R., 11227, February 6, 1981, which "froze" the effective dates of all rules for 60 days.

    b. Minor changes typically involved clarifications in the preamble to the *Federal Register* notice rather than substantive changes to the rule.

    c. No data are provided to identify the number of major rules approved as submitted, after minor changes, or after substantial changes.

    d. Withdrawn by the agency before review by OMB was completed.

    e. This category applies only to the "frozen rules" because the first two columns list only rules for which OMB has completed review.

    f. As of April 23, 1982.

    g. A total of 2,803 rules were submitted to OMB for review, but 124 were exempted or improperly submitted and therefore not reviewed.

    h. Although 62 major rules were submitted to OMB for review, only 43 were published in 1981.

    i. Percentages do not add to 100 percent because of rounding.

still pending. An exception was the "frozen" rules. Approximately one year after the freeze had been imposed, 17 percent of the 172 frozen rules still fell into this category.

What are we to make of this picture? One possible interpretation—the one obviously favored by the White House—is of an active, open, smoothly operating review process that was significantly improving regulatory coordination and reducing costs with a minimum of delay. Critics of the Reagan oversight process interpreted the same information quite differently. For example, in late 1982, the General Accounting Office (GAO) published the results of a comprehensive review of OMB's regulatory relief activities.[19] GAO interviewed officials at eleven different regulatory agencies and at OMB and reviewed thirty-eight regulatory analyses conducted under Executive Order 12044 (the Carter order) and nineteen conducted under Executive Order 12291 (the Reagan order).

Commenting on the data contained in table 5 (which the GAO report reproduced, together with additional explanatory detail), GAO noted that because OMB generally avoided recording its objections to regulations, the data shown were of little value in evaluating OMB's activities or influence on the rule-making process.[20] The reader will recall that under the executive order, OMB was empowered to discuss proposed rules both before and after it received them for formal review. As GAO noted, the data in table 5 only indicate the disposition of the rules that were formally proposed. But what of those that might never have seen the light of day because of actual or anticipated OMB objection? Apparently no publicly available information on these existed. GAO's interviews determined that written information detailing OMB's objections to specific rules and agency responses to these objections was confined to those rare cases in which agreement could not be reached between OMB and an agency and the dispute had to be settled by the task force.

The typical case generated no written record, even if OMB had demanded—and obtained—significant changes in a rule or had acquiesced without taking the matter to the task force. OMB responded to a specific GAO question on this point as follows:

> Communications [between OMB and agencies] generally are through telephone conversations or meetings at the staff level. We find that the exchange of the kind of technical information needed in producing and reviewing regulatory impact analyses is generally more efficiently and productively carried out informally by staff rather than by formal, written memoranda. Therefore, we do not have a written record of such communications.[21]

OMB's response to GAO's question seems to refer to regulations for which a regulatory analysis had been prepared—although there is no indication that GAO intended to limit its question to such instances. Indeed, most regulations did not include regulatory analyses. Table 5 shows that of the almost 2,700 new rules proposed during 1981, nearly 98 percent were not designated as "major," and therefore were not, even in principle, subject to the regulatory analysis requirement. These "nonmajor" rules were apparently dealt with—again with no paper record—by OIRA desk officers, who were assigned to monitor the rule-making activities of various executive branch agencies.

OIRA desk officers also apparently played an important role in deciding whether a "major" rule might be exempted from the provisions of the executive order under OMB's broad exemption powers. According to GAO, these exemption powers were frequently used. Between February 17 and December 31, 1981, OMB waived the regulatory analyses requirement for twenty-one of the forty-three rules designated as "major" and published by executive branch regulatory agencies. In many cases, the reason for the waiver could not be determined from the documentation provided, but declaration by the agency proposing a rule that its aim was to reduce costs was often reason enough to secure an exemption. On this point, GAO remarked: "Insofar as 'deregulation' simply means making regulation more efficient, we believe the regulatory impact requirement can contribute to—rather than detract from—that goal."[22]

It was fortunate for OMB that so many of the rules submitted to it during 1981 could be judged to comply with the executive order and the Paperwork Reduction Act (or could be made to comply by only minor technical amendments.) Table 5 shows that during 1981, a year that by the administration's own accounts was one of extremely light rule-making activity, new rules were being sent to OMB at a rate of approximately ten per working day. Given the extremely small number of technically qualified analysts, a significantly larger number of "major" rules, accompanied by detailed regulatory analyses that themselves had to be subjected to scrutiny, would have swamped the agency.

But how *were* priorities set within OMB? GAO apparently had a hard time telling. Certainly OMB analysts did not seem to be devoting their time to some of the issues that one might have expected, given the wording of the executive order:

> OMB does not appear to exercise its powers under E.O. 12291 to reduce conflicts among regulations or to insure consistent application of the regulatory analysis process. . . .OMB has not issued standards for identifying major rules beyond the standards given in the Executive Order, which are subject to varying interpretations. . . . There is also potential for inconsistency in initiating reviews of existing rules and in waiving RIA (Regulatory Impact Analysis) requirements for major rules. OMB has neither announced nor published criteria for selecting rules targeted for review. . . .There also seems to be no explicit policy on waiving the RIA requirement for major rules. . . . The provisions of the executive order that authorize the development of procedures for compiling a regulatory budget . . . and that require agencies to take into account other

regulatory actions contemplated for the future . . . imply a need for achieving consistent methodologies for measuring regulatory impacts. . . . [However,] problems of coordinating methodologies for estimating the costs and benefits in any given industry have not been addressed.[23]

GAO concluded that although OMB's overall impact on the rule-making process was difficult to discern, in those instances in which OMB returned rules to the agencies for major changes (in effect rejecting them in their proposed form), OMB's actions clearly had a significant effect. In 1981, for example, OMB returned forty-five rules to agencies for major revisions, but no agency appealed any of these rejections to the task force.[24]

GAO's ultimate judgment of OMB's regulatory oversight role was, however, harsh:

OMB's approach to regulatory oversight under E.O. 12291 blurs the source of regulatory decisions. Not only does OMB generally communicate with agencies orally rather than in writing, but in at least one case, OMB resisted putting its opinions on paper even when the agency asked it to do so. When OMB opinions are put in writing, they generally do not provide a full explanation of OMB's objections. Instead, the opinions frequently refer to earlier staff discussions. The result of this non-documented approach to rulemaking is that the public cannot determine at whose initiative a rule was issued. While the agency formally remains accountable for its rules, the record does not show whether the agency made its decisions primarily on the basis of its interpretation of the evidence available to it or in response to OMB directives. The lack of documentation also makes it impossible for others in the Federal Government to comment on the basis for a rulemaking decision and to play a ''peer review'' role.

Because OMB's influence is potentially great, its apparent openness to *ex parte* communications (communications with interested parties that are not recorded in the public record and for which public notice to all parties is not given) about pending rules raises similar disclosure concerns. While OMB's expressed policy is to encourage those who contact it about a rule to submit a notice to the agency for the public record, OMB has no monitoring system to ensure that this takes place. Thus not only may OMB's views be communicated to the agency without being placed on the public record, but the views of outside parties may be communicated, using OMB as a conduit, without being placed on the public record. The public cannot determine either who made the regulatory decision or on what basis it was made.[25]

GAO's report suggests, then, that the Reagan oversight program did not take as its central objective the coordinating, conflict-reducing goals advanced by former administrations. Furthermore, the program did not seem to observe the cardinal political rules that other administrations found to apply to such an inherently controversial program. In the first place, the uniform application of neutral evaluative principles was not apparent; in fact the new procedures' design had few, if any, elements to discourage arbitrary interventions. Second, the rule-making record was unlikely to reveal the frequency or nature of contacts between executive department decision makers, interested parties, and agency officials. As a result, the new procedures provided OMB and the White House with a suspect and somewhat larger-than-life look.

The Auto Package: Regulatory Oversight Delivers

Probably the most significant single regulatory "event" during the administration's first year in office was the president's announcement in April of thirty-four specific regulatory actions (principally rescissions or relaxations of existing rules) that he believed would "save" the domestic automobile industry $1.4 billion in capital costs and consumers more than $9.3 billion over five years. Table 6 lists the most important of these regulatory actions, shows their status as of mid-1983, and reports administration estimates of the savings that they were intended to generate.

The president's announcement itself accomplished nothing other than to inform the public that the agencies involved—the National Highway Traffic Safety Administration and the Environmental Protection Agency—had submitted a series of notices to the *Federal Register* initiating a series of rule makings. Although the White House "fact sheet" accompanying the announcement attempted to make the actions seem to be faits accomplis, no specific outcomes could actually be guaranteed. Both NHTSA and EPA would have to hold public hearings on the proposed changes, and the standards they would apply in reaching their decisions would, in theory, be unchanged from those that Carter administration officials had employed in putting the regulations into place initially. To be sure, the new Reagan executive order did contain a new set of "general requirements" for rule making, but these were to apply only "to the extent permitted by law." And the "law" in question had not been modified.

Yet the way in which the Reagan auto package was assembled, announced, and monitored illustrates quite well how the administration hoped that the new oversight process would work. In a real sense, the presentation was the most strikingly successful part of the process.

To illustrate this fact, it is useful to contrast the Reagan auto package with one announced by Carter approximately a year earlier. The political and economic circumstances surrounding each plan's announcement were similar. The American automobile industry was in considerable financial difficulty. Sales had plummeted, and even the strongest of the companies were reporting

TABLE 6
MAJOR ELEMENTS OF THE REAGAN ADMINISTRATION'S AUTO PACKAGE

		5-Year Savings (millions)	
Issue	Action (date of completion)	Industry	Public
	RULES ACTED ON		
Gas-tank vapors	Declined to order new controls on cars (April 1981).	$103	$1,300
Emissions tests	Streamlined certification of industry tests on vehicles (October 1981, November 1982).	5	—
	Raised the allowable "failure rate" for test of light trucks and heavy-duty engines from 10 to 40 percent (January 1983).	19	129
	Reduced spot checks of emissions of vehicles on assembly lines by 42 percent; delayed assembly-line tests of heavy-duty trucks until 1986 (January 1983).	1	1
High-altitude autos	Ended assembly-line tests at high altitude, relying instead on industry data (April 1981).	0.2	—
	Allowed industry to self-certify vehicles as meeting high-altitude emission standards (April 1981).		
Pollution waivers	Consolidated industry applications for temporary exemptions from tougher emissions standards for nitrogen oxide and carbon monoxide (September 1981).	—	—
Paint shops	Delayed until 1983 tougher hydrocarbon pollution standards for auto paint shops (October 1981).	300	—
Test vehicles	Cut paperwork required to exempt prototype vehicles from environmental standards (July 1982).	—	—
Driver vision	Scrapped existing 1981 rule and second proposed rule setting standards for driver's field of view (June 1982).	160	—
Fuel economy	Decided not to set stiffer fuel economy standards to replace those expiring in 1985 (April 1981).	—	—
Speedometers	Revoked rule setting standards for speedometers and tamper-resistant odometers (February 1982).	—	20

TABLE 6 (continued)

Issue	Action (date of completion)	5-Year Savings (millions)	
		Industry	Public
Tire rims	Scrapped proposal to set safety standards for explosive multipiece tire rims (February 1982).	$300	$ 75
Brake tests	Eased from 30 to 20 percent the steepness of grades on which post-1984 truck and bus brakes must hold (December 1981).	—	1.8
Tire pressure	Scrapped proposal to equip vehicles with low tire pressure indicators (August 1981).	—	130
Battery safety	Scrapped proposal to set standards to prevent auto battery explosions (August 1981).	—	—
Tire safety	Revoked requirement that consumers be told of reserve load capacity of tires; eased tire makers' reporting requirements (June 1982).	—	—
Antitheft protection	Eased antitheft and locking steering wheel standards for open-body vehicles (June 1981).	—	—
Fuel economy	Streamlined semiannual reports of auto makers on their progress in meeting fuel economy goals (August 1982).	—	0.1
Tire ratings	Suspended rule requiring industry to rate tires according to tread wear, traction, and heat resistance (February 1983).	—	10
Vehicle IDs	Downgraded from standard to administrative rule the requirement that all vehicles have ID numbers as an aid to police (May 1983).	—	—
Seat belt comfort	Scrapped proposal to set standards for seat belt comfort and convenience (June 1983).	—	—
RULES WITH UNCERTAIN FUTURES			
High-altitude emissions	Failed to revise Clean Air Act order ending weaker high-altitude emissions standards in 1984; eased through regulatory changes.	37	1,300

TABLE 6 (continued)

MAJOR ELEMENTS OF THE REAGAN ADMINISTRATION'S AUTO PACKAGE

		5-Year Savings (millions)	
Issue	Action (date of completion)	Industry	Public
Emissions reductions	Failed to revise Clean Air Act order to cut large trucks' hydrocarbon and carbon monoxide emissions by 90 percent by 1984; standard was delayed until 1985.	$105	$536
	Failed to ease Clean Air Act order reducing nitrogen oxide emissions from light trucks and heavy-duty engines by 75 percent by 1984. Regulatory changes under study.	150	563
Particulate pollution	Delayed a proposal to scrap specific particulate standards for some diesels in favor of an average standard for all diesels. Stiffer standards delayed from 1985 to 1987.	40	523
Methane standards	Shelved because of "serious" cost; questions a plan to drop methane as a regulated hydrocarbon.	—	—
Passive restraints	Delayed and then revoked requirement that post-1982 autos be equipped with passive restraints; revocation overturned by Supreme Court in June 1983.	428	981
Bumper damage	Cut from 5 to 2.5 mph the speed at which bumpers must resist damage; change is on appeal.	—	308

SOURCE: Michael Wines, "Reagan Plan to Relieve Auto Industry of Regulatory Burden Gets Mixed Grades," *National Journal*, July 23, 1983, pp. 1534–1535.

substantial losses. Unemployment in the industry was extremely high and concentrated in a few important industrial states. Imports, especially from Japan, were taking a growing share of the domestic market. Both administrations had been under great pressure to do something to help the industry, and both had been reluctant to turn to either general financial assistance or limiting imports. Both seized upon changes in regulations as a way to obtain some breathing space for the industry.

Since the late 1960s, the auto industry had been subject to an increasingly stringent set of regulations governing fuel economy, emissions, safety, and overall product performance. Although no auto regulatory commission had been set up, the industry had, by the late 1970s, truly become a "regulated" industry in the strictest sense of the word.

The role that these various regulations were playing in the industry's financial difficulties was in dispute. Industry argued that the regulations were a massive burden from which relief was clearly warranted. Government regulators heatedly denied this.[26] Perhaps the most extreme claim was made in a study commissioned by the Chrysler Corporation which concluded that regulations were the principal factor in Chrysler's near demise.[27]

Regardless of who was right, it seemed clear to the Carter administration by early 1980 that some interim relief would have to be given, if only from political necessity. But how to do it? The Office of Management and Budget and the Regulatory Council had compiled a list of regulations affecting the industry and estimates of their associated costs.[28] During the late winter and early spring of 1980, officials in OMB, the CEA, the domestic policy staff, and the secretary of transportation's office worked with NHTSA (itself a unit of DOT) and EPA to develop a package of regulatory actions the president could announce that would provide the industry with a measure of "regulatory relief." (The "relief" component was explicit in this case.) The effort was painful, provoking considerable resistance, especially from NHTSA. Eventually a modest auto package was assembled and announced by President Carter at a meeting with auto industry executives on July 8, 1980.

The Carter administration estimated that its auto package could increase the auto industry's cash flow by "more than $500 million in the next three years." Moreover, the announcement committed "the Department of Transportation to *make certain* that regulations to be issued in the coming year will . . . reflect a sensitivity to the industry's cash flow problems."[29] (Emphasis added.)

Why did the development of this auto package prove so laborious for the Carter administration and the results so modest? For one thing, the administration was acutely sensitive to its limited ability to control agency behavior. It could ask agencies to reexamine regulations to see if any could be rescinded or modified, but, as noted in previous chapters, it did not believe that it had the power to dictate outcomes. Indeed, under the Carter executive order, officials in charge of regulatory oversight could not even formally require an agency to initiate a review of existing regulations; they could *request* such a review, but the agency was free to turn them down.

But could not Carter administration officials have used indirect pressure to force NHTSA and EPA to comply with their wishes? Perhaps. But even though many Carter aides considered "doing something" to ease the regulatory plight of the auto industry to be both economically justified and politically expedient, there were other important constituencies, such as the environmentalists and consumer activists, to consider with an election approaching. Therefore, the Carter auto package could not make any changes that might appear to suspend important regulatory protections. Even the "fact sheet" issued at the time of Carter's meeting with the industry to announce the various elements of his package went out of its way to stress the administration's continuing commitment to environmental, auto safety, and fuel economy goals.[30]

What did the Carter auto package actually contain? EPA made three commitments: to submit legislative proposals to Congress designed to reduce the stringency of high-altitude emissions standards scheduled to go into effect in 1984 (this was the only "big ticket" item in the package—the entire $500 million savings mentioned in the president's "talking points" was attributable to this one change); to implement a voluntary pilot program that would have reduced the cost of verifying the durability of vehicle emissions-control devices and to expedite consideration of requests to waive requirements of the carbon monoxide emissions standard. OSHA even contributed something. It announced that it would permit General Motors and the United Auto Workers to develop a less costly way of complying with newly promulgated lead and arsenic exposure standards "while still protecting worker health," and would "consider" similar proposals from Ford and Chrysler.

NHTSA's principal commitment was to refrain from issuing any "major" safety rules during the remainder of calendar 1980, but it also promised to "review again" fuel economy standards for light trucks for 1983 through 1985 "pursuant to comments from the president's Regulatory Analysis Review Group" (which had strongly criticized the proposed standards). NHTSA also agreed to "thoroughly consider" post-1985 fuel economy standards as part of a DOT study of the auto industry in progress and to refrain from pursuing such standards in rule making "until that study is complete and submitted to the president."[31]

Even more significant was what the Carter auto package did *not* contain. During late 1979 and early 1980, Ford and General Motors had individually approached the Carter administration with extensive regulatory "wish lists." These lists included some extremely significant regulatory changes, including substantive modifications of the Clear Air Act and a rollback of regulations that the Carter administration had just put into place—often after substantial internal dissent among the president's advisers. The administration rejected most of the industry's proposals out of hand. Certain others were taken up by those of Carter's advisers who previously had supported them, but none ultimately found its way into the July 8 announcement.

Another important characteristic of the Carter auto package was that the significant elements in it were going to occur anyway. EPA had already decided that the definition of "high altitude" embodied in the Clean Air Act Amendments of 1977 was unreasonably burdensome and was planning to change it. The only question was whether the change could be accomplished administratively or whether legislation would be required.

In short, the Carter auto package was an empty box. It provided no regulatory savings for the auto industry beyond what the industry was already going to get. What was worse politically, the industry was aware of this fact and reacted accordingly. The long, frustrating, sometimes bitter struggle that accompanied the development of the package thus did not even accomplish its *political* objective—to indicate to the industry and to the United Auto Workers, who were also concerned with the issue, that the administration was sympathetic to their plight.

Contrast these limited proposals with the Reagan effort. Development of a substantial auto regulatory relief package began almost as soon as the administration took office. The continuing plight of the domestic industry plus the obvious interest of OMB Director Stockman (he had represented a district in western Michigan in Congress and had long been critical of automotive regulations) made development of such a package almost inevitable. The administration had the same industry regulatory "wish lists" to work from as had the Carter administration. They had the analyses that Carter's advisers had prepared arguing against the initial adoption of the regulations and seeking their relaxation during the fight over the Carter auto package. Thus, the analytical effort required to put together a substantial Reagan auto package was minimal.

The Reagan administration also was happy to claim credit for actions the Carter administration had already taken. Recall that the only significant item in the Carter package was the commitment to ease what even EPA acknowledged was an overly stringent definition of "high altitude." The Reagan administration not only included this item in its package but raised the claimed savings from the $500 million estimated by EPA under Carter to $1.3 billion.

One item that made its way into the Reagan auto package illustrates the sharply contrasting criteria that the two administrations employed in deciding whether to modify regulations affecting the auto industry. The "paint shop" item in table 3 had been on the auto industry's regulatory wish lists given to the Carter administration, but had received no support even from the most dedicated of Carter's regulatory reformers. The explanation was simple: paint shops were extremely significant, concentrated sources of hydrocarbon emissions. If the Clean Air Act standards for hydrocarbon emissions were to be met (and neither the Carter nor the Reagan administration proposed changes either in their stringency or in the timetables for their attainment), a certain volume of hydrocarbon emissions would have to be eliminated. Although costly to the auto industry (the industry put the cost of meeting these regulations at $300 million), the regulations appeared to represent by far the most cost-effective method of controlling hydrocarbon emissions. In other words, removing an equivalent volume of emissions from other sources would have cost far more. However, this higher cost would have fallen not on the auto industry but on other industries in the vicinity of the auto industry's paint shops (e.g., dry-cleaning establishments and gasoline stations.) The Carter administration stressed the overall cost-effectiveness of the regulations in refusing to consider changing them; the Reagan administration was more concerned with the auto industry's claimed $300 million investment impact.[32]

The change in oversight procedures that Reagan had made, plus the fact that the auto package was put together early in the administration, assured that there would be little of the bickering that had accompanied the assembling of Carter's auto package. The powers that the OMB had under the Reagan executive order made certain that rules targeted by the White House would be reviewed. The OMB's new "gatekeeping" powers, plus its ability to exempt "major" rules from the requirements of the executive order, assured minimal bureaucratic delay in getting the required rule makings completed. If any trouble did develop, the task force could help bring recalcitrants into line, but serious resistance from the agencies was unlikely. During much of the time the package was being developed, both NHTSA and EPA were leaderless. And when leaders for these two agencies were chosen, special care was taken to assure that they were committed to regulatory relief.

Not surprisingly, therefore, most of the elements in the Reagan auto package moved smoothly through the rule-making process and produced the outcomes that the president had forecast in April. However, as table 6 shows, not every promised action was taken. In particular, actions requiring legislation—such as the change in the 1984 high-altitude standards—did not go through. (The administration attempted to make this change administratively, thereby risking having it overturned in the courts.) But many of the major items in which industry was interested were there. Although one can dispute the specifics of the administration's savings claims, the volume of relief provided industry was clearly substantial—provided the changes eventually held up under the inevitable court challenges.

In the spring and summer of 1981, challenges in the courts seemed a long way off. As far as the administration, the auto industry, and industry in general were concerned, the auto package signaled that there was indeed a new regulatory game in town—one that might be capable of delivering significant regulatory relief.

The Lead-in-Gasoline Decision

The auto package was announced when presidential attention was focused on regulatory relief and agency heads were new in their jobs and anxious to please. It is instructive to contrast the outcome then with what occurred approximately eighteen months later when EPA tried to "end run" OMB in order to thwart OMB's efforts to hold up proposed EPA regulations revising the amount of lead that refiners could add to gasoline to boost its octane level.

As was the case in the auto package, the review of the lead-in-gasoline rule was initiated by a request from the task force. (The Carter administration had several times considered changing the rule but had declined to.) To comply with the task force's request, EPA proposed easing the regulation in February 1982, but environmentalists and public health officials strongly objected to the EPA proposal. EPA had second thoughts about the wisdom of the change, and in July informed OMB that it was preparing a new proposal which, in effect, would tighten the existing standard. When EPA completed this proposal at the end of July, it sent a copy to OMB for its review, and, according to the *Washington Post*, simultaneously leaked a copy of it to the press. OMB objected to the EPA proposal, and those objections were also leaked to the press (one story asserts that the leaking was done by OMB). OMB requested that EPA reconsider its decision not to relax the basic rule. But what drew the most criticism was OMB's objection to the part of the EPA proposal that would have issued an interim rule narrowing an exemption that previously had been granted to small refiners.

Under the existing regulations, small refiners had been permitted to put substantially larger amounts of lead into gasoline than the larger refiners. This gave them a cost advantage that helped offset their higher refining costs. The result was a larger supply of gasoline—an important concern at the time the regulation had first been issued. But the "small refiner" exemption also encouraged the growth of blenders—firms that were not refiners but purchased low-octane gasoline (often overseas) at a substantial discount and added the maximum permissible amount of lead to it as a cheap method of boosting its octane to commercial levels. The narrowing of the definition of small refiner was aimed primarily at these blenders, whom both the large refiners and environmentalists referred to as "regulatory entrepreneurs."

Eventually the dispute was resolved, with EPA the apparent winner. Characterized as an attempt to "salvage what has been a public relations disaster for the agency and to end the long-running lead soap opera," the compromise agreed to by OMB and EPA committed the administration to issue final rules by November 1, 1982, somewhat earlier than OMB had wished. The basic standard of 1.1 gram per gallon was retained, and the small-refiner definition was narrowed. Some elements of increased flexibility favored by OMB were included in EPA's final proposal, among which was a so-called "lead bubble" that permitted refiners to trade lead reduction credits among themselves.

Subsequently, the administration sought to turn lemons into lemonade by citing the lead phase-down decision as a significant victory for the oversight process. Its official account as published in the task force's final (August 1983) report reads as follows:

> The lead phasedown rule . . . [is one example] of how OMB oversight under the Executive Order and its policies have improved rulemaking by making it quicker and more responsive to the concerns—here environmental—at issue. . . .The lead phasedown regulations . . . grew out of one of the Task Force's designated reviews which resulted not in the elimination or cut-back of a rule, but rather in the expansion of a regulatory program that introduced new concepts of general applicability to reduce compliance costs. When the existing phasedown rule was initially targeted for review, questions had been raised both about the evenness of the rule's application to disparate segments of the refining and distribution industry, as well as its continued need in view of virtually universal compliance with the lead ambient air standard and the declining sales of cars that use leaded gasoline. During the review, however, the Center for Disease Control developed information that more strongly linked leaded gasoline usage with unhealthy blood-lead levels. Moreover, lead usage began to increase rather than decrease as the result of growing exploitation of a loophole in the existing regulations that did not apply evenly to all segments of the industry. As a result of the ongoing review, the Administration was able to respond quickly to accelerate the phasedown while introducing a new trading policy that assured that all segments of the industry were treated equally and that the lead reductions would be achieved at the lowest cost.[33]

Although we cannot know for certain, in this as in subsequent instances of agency-OMB conflict, the monolithic image of the new oversight process may have played into the hands of agency bureaucrats. Political points could be made from a well-publicized division between agency regulators and their overseers at the White House. How often an agency head could exploit this strategy and remain a valued team player was unclear, but the tactic certainly proved effective when selectively deployed.

More Sour Notes

The spectacle of OMB and an agency publicly squabbling over a proposed regulation or regulatory revision was not confined to this one incident. Indeed, relations between OMB and the Occupational Safety and Health Administration seem to have been rocky throughout the Reagan administration. In the spring of 1982 OSHA Administrator Thorne Auchter refused to accept an OMB rejection of OSHA's proposed chemical-labeling rule. Auchter insisted on appealing OMB's decision to the task force, and he prevailed.[34] In March 1983, *Business Week* described several instances in which OSHA and OMB had disagreed strongly on proposed OSHA standards. In one, Auchter was reported to have ordered the publication—despite OMB objections—of a standard that had been held up by six months of "bickering." He pulled the standard back only after OIRA Administrator DeMuth protested directly to Labor Secretary Raymond Donovan.[35] Auchter also prevailed over OMB in an argument about how far the Carter administration's cotton dust regulations should be relaxed. Auchter argued that the regulations then in place were cost-effective and had boosted productivity.[36] In July of 1983, a *Wall Street Journal* story indicated that OSHA was "reevaluating" an earlier decision to loosen its standard for workplace exposure to lead—an action the task force's August 1982 "Progress Report" had credited with saving industry $50 million.[37]

Although other examples of OMB-agency conflict could be cited—examples not involving OSHA—it would be a mistake to conclude that OMB generally forced unwilling agencies into granting regulatory relief. Most of President Reagan's regulatory appointees strongly supported his regulatory relief effort. They worked hard to deliver on the regulatory revisions that the task force and OMB committed them to.

It was a good thing for him that they did, for the OSHA and EPA examples illustrate once again the limited powers, even under the broad Reagan executive order, that the White House actually has to force regulatory changes on unwilling agencies if such agencies are prepared to protest the changes all the way to the president and to leak word of their protest to the press. The examples raise anew the question DeMuth posed in his critique of the Carter oversight process: whether any such process can reasonably claim to be exerting overall control over something as complex as executive branch rule-making activity if it does not somehow fundamentally alter the incentives facing the agencies.

Perceptions of the Reagan Oversight Process as a Political Filter

Whether the Reagan oversight process has continued to impose more coherence and consistency on the regulatory process is open to question, but there can be no doubt that the process's operation has evoked considerable controversy. The main controversy stems from the perception that the process was intended not to make social regulation more cost-effective and coherent, but to serve as a political filter.

At the beginning of chapter 3, we noted the inevitable tension that exists in *any* White House regulatory oversight operation between (1) intervention to promote policy consistency and coordination and (2) intervention to promote political favoritism. The power to do one inevitably implies the power to do the other. The public, its view colored by reports generated by congressional hearings and sensational newspaper stories, is not always able to tell the difference. At times, even when intervention is undertaken for legitimate purposes and carried out in a legally acceptable manner, it may be painted as politically motivated.

Earlier in this chapter, we stressed the differences between the Reagan and Carter oversight programs, and especially the greater chances inherent in the design and operating methods of the Reagan program for suspicions to emerge. The concerns were reinforced by the abandonment of public filings by executive office agencies; the apparently casual attitude taken toward contacts with industry and toward comments made to agencies (especially during the postcomment period); and the establishment of OMB as the regulatory gatekeeper without adequate resources to conduct substantive oversight.

We have also contrasted the outcomes of the auto package and the lead-in-gasoline decision. The former revealed the usefulness of a comparatively strong, centralized oversight process—at least until the courts began to overturn major elements of the package. The latter turned into a messy, politically embarrassing squabble between White House regulatory overseers and a supposedly docile EPA—a feud that the White House clearly lost.

Crucial to this latter loss, it seems, was the suspicion that the White House was willing to risk public health in order to play political favorites. During the long squabble between OMB and EPA over the lead phasedown regulations, the press revealed that OMB had been approached by a California attorney, John Diepenbrock, who represented one of the blenders who would be hurt by the proposal. Diepenbrock had been California finance chairman for Ronald Reagan's 1980 campaign and was a close friend of White House Counselor Edwin Meese. Diepenbrock admitted to the *Washington Post* that he had contacted OMB (as well as the task force and EPA itself) and had found OMB "very sympathetic."[38] OIRA Administrator DeMuth challenged the assertion that OMB's stand was influenced by pressure from Diepenbrock, stating, "There have been people in there on every side of this issue."[39] But given OMB's operating procedures, especially its unwillingness to provide documentation for its actions, such charges were hard to disprove.

In some instances, OMB's involvement in a regulation was *clearly* political—and nothing else. The most amusing of these was the so-called "catsup and tofu incident." In the late summer of 1981, just before James Miller left OIRA to become chairman of the Federal Trade Commission, the Department of Agriculture, in an effort to increase the flexibility of school districts struggling with budget cutbacks affecting school lunch programs, sought to redefine what would qualify as an acceptable lunch. The proposed regulations included a number of controversial changes, but the one that caught the attention of the news media—and subjected the administration to public ridicule—was Agriculture's attempt to define catsup as a vegetable and tofu (bean curd) as meat.

The Democrats made full use of the opportunity to "embarrass the administration as rarely before."[40] The editorial cartoonists also had a field day. After nearly a month of controversy, OMB Director Stockman moved to contain the political damage to the administration. Acting apparently on direct orders of the president (the president has been quoted as saying that he gave the order), Stockman told Miller to direct the Agriculture Department to withdraw the regulations because "they violated the regulatory review procedure." According to the *Washington Post* this action left Agriculture Secretary John R. Block "sorely miffed."[41]

This is hardly an example of massive presidential intervention to support regulatory relief. (It is, however, the only example we are aware of in which President Reagan has publicly acknowledged intervening to change a regulation.) But it was an early sign that OMB would, if the situation warranted it, use its 'gatekeeping' powers to demand specific changes in regulations. What is more, the situation calling forth OMB's powers in this case was the desire to control a politically embarrassing situation—understandable from the White House's point of view, but not something calculated to send a signal to the agencies that OMB intended to base its decisions primarily on the technical (as opposed to the political) merits of regulatory proposals.

Certainly attorneys for private industry have come to view OMB and the task force as "the place to go" to get their point across concerning regulations they do not like. In April 1981, William Warfield Ross, writing in the *National Law Journal*, advised his fellow attorneys (who were just beginning to gain experience with the new Reagan oversight process):

Practitioners should . . . be alert to the possibility of direct intercession with the White House itself, that is, with the [OMB] director and his staff. Given the very considerable powers vested in the director—and the fact that the

executive order is completely silent as to any restrictions on communication
with OMB or the task force with respect to the review of major rules—the
practitioner should make every effort where appropriate to communicate with
the director to attempt to influence his "views" on a proposed rule in the
direction of the client's preference.

In the absence of any ground rules, the possible approaches are limited
only by the extent of the practitioner's ingenuity or effrontery. One can assume
that the director and his policy staff will soon have unlisted telephone numbers
if they do not already.

Ross concluded his article with this observation: "Now more than ever, it
can be expected that the race will be to the swift, the enterprising and to those
with access to the levers of power, not only in the Congress and the regulatory
agencies, but also in the presidential office.[42]

A similar but more succinct statement of this viewpoint was quoted in
the *Washington Post* in November 1982, long after the Stockman memo had
been issued. The story concerned another feud between OMB and EPA, this
one relating to some regulations involving the discharge of toxic effluents
into water by twenty-seven major industries. In this instance it was the phar-
maceutical industry that was upset, and to convey its view, its representatives
went to Associate OIRA Administrator James Tozzi and to Boyden Gray of
the task force. Commenting on the reason for this, the attorney for Pfizer,
Joan Bernstein, who had been EPA's general counsel during part of the Carter
administration, remarked: "Anybody representing a client who didn't use that
route would be damn negligent."[43]

Certainly many people—and not just opponents of the administration's
regulatory relief effort—perceived the role of OMB and the task force as
primarily that of a political filter. The perception may have been incorrect,
but OMB's methods of operation—plus the insensitivity of the officials running the regulatory relief program to the longer-term adverse consequences
of being perceived as overwhelmingly pro-business—certainly did little to
alter perceptions of politicization. As a result, concerns that had been first
raised by the oversight activities of the Nixon White House—concerns that
the Ford and Carter oversight processes had begun to quiet—reappeared with
a vengeance. If the Reagan oversight activities had indeed proved as effective
as originally hoped in helping to revitalize the economy, this trade-off might
have been acceptable, at least from the president's perspective. But in view
of the program's marginal contribution (see Chapter 2), its political costs
almost certainly have outweighed any of its benefits.

7

Agency Management Strategies

The officials who designed the expansion of the White House regulatory oversight process for the Reagan administration realized that it could not, by itself, "turn around" regulation to the degree that the president intended. As both James Miller and Murray Weidenbaum acknowledged in an interview, the agencies would have to be "the first line of defense against overregulation" and "the first line of *offense* in ferreting out ineffective and excessively burdensome regulations."[1] To play this dual role, the agencies needed to be headed by and staffed with people sympathetic to the president's regulatory relief aims.

The administration could immediately designate the heads of the executive branch regulatory agencies and their principal aides, and the chairmen of independent regulatory agencies. Although the president could not fire a sitting commissioner to make way for his own appointee on independent commissions, numerous unfilled vacancies in effect allowed the president to put his stamp on most of these commissions from the start of his term. Moreover, the civil service reforms championed by the Carter administration had the unintended consequence of permitting Reagan to make more appointments in what had been senior career civil service positions than previously would have been possible.

As Miller notes in the interview just mentioned, it was critical that the "GS-13s and GS-14s who write [and, incidentally, enforce] the regulations"[2] understand that regulatory matters would no longer be handled in a "business as usual" fashion. The OMB oversight process could help, but other tech-

139

niques would be necessary to convince career staff that the regulation game really had changed.

This chapter explores means other than the direct oversight of the rule-making process which the Reagan administration used to bring, in the president's words, the regulatory agencies "to heel." We review the high-level regulatory appointments the administration made, the sizable cuts in regulatory agency budgets, and the various reorganizations proposed—and in some cases, effected—for several of the more activist agencies.

Viewed collectively, these management strategies were designed to send a clear message to the general public and the bureaucracy that regulatory policy was undergoing a sharp change. Old activist tactics would no longer be acceptable in the government, and the defensive responses they triggered within the private sector would no longer be necessary. Unapologetically probusiness regulatory leaders, armed with the disciplining weapons of real and feared staff reductions and reorganizations, were to forcefully restrict new regulatory initiatives.

But the administration faced a fundamental dilemma upon assuming office. On the one hand, the architects of regulatory policy plainly wanted to improve the efficiency of regulatory management. In fact, Executive Order 12291, which vested increased regulatory oversight responsibilities in OMB and mandated that all proposed regulations undergo cost-benefit analysis, can be viewed as a management instrument. On the other hand, management strategies aimed toward the conventional goals of enhanced agency competence and productivity might not serve the overall goals of the regulatory relief program. Since many of the president's supporters—particularly those in the libertarian camp—questioned the validity of regulation per se, increasing agency efficiency appeared a dubious goal. Hence, administration management strategies focused less on improving agency competence than on sending a clear signal to the regulatory bureaucracy. Over time, however, the appeal of more conventional strategies—and managers—grew. Although a short-run bureaucratic paralysis may have been acceptable, over the longer term it became clear that (1) the process of regulatory relief or reform would prove procedurally and technically complex; (2) many of the responsibilities of the agencies administering social regulation were politically and practically fixed; and (3) the administration would be required by the media, Congress, and the electorate to enforce the rules and laws it had been unable to change.

Regulatory Appointments

The history of presidential appointments suggests that they are made with three distinct, but not mutually exclusive, objectives in mind: rewarding political patronage, deploying a set of political symbols, and obtaining managerial or technical competence.[3] Like the appointees of all presidents, Reagan's regulatory appointees served each of these objectives; as is the case in many administrations, symbolism and patronage were given special emphasis at the outset.

In fact, Reagan may have outdone his predecessors in the clarity of the political signals he communicated through his regulatory appointments. At least in terms of their publicly expressed principles and ideologies, Reagan's regulatory appointees presented an unusually uniform probusiness and antiregulation image. One political scientist, reviewing the administration's appointments process, noted: "There was achieved in [these] appointments an uncommon degree of ideological consistency and intensity."[4] Only in the wake of the resignation of twenty-one political appointees at EPA did the administration attempt to demonstrate more interest in managerial competence.

The administrative dilemma posed by regulatory policy was nowhere more apparent than in the appointments process. The archetypical effective agency manager is someone with experience in a government organization or extensive knowledge of agency operations. The most frequently cited attribute of this model manager is an ability to inspire high employee morale, and hence productivity, in the bureaucracy—principally by keeping lines of communication open between career and political staff.[5]

Clearly this approach suggests a measure of faith in the regulatory process and in regulators not shared by a number of the administration's chief policy architects. In fact, Reagan had campaigned against Washington and had taken every opportunity to pillory the stereotypical, do-nothing federal bureaucrat. Accordingly it was not surprising that wide divisions between career and political staffs developed in many regulatory agencies during the administration's first years.

Although all incoming administrations view the bureaucracy they have been elected to manage with some suspicion, it appears that few administrations have distanced themselves from the career bureaucracy as the Reagan administration did. Even relations between most career and political staffs in the Nixon administration offer a contrast in their comparative openness. Richard Nathan, a senior member of Nixon's OMB staff, has written:

> Both Nixon's Cabinet and sub-Cabinet appointees, particularly if they were new to the programs or agency that they had been named to head, entered on their appointment into an almost ritualistic courting and mating process with the bureaucracy. They were closeted for long hours in orientation sessions with career program officials, the purpose being for these career officials to explain to them program goals and accomplishments and to warn them about the need

for support from powerful outside interests. . . . Thereafter, in many obvious
and subtle ways, the praise and respect of the agency's permanent staff was
[sic] increasingly made a function of the performance of these presidentially
appointed officials as spokesmen and advocates for the agency's interests.[6]

The common characteristics of the Reagan administration's political appointees—their ideological leanings and suspicions of the bureaucracy—are
likely to produce both efficient and inefficient results. On the one hand,
relations between agencies (horizontal relations) are likely to be conducted
harmoniously. This reduction in interagency tension theoretically should lead
to regulatory policies that are consistent and relatively quickly produced. On
the other hand, relations between political and career staffs within agencies
(vertical relations) have suffered, creating morale and communication problems that rarely promote efficient outcomes.

Even with the most straightforward and unambitious of political agendas,
it is always hard for a new administration to find suitable regulatory appointees. There are more than 600 positions to be filled within a matter of weeks.
An enormous pool of talented, available, politically attuned, and politically
acceptable individuals must be identified and placed in positions where their
skills and experience can be put to good use. Complicating matters is the fact
that government service and the management of regulatory agencies have few,
if any, analogs in private life. Evaluating potential performance is at least
partially guesswork. In addition, personnel matters are not the only issues
competing for White House attention during the first weeks of a new administration.

We have already commented on the key role that skilled personnel played
in the efforts of Presidents Ford and Carter to reform economic regulation.
President Reagan's proposed attack on social regulation posed far greater
technical, administrative, and political problems. For one thing, the generally
acknowledged objective was not to eliminate the programs of social regulation
themselves but to find ways of paring them back and making them work more
effectively. As we pointed out in chapter 5, exactly how this might be done
was a matter of considerable dispute, but virtually any solution required
managerial competence. If regulations were to be modified administratively
in ways that could withstand court challenges, if economic incentives of
various types were to be successfully introduced, or if statutes were to be
changed to permit greater administrative discretion and flexibility, managers
of social regulatory agencies had to possess—and be seen to possess—significant technical, legal, political, and bureaucratic skills.

The dilemma the administration faced concerning appointments, then,
was this: Obtaining *rapid* regulatory change required the appointment of

administrators who passionately shared the president's commitment to regulatory relief. In fact, these appointees should actively support efforts to modify statutes or to cut the budgets of their agencies. Obtaining *durable* regulatory reform, however, required the appointment of technically skilled, managerially competent administrators who, although they might wish to see social regulation pared back, basically were sympathetic to its aims and wished to see it work. These administrators might be expected to balk at efforts to strip them of effective decision-making powers and to eliminate their agencies' resources.

A simple interest in rolling back agency regulations would permit the appointment of modestly talented people—the kind often selected through political patronage channels—to serve as agency caretakers. Similarly, controversial, high-visibility leaders could be appointed to embody the new era in regulatory policy. Each type of appointee appeared acceptable at the outset, in part because the administration may have underestimated the extent to which substantive change could be accomplished by executive fiat. In addition, administration planners had little fear of agency paralysis resulting from deep divisions between appointed and career staff; indeed, such paralysis might have appeared desirable to some people in the administration. But the planners obviously did not take into consideration the extent to which controversial appointees could generate negative political fallout beyond the relatively parochial boundaries of an individual agency's regulatory affairs. Administration planners may also have underestimated the ability of certain "symbolic" appointees to develop their own constituencies with agendas that did not always parallel those of the president.

On the one hand, then, there was no appreciable fear of the damage controversial appointees could generate. There did, however, appear to be some concern that the appointment of recognized regulatory managers—even those with a bias toward regulatory reform—could be interpreted as sanctioning the regulatory enterprise. Appointees who advocated the use of market-based mechanisms and other recognized reform tools might be seen by agency staffs and representatives of regulated enterprises as regulatory mechanics, and not sufficiently committed to regulatory relief.

Thus, leaders selected for their symbolic value rather than their administrative skills predominated in the president's first round of regulatory appointments. A number of these appointees were drawn from the industry they had been chosen to regulate; others were identified as critics of the missions of their designated agencies (one, James Watt, had explicitly challenged his agency's mission). Still others were relatively obscure professionals with little or no knowledge of the agencies they were to manage or industries they were to regulate. Appointments of this last type appear to have been intended to broadcast White House indifference to the missions of certain agencies and independent commissions.

Examples of appointees drawn directly from regulated industries were John Shad, executive vice president of the E.F. Hutton Company, who was selected to head the Securities and Exchange Commission (SEC), and Thorne Auchter, vice president of his family's Jacksonville, Florida, construction company, who was appointed to head the Occupational Safety and Health Administration (OSHA). Shad's and Auchter's tenures were not free of controversy, but their comparatively successful leadership underscores the distinction scholars have long made between appointees who are simply drawn from industry and appointees who perform their duties in a manner "friendly to industry."[7] Examples of the latter were, of course, exposed by congressional probes of management practices at the Environmental Protection Agency (EPA) when Rita Lavelle, chief of the agency's Superfund program and a former official of the Aerojet General Corporation, is said to have participated in EPA decisions affecting her former employer as late as March 1, 1983. Similarly, James Sanderson, an adviser to the EPA administrator and a one-time nominee for the agency's third-highest-ranking position, was accused of participating in agency decisions that would affect corporations he represented in his Denver law practice.

In addition to appointing as agency heads some people who symbolized a pro-industry stance, the administration placed a number of prominent agency and regulatory critics in important regulatory positions—the most notable example being James Watt as Secretary of the Interior. The Interior Department, like other multifunctional cabinet departments, is responsible for a number of regulatory activities, including regulation of surface mining. As president of the conservative public-interest litigation group, the Mountain States Legal Foundation, Watt had played a key role in a suit to declare the 1977 Surface Mining Control and Reclamation Act unconstitutional. That act set out the federal role in regulating surface mining and established the Office of Surface Mining Reclamation and Enforcement within the Interior Department.[8]

The administration also elevated some prominent academic critics of federal regulatory activities to positions from which they could influence governmentwide regulatory policy. For example, Murray Weidenbaum was selected to head the Council of Economic Advisers, James Miller was named the first director of OMB's Office of Information and Regulatory Affairs, and Christopher DeMuth was designated as Miller's successor. All are academics who had participated in previous Republican administrations and were known to be critics of the excesses of federal regulation. All could be viewed as "principled deregulators," to use Antonin Scalia's phrase.[9] That is, their chief concerns were that regulations adopt market-based solutions, eliminate entry and exit barriers, and generally rely more heavily on cost-benefit analysis. This predisposition was demonstrated by James Miller's fight to retain the jurisdiction of the Federal Trade Commission (FTC) over the legal and medical professions despite strong interest-group lobbying of the agency and Congress. Indeed, to some degree Miller and Weidenbaum provided the original shape of the administration's regulatory relief effort.

Administration attitudes toward social regulation and the agencies that administer it were also conveyed by the appointment of managers with surprisingly little experience in the technical fields regulated by their agencies or offices. In such instances, an appointment could be made in recognition of the appointee's general management skill, could be a political payoff, or could simply be a signal of the administration's indifference to an agency's mission or the quality of its performance.

A number of examples of inexperienced directors come to mind. Raymond Peck, known as an aggressive advocate for mineral producers and a general foe of federal regulation, was named to head the controversial National Highway Traffic Safety Administration (NHTSA)—ostensibly because he had no track record in the field. William Bradford Reynolds, a Washington attorney specializing in commercial law with little background in the statutorily complex field of civil rights, was appointed to head the Department of Justice's Office of Civil Rights—arguably the most important civil rights enforcement position in the federal government.

In other instances, efforts to name unqualified people to some regulatory posts revealed a cavalier attitude toward some posts early in the Reagan administration. Before finally appointing Clarence Thomas to head the Equal Employment Opportunity Commission (EEOC), Reagan officials lobbied first for an unknown and disastrously impolitic radio preacher, and then for the head of a personnel firm who had never administered more than four employees.

In a number of instances, however, administration appointees have clearly been selected primarily for their technical expertise. Two such persons are Dr. Nunzio Palladino, who heads the Nuclear Regulatory Commission (NRC), and Dr. Arthur Hull Hayes, who directed the Food and Drug Administration (FDA) through mid-1983. At the time of his appointment, Dr. Palladino was dean of Penn State University's College of Engineering; he had served on the NRC's Advisory Committee on Reactor Safety and was a former president of the American Nuclear Society. Dr. Hayes was also a Penn State professor before joining the Reagan administration, having served as Hershey Professor of Medicine and Pharmacology. A former Rhodes scholar, Dr. Hayes is one of the most prominent clinical pharmacologists in the United States. Although

Dr. Hayes earned wide respect among members of the private- and public-interest bar who work on FDA matters, no other recent director of FDA had his discretion so limited by the secretary of the Department of Health and Human Services (HHS) and by the director of the the Office of Management and Budget. Indeed, formal, routinely delegated grants of authority from the secretary of HHS to the FDA director were repealed early in the administration.

The Consequences of the Administration's Appointment Strategy

Given the president's basic attitude toward regulation and the role that regulatory relief was to play in the administration's game plan, it is not surprising that political acceptability rather than administrative skill was a candidate's most valuable asset in obtaining an appointment to a major regulatory post during the early days of the Reagan administration. How did these appointees perform?

By shortly after midterm, it was becoming increasingly clear that a substantial number had failed to overcome the technical, procedural, and political hurdles that had earlier confronted the Ford and Carter reformers. In areas ranging from air bags to clean air and teenage birth control, the appointees frequently had proved unable to convince the Congress, the public, or the federal judiciary of the merits of the administration's positions. Furthermore, budget cuts, personnel reductions, and deepening divisions between career and political staffs kept morale and productivity low and attrition high at a number of agencies—most notably EPA.

Certainly, frequent legal challenges and defeats, mounting complaints of mismanagement and deception, and frequent public controversies were not the desired products of the administration's regulatory leadership. Were these results inevitable? One writer, generally favorable to the administration's regulatory objectives, summarized the results—and the reason for them—as follows:

> The fact is that regulation has gotten a bad name because it has always been a haphazard, ill-considered, sloppy process. Without careful factual, analytical, and political work, regulations will remain a disgrace.
>
> To improve the process will take explaining what is required, training so staff members know how to improve their product, and improved management.
>
> With precious few exceptions, this Administration has not done a good job of putting managers in key positions. The complex task of developing well-reasoned, on-the-record regulatory positions has been difficult for many of them.

Until they master the nuts-and-bolts of the process, it is unlikely that we will see greatly improved products.[10]

A similar, even more telling assessment of the fundamental failing of one of President Reagan's most controversial appointees, Anne Burford, was given by Rita Lavelle, herself a dismissed EPA official:

> She's a beautiful woman, very dramatic with a strong personality. . . . She's a brilliant attorney and a consummate politician, but she's not a manager. It's a case of a politician in a job that calls for a manager. When she couldn't make decisions based on good management principles, she became vulnerable to rumors, innuendo, and political plays. Disagreements on policy . . . she equated with personal disloyalty.[11]

From the perspective of regulatory reform, the problems with using the appointments process to project political images were brought home by the continuing problems at EPA and the resulting deterioration of relations between the White House and key House committees. This situation in turn led to growing mistrust and persistent congressional efforts to constrain the discretion of regulatory officials—particularly those within EPA. These efforts are likely to result in a return to overly stringent regulations and a reduction in agency discretion. The probable results are more regulatory mismatches and increased examples of regulatory unreasonableness—the reverse of the administration's goals.

The upshot was that many of the administration's regulatory reforms that required greater vesting of discretion in agency heads found little congressional support. An example was EPA's proposed environmental integration program, designed to assess the cumulative impacts of existing environmental laws on individual industries and regions. Analysis was to determine the most efficient health and economic trade-offs and would, in effect, look across the media (air, water, land) at particular pollutants. Despite the fact that the effort ranked at the top of EPA's list of regulatory reform measures, its prospects soon became quite dim. Effective implementation would have required revision of most major legislative initiatives assigned to EPA and a substantial increase in discretion for the agency's administrator. An increased grant of discretion was unlikely, given congressional distrust of the then EPA administrator, Anne Burford.[12]

The replacement of Burford with William Ruckelshaus partially restored Congress's faith in the agency and its leadership. Recent budgetary actions have provided Ruckelshaus unfettered discretion in spending the increased appropriations the Congress had made available to the agency—as one journal noted, a measure of independence Congress would never have granted Burford.[13] It is doubtful, however, that the Ruckelshaus appointment foretells a honeymoon between Congress and Reagan's regulatory chiefs.

Budgeting for Deregulation

Despite critics' skepticism, Reagan administration officials often contend that reductions in regulatory agency budgets have not been driven by deregulatory motives. Rather, they assert that (1) federal regulatory bodies— particularly those engaged in economic regulation—have outlived their usefulness and should be phased out of existence; (2) federal regulatory programs (for example, monitoring nontoxic discharges regulated under the Clean Water Act) have matured to a point at which expenditures are likely to be lower than those previously required during start-up and early implementation phases; (3) federal regulatory responsibility will be increasingly delegated to the states; and (4) more efficient management of federal regulatory programs will provide significant savings.[14]

Budget cuts and the personnel reductions they trigger were obviously not invoked simply for programmatic reasons. At one level they could be viewed as responses to a governmentwide imperative to curb federal spending and reduce mounting deficits. More realistically, however, they were rooted in the way the architects of the regulatory relief program viewed regulatory costs (or costs borne by the private sector) to be a function of federal regulatory expenditures. As we discussed in chapter 2, Murray Weidenbaum's estimates of how much regulations cost the economy were obtained by applying a simple multiplier to total federal regulatory expenditures. Thus the impression could be created that simply reducing agency budgets would reduce regulatory activities as well as overall costs. One derived benefit of reducing agency budgets was the increased control over otherwise independent bureaucrats that fear instilled by widespread personnel reductions could generate.

As regulatory responsibilities and resources became increasingly unbalanced, several problems arose, particularly in the politically sensitive area of environmental protection: (1) Congress refused to accept significant revisions in the nation's environmental laws that would reduce agency responsibilities at the same time that a host of previously enacted laws arrived at the full-implementation stage. (2) Although regulations that relied on market-based mechanisms might in the long run have offered real cost savings, getting them operational was clearly expensive. As a result, cutbacks in agency resources were likely to impede the full development of these important regulatory innovations. (3) Administration-sponsored budget reductions seemed to be inconsistent with the administration's expressed interest in requiring agencies to determine regulatory costs and benefits.

These problems were complicated by the somewhat unrealistic belief on the part of administration officials that they could delegate federal regulatory responsibility at an unprecedented rate without antagonizing the potent political force of state and local governments. Although these governments were clearly interested in obtaining increased program authority (see chapter 10), they were also unwilling to accept the administration's proposed "zero funding" option, which would have eliminated federal financial support for environmental enforcement activities.

Accounting for inflation, the regulatory components of the budgets for the agencies listed in table 7 would have fallen approximately 28 percent from the actual level in fiscal year 1980 if the administration's proposed budget for fiscal year 1984 had been approved. When inflation is not considered, total aggregate expenditures would have fallen by 10 percent between 1980 and 1984. Although a few proposals were vigorously contested—EPA's proposed budget being an example—most were accepted at levels approximating those requested by the administration. (For the purposes of this chapter, we will make no effort to "read" the political viability of most elements of the president's budget. Some discussion of congressional action on EPA's budget is included, however.)

Table 8 presents an important companion finding to these figures: that personnel levels within selected federal regulatory agencies were scheduled to fall at a rate that exceeded nominal budget reductions and roughly equaled inflation-adjusted budget reductions. Thus, although budget reductions were themselves substantial, they understate changes in federal staffing levels and, as a result, federal enforcement capacity. Although several regulatory agencies, such as the Securities and Exchange Commission, registered real (if minor) budget increases between fiscal year 1980 and fiscal year 1984, no agency listed in table 8 enjoyed personnel gains.

Even in this declining area of federal involvement, relative winners and losers can be singled out. As tables 7 and 8 indicate, budget reductions were not evenly distributed among regulatory agencies. Differences obviously reflected a mix of the political pressures on and preferences of administration officials and, to some degree, the dictates of prior congressional action. Accordingly, a review of the figures in tables 7 and 8 reveals the following information:

- *The agencies regulating financial markets*—the SEC and the Commodity Futures Trading Commission (CFTC)—were the only agencies represented that enjoyed net budget gains between FY 1980 and FY

TABLE 7
BUDGETS OF SELECTED REGULATORY AGENCIES

Agency/Division	Budgets		Percentage Change, 1980–1984	
	FY 1980 Actual	FY 1984 Proposed	Not Accounting for Inflation	Accounting for Inflation[a]
A. Budget Authority for Selected Executive Branch Regulatory Agencies, Divisions, Functions				
Environmental Protection Agency[b]				
(Total)	1,264,684	946,021	−25	−40
Salaries and Expenses	524,773	540,389	3	−17
Research and Development	233,481	111,699	−52	−62
Abatement Control and Compliance	506,430	293,933	−23	−53
Federal Grain Inspection Services (Agriculture)	23,971	6,861	−71	−77
Food and Drug Administration (Health and Human Services)	325,224	385,933	19	−5
Mine Safety and Health Administration (Labor)	143,637	148,032	3	−17
National Highway Traffic Safety Administration (Operations and Research) (Transportation)	57,400	55,784	−3	−22
Occupational Safety and Health Administration (Labor)	186,394	210,860	13	−9
Office of Surface Mining (Total: Regulation and Technology) (Interior)	84,687	63,497	−25	−40

B. Budget Authority for Selected Independent Agencies

Civil Aeronautics Board (Salaries and Expenses)	29,492	20,890	−29	−43
Commission on Civil Rights	11,719	12,180	4	−17
Commodity Futures Trading Commission	16,612	24,680	49	19
Consumer Product Safety Commission	41,328	32,000	−23	−38
Equal Employment Opportunity Commission	124,562	155,300	25	0
Federal Trade Commission	66,059	59,517	−10	−28
Interstate Commerce Commission (Salaries and Expenses)	79,063	58,038	−27	−41
Securities and Exchange Commission	72,739	91,935	26	1
Total A + B	2,517,571	2,271,528	−10	−8

SOURCE: Budget of the United States Government, Fiscal Year 1982 and Fiscal Year 1984, Executive Office of the President, Office of Management and Budget.

a. Budget figures for 1984 have been converted to 1980 constant dollars using the GNP Implicit Price Deflator. Inflation for 1983 and 1984 has been assumed to be 3.3 percent annually.

b. Subsequent congressional action on the administration's proposed budget for EPA is discussed later in this chapter.

TABLE 8

PERSONNEL: AUTHORIZED PERMANENT POSITIONS FOR SELECTED EXECUTIVE AND
INDEPENDENT AGENCIES

	Actual		Estimated		Percentage Change
Agency/Division	FY 1980	FY 1982	FY 1983	FY 1984	1980–1984
Executive Branch Agencies					
Environmental Protection Agency	11,015	9,821	9,125	8,669	−21
Federal Grain Inspection Service (Agriculture)	2,242	1,089	1,045	1,045	−53
Food and Drug Administration (Health and Human Services)	7,190	7,142	7,140	7,139	−1
Mine Safety and Health Administration (Labor)	3,857	3,763	3,408	3,184	−17
National Highway Traffic Safety Administration (Transportation)	874	686	617	617	−29
Occupational Safety and Health Administration (Labor)	3,015	2,354	2,354	2,355	−22
Office of Surface Mining (Interior)	1,025	735	731	731	−29
Civil Aeronautics Board	743	498	434	366	−51
Commission on Civil Rights	285	248	237	236	−17
Commodity Futures Trading Commission	550	550	550	550	0[a]
Consumer Product Safety Commission	880	631	577	542	−38
Equal Employment Opportunity Commission	3,777	3,326	3,185	3,185	−16
Federal Communications Commission	2,153	1,862	1,896	1,896	−12
Federal Trade Commission	1,665	1,380	1,265	1,131	−32
Interstate Commerce Commission	2,024	1,662	1,378	1,200	−41
Securities and Exchange Commission	2,102	2,021	2,021	1,896	−10

SOURCE: Budget of the United States Government, Fiscal Year 1982 and Fiscal Year 1984,
Executive Office of the President, Office of Management and Budget.

a. The fact that CFTC position authorizations remained unchanged in FY 1980–1984 is
partially explained by expansion of the agency's regulatory responsibilities resulting from the
introduction of trading in at least one major new area: i.e., stock futures.

1984. SEC staff, however, were budgeted by the administration to fall by 10 percent in FY 1984.

- Despite claims that their effectiveness has been substantially reduced, *organizations devoted to the enforcement of federal civil rights laws* also suffered comparatively small budget or staff reductions. The FY 1984 budget of the Equal Employment Opportunity Commission (EEOC) was to remain the same, but its staff was to fall by 16 percent.[15]
- *Health and safety agencies* in aggregate were also to be relatively modest losers in the regulatory budget battles. The Food and Drug Administration would suffer a 5 percent budget loss and a 1 percent staffing reduction; the Occupational Safety and Health Administration, a 9 percent real budget loss but a 22 percent staffing reduction; the Mine Safety and Health Administration, a 17 percent budget loss and a 17 percent staff reduction; and the National Highway Traffic Safety Administration, a 22 percent budget loss and a 29 percent staffing reduction.
- *Agencies concentrating on the environment* and, in large part, on natural resource regulation (the EPA and the Interior Department's Office of Surface Mining) fared relatively badly—even by regulatory agency standards. In the president's FY 1984 budget, EPA was to suffer a staff reduction and a 40 percent real funding cut for the three major categories listed in table 7. At the Office of Surface Mining, real budget cuts of 40 percent were proposed along with a 29 percent staff reduction.
- *Agencies identified with consumer protection* issues saw their budgets severely reduced. The Consumer Product Safety Commission was scheduled to suffer a 38 percent reduction in both budget and staff, and the beleaguered Federal Trade Commission, a 28 percent budget cut and a 32 percent staff reduction.
- The biggest losers, however, were *agencies involved in old-style economic regulation*, which are being phased out of business. For example, the Civil Aeronautics Board and the Interstate Commerce Commission were slated to suffer 43 percent and 41 percent budget cuts, respectively. The CAB staff was to be reduced by 51 percent and the ICC staff by 41 percent.

Until summer of 1983, Congress generally was willing to go along with administration efforts to reduce regulatory spending. After all, its members were extremely sensitive to the public's complaints about overregulation and excessive government spending. However, the turmoil at EPA, which aggravated fears over the health impacts of toxic waste disposal as well as air and water pollution, coupled with the installation of a new EPA administrator, gave Congress the impetus it needed to recast the administration's proposed FY 1984 EPA budget. Although congressional efforts to increase EPA's budget began independently, Ruckelshaus and the Office of Management and Budget became involved, and the amended budget won the approval of Congress and the White House. Major agreed-upon changes were:[16]

	Original Administration-Proposed Budget	Amended Budget
	($ millions)	
Salaries and Expenses	540.3	574.9
Research and Development	111.7	142.7
Abatement Control and Compliance	293.9	393.9
Total	945.9	1,111.5

Whether this marked a watershed in the constant decline in administration funding of social regulation or was simply a political anomaly remains uncertain at the time of this writing.

One rationale for these changes was that the disruptive impact of budget reductions cannot be gauged only by their relative size. Agencies with shrinking mandates—agencies enforcing old-style economic regulations such as the CAB and the ICC—will not face the administrative problems of agencies with expanding or stable mandates. EPA, for example, with its new responsibilities for attacking toxic waste generation and disposal, would have had far fewer resources to accomplish its increasingly complex assignments. A brief summary of those new responsibilities may help illustrate the point.

Beginning in 1976 with the enactment of the Resource Conservation and Recovery Act and the Toxic Substances Control Act (TOSCA), EPA's legislative mandate to mitigate the dangers posed by toxic substances expanded rapidly. Among the new responsibilities that have fallen to the agency are these:

- The tracking of hazardous wastes from their origin to ensure their safe ultimate disposal (Resource Conservation and Recovery Act);
- The analysis, testing, and regulation of toxic chemicals before they are introduced to the market (TOSCA);
- The review and analysis of chemicals currently in use in order to identify and regulate those that pose unreasonable health risks (TOSCA);
- The control of discharged toxic chemicals into the nation's waters, sewers, and wastewater treatment plants (Clean Water Act Amendments of 1977);
- The identification, analysis, and regulation of the emission of toxic compounds into the atmosphere (Clean Air Act Amendments of 1977);

- The protection of underground drinking water from the injection of toxic and other wastes (Safe Drinking Water Act);
- The identification and cleanup of abandoned hazardous waste disposal sites (Superfund).

Although some of these responsibilities have been pending for some time, in most instances administrative regulations implementing congressional action have only recently been promulgated. Thus, given EPA's ongoing responsibilities under federal air, water, and pesticides legislation, along with its new obligations under Congress's toxic agenda, budget cuts might seriously restrict the agency's capacity to carry out its legislative mission.[17]

In their efforts to justify regulatory budget cuts, administration officials have stressed their commitment to the delegation of federal program authority to state and local governments. Given the current weakened fiscal health of most states, to what extent does the federal budget provide the funds to permit state and local governments to assume new regulatory responsibilities? On the whole, changes over the four years in sample federal programs where there has been comparatively extensive delegation to state and local governments (see table 9) do not appear to reflect the fiscal implications of the wholesale transfer contemplated by the administration.

One apparent exception is grants to state and local governments for enforcement of regulations promulgated by the Office of Surface Mining. The increase in these grants from $189,000 in fiscal 1980 to $37.6 million in fiscal 1984 would seem to reflect the current shift in responsibility. While critics challenge the adequacy of these funds, other program grants provide states even fewer program dollars. Despite the dramatic expansion of EPA's regulatory responsibilities and EPA's efforts to accelerate program delegation, the administration at one time had proposed to cut the agency's grants to abatement, control, and compliance programs in the states by 43 percent in nominal terms and 55 percent in real terms.

The relative willingness of the administration's regulatory leaders to accept—at least publicly—budget and personnel reductions within their agencies testifies to the president's success in finding team players and their shared antipathy to federal regulation. This dispassionate view of the proper size and configuration of federal agencies is nowhere more in evidence than in a series of proposed and accomplished major agency reorganizations advanced by the administration's regulatory leadership.

Reorganization

In theory, reorganization is a "neutral" management strategy that can be used to accomplish substantive policy ends that might otherwise be polit-

TABLE 9

FEDERAL GRANTS TO STATE AND LOCAL GOVERNMENTS RELATING TO
ENFORCEMENT OF SELECTED FEDERAL LAWS

| Agency/Division | Grants ($ thousands) | | | Percentage Change 1980–1984 | Percentage Change Accounting for Inflation |
	FY 1980 Actual	FY 1982 Actual	FY 1984 Proposed		
Office of Surface Mining: state regulatory program grants	189	32,797	37,600	+ 15[a]	+ 7[a]
Occupation Safety and Health Administration: support of state enforcement programs	42,785	47,238	54,107	+ 26	+ 1
EPA: grants, subsidies, and contributions, abatement control compliance	305,776	249,683	172,994	− 43	− 55

SOURCE: Budget of the United States Government, Fiscal Year 1982 and Fiscal Year 1984,
Executive Office of the President, Office of Management and Budget.

a. For period 1982–1984 only. Program beginning in 1980, so figures would not be
meaningful.

ically unachievable. This tool has proved attractive to agency reformers for
two principal reasons. First, congressional support is rarely required. (By
contrast, all agency budgets and most high-level appointments require
congressional assent.) Second, reorganizations and the personnel transfers
they involve can be quite useful to administrators who must operate within
the confines of rigid, highly regulated personnel systems such as the federal
civil service. The political utility of reorganizations is an unquestioned, but
rarely (if ever) announced, rationale. However, the aims of reorganizations
are typically declared to be to maximize efficiency and economy, promote
effective planning and coordination, reduce program fragmentation and overlap, eliminate unnecessary paperwork, and increase accountability.[18]

In this section we briefly examine the proposed reorganizations of two
federal regulatory agencies: the closing of the Federal Trade Commission's
ten regional offices and the reorganization of the Interior Department's Office

of Surface Mining. Critics—and there have been many—have alleged that the FTC and OSM moves were motivated by a desire to restrain or redirect those agencies' enforcement activities in a way that would reduce, not enhance, their overall effectiveness.

FTC Regional Offices. James Miller, the current director of the Federal Trade Commission, wrote the controversial report on the FTC for the administration's transition team—the report that called for the closing of the ten FTC regional offices on grounds that they were responsible for "a disproportionate share of the problems that allegedly plague the FTC, such as delay and lack of priority setting."[19] The report also characterized the regional offices' efforts as "misguided" and "mismanaged" and suggested that trivial cases made up a disproportionate share of the caseload. The "geographic and psychological" distance between these offices and Washington headquarters was cited as an obstacle to the kind of effective, centralized control the Reagan administration sought.

Many supporters of the FTC's regional offices disagreed, pointing out that between FY 1977 and FY 1982 the regional offices, working with only 17 percent of FTC's total budget, had—

- Initiated 62 percent of the commission's initial phase investigations;
- Conducted 59 percent of the commission's full investigations;
- Been responsible for 38 percent of all complaints issued;
- Obtained 50 percent of all final consent orders (and 45 percent of those pending as of March 31, 1982);
- Obtained 32 percent of decisions by administrative law judges;
- Obtained 25 percent of orders in litigated cases;
- Obtained 40 percent of civil penalty judgments;
- Obtained 55 percent of injunctions;
- Obtained $218 million in direct restitution to injured consumers and small businesses, or 84 percent of all restitution obtained by the commission.[20]

Furthermore, critics of the chairman's efforts to close agency offices noted that the regional structure of the FTC had been established by Caspar Weinberger, chairman from 1969 to 1970, in an attempt to make the FTC more responsive to local needs, and that no systematic cost-benefit analysis had been conducted to determine the proposed move's efficiency.

Congress, despite its animosity toward the FTC in recent years, was not receptive to Chairman Miller's proposals—rejecting out of hand his initial suggestion to close all ten. In April 1982, responding to severe proposed budget cuts by both Miller and OMB, the agency's commissioners voted to close four of its ten regional offices, but congressional opposition forced a suspension of the plan; in December 1982, Congress provided additional funds to the agency to keep seven regional offices open for the remainder of the fiscal year.

Chairman Miller's persistent efforts to limit regional enforcement strength were eventually rewarded in late February 1983, even if his petition for a formal reorganization was not. At that time the Senate Appropriations Committee, while restating its support for a full regional office structure, authorized a reduction of personnel in each office to eighteen slots. With this agreement, the FTC promptly eliminated all GS-15 positions in the New York and Chicago regional offices, thereby reducing to eighteen the New York staff (from thirty-nine) and the Chicago staff (from thirty-four), and eliminating the most experienced attorneys in both—most of whom chose to leave the agency rather than accept the offer to all professionals to join the Washington headquarters staff.

An organizational analysis of staff reductions within the FTC reveals the administration's preference for Washington-based economic analysis rather than regionally based enforcement activity when consumer protection or competition problems are raised. Total enforcement-related employee time within the agency's Bureaus of Competition, Consumer Protection, and Economics fell 15 percent between 1982 and 1984 (excluding the reductions in personnel already described). Employee time devoted to economic activities not related to enforcement within the three bureaus, however, remained constant. Moreover, approximately 90 percent of the lost enforcement time was taken from the regional office staffs.

In sum, then, given the size and nature of recent regional staff reductions, it appears the administration has won a real, if not formally declared, victory in the reorganization of the Federal Trade Commission. Thus, while a budget-induced rationale for reorganization may not have succeeded in reducing or eliminating FTC's regional offices, the mechanism has proved useful for justifying a significant reduction in FTC's senior enforcement staff.

The Office of Surface Mining. One of the most far-reaching proposed reorganizations of a regulatory agency was announced in 1982 at the Department of the Interior's Office of Surface Mining. The office is charged with implementing the Surface Mining Control and Reclamation Act of 1977, which calls for the regulation of all coal and surface mining operations.[21] The act established separate compliance programs for operations on federal land and operations on privately held land. For the latter, an interim federal program was established, which provided for eventual delegation to the states.

Once the new administration assumed office, the Office of Surface Mining was singled out by a Heritage Foundation report for especially rough treatment. Accusing the office of "zealotry," the report called for the in-coming administration to "move quickly to reduce OSM enforcement staff and cut budget requests significantly in the regulatory program." It continued, "Of course the success of many of these short-term efforts depends on the replacement of current OSM senior staff and regional directors with profes-sionals more attuned to a rational program of ensuring rehabilitation of mined lands."[22]

The administration responded by proposing a reorganization that would have replaced OSM's network of five regional, thirteen district, and twenty-four field offices with fourteen state and six field offices and two technical centers. The overall number of OSM offices outside Washington would fall from forty-two to twenty-two as the total number of agency personnel would be reduced from 1,000 to 628 permanent employees. The administration maintained that the changes reflected a shift in regulatory responsibility to the states. Among other things, the reorganization was to entail closing the agency's Denver regional office and reshuffling the staff, many of whom would be reassigned to a new office to be opened in Casper, Wyoming. Ironically, like the FTC reorganization discussed earlier, the OSM move would result in a net increase in the agency's Washington staff.

While the relocation to Casper never materialized, the Interior Depart-ment's handling of the reorganization resulted, in the words of Representative Patricia Schroeder, who heads the House Subcommittee on Post Office and Civil Service, in "total agency chaos and employee panic."[23] More signif-icantly, it contributed to a mass exodus from the agency. In a letter to Secretary Watt, Schroeder contended that between January 1981 and June 1982, OSM's staff fell from 948 employees to 478; 228 of OSM's 565 employees in grades GS-7 through GS-13 either resigned or were fired by the agency, and 88 percent, or 149, of the agency's 170 employees in the West left OSM.[24] Agency insiders, members of Congress, and environmental critics have chal-lenged the overall efficiency of OSM since its reorganization. One attorney who works extensively with OSM's Denver staff has noted that permit review for all western mines on federal property are, at the time of this writing, undertaken by a greatly reduced number of hydrologists.[25] A former OSM employee testified in a written statement presented to the House Interior and Insular Affairs Committee that he constantly received complaints from in-dustry, states, and other federal agencies about the quality of the agency's new staff.[26] Indeed, representatives of the states of Colorado, Montana, and Wyoming testified before the House Civil Service Subcommittee that they had not been consulted about the proposed reorganization and that they op-posed any move on the part of the Interior Department that would reduce the quality of OSM staff.[27]

The complexity of the new Surface Mining Act and its controversial implementing regulations make federal oversight of state efforts during the transition from federal to state authority critical. As testimony by the heads of three important western surface mining programs has indicated, the states need federal oversight and technical assistance.[28] Moreover, of the approximately 180 mines in the West, 125 are located on federal lands. The Surface Mining Act allows the states to participate in regulating mining on federal land, but primary responsibility for permits and enforcement will remain at the federal level for at least a year or two. Thus, although OSM's western office continues to carry the agency's heaviest regulatory burden, its staff has experienced an 88 percent attrition rate.

It is difficult to conclude that the two reorganizations proposed here could have enhanced agency efficiency and economy—the standard rationale for institutional reorganization. Indeed, the most visible result of each was the high attrition rate generated among experienced professionals in technically demanding fields. Although some paperwork and short-run costs may have been reduced, it is unlikely that the savings offset the inefficiencies associated with the loss of technical competence. Finally, we should note that the Office of Surface Mining's announced shift from design to performance standards will, by the agency's own admission, require greater technical expertise on the part of field enforcement staff.

Conclusion

In this chapter we have surveyed three key deregulatory strategies the administration has relied on to "get a hold on government." Ronald Reagan came to office with the view that the federal government and its employees were alien to his philosophical mission. Accordingly he has gone about his promised regulatory relief campaign using recognized management strategies specifically aimed at federal regulatory personnel. As this chapter has indicated, those strategies include the appointment of new, philosophically uniform regulatory leaders who feel little kinship to the staff they administer; deep cuts in federal regulatory budgets and personnel; and internal reorganizations that have reduced the number of experienced technicians on agency enforcement staffs. In addition, career staff people holding positions usually left undisturbed by changes in administration have been replaced by more politically attuned individuals.[29] And performance criteria that serve the administration's political goals have been developed to assess the performance of job holders.[30] In sum, the rules have apparently changed for regulators and regulated alike.

As we have suggested, the administration's professed objective for these management initiatives has been the achievement of greater efficiency. We do not doubt that some management improvements have resulted, but we believe that the efficiency gains that have been claimed are likely to have been substantially offset by the loss or demoralization of many experienced, technically proficient career civil service staff.

In addition, although sharp budget cuts in some regulatory agencies may have gone relatively unnoticed during the deeper phases of the recession, as the economy picks up, so too will the demand for permits and other necessary regulatory agency services. Personnel shortages may lead either to a lengthening of the time it takes to obtain a permit or to a disproportionate number of legally vulnerable administrative actions. Staff reductions are also likely to hamper the administration's efforts to base regulatory decision making on better information, since technically competent cost-benefit analyses are quite labor intensive.

As the case studies of reorganizations within FTC and OSM suggest, agency management policies have often led to the removal or exodus of the most seasoned and technically expert bureaucrats. Where these people are to be replaced, their successors must traverse the same slow learning curve—with efficiency losses being borne by the agency and the regulated community alike. Moreover, forcing lawyers in the FTC's respected San Francisco regional office to type their own briefs and assigning permit review responsibility for all western surface mines on federal property to a handful of overworked hydrologists do not appear to be a cost-effective use of resources.

Finally, it appears that for a significant number of agencies, divisions between career staff and administration officials have never been deeper.[31] As an unnamed source noted regarding the travails of former EPA administrator Anne Burford, ''Anne and other political appointees came in and alienated the career people by treating them like enemies. . . . Now she likes them and trusts them but it is too late.''[32]

The replacement of Burford by Ruckelshaus—apparently a model appointment from the perspective of regulatory reform—raises the question whether the appointment (and the administration-supported increases in EPA's budget that followed) represents a watershed in administration regulatory management policy or simply an isolated political fix to a specific and potentially dangerous political problem.

We believe the answer lies in the middle. The deep cuts in agency budgets and personnel appear to have abated, and future cuts may be far less severe than those absorbed during the administration's first two years. Deregulation efforts are likely to continue, particularly in fields that do not receive close congressional oversight—but second-round regulatory appointees will probably be selected more for their managerial or technical competence than for their symbolic utility. In addition, budget cutting will moderate for agencies engaged in social regulation (in part, as a result of congressional resistance), whereas the budgets of agencies engaged in "old-style" economic regulation, such as the CAB and ICC, will continue to decline sharply.

8

Changing Regulatory Standards

Two separate but ultimately complementary paths to regulatory relief lay before the Reagan administration upon taking office. One would have led to a broad revision of the nation's principal regulatory statutes, the other to an assault on the administrative regulations that interpreted and implemented those statutes. As this chapter demonstrates, the administration has chosen so far to pursue an administrative agenda—that is, one directed more at rules than laws. However, this strategy—and the irregular manner in which it was implemented—has led to a number of highly visible political and legal setbacks. Moreover, as time has passed, the effort to recast regulatory standards has seemed to offer considerably less than the sea change in regulatory affairs the confident new administration promised.

Reliance primarily on an administrative strategy was clearly deliberate. Rule changes early in 1981 gave administration officials an opportunity to claim they had saved consumers, industry, and lower levels of government billions of dollars, and to signal that regulatory philosophy had sharply shifted. The strategy also gave the administration the look of a team that had "hit the ground running" to turn around a disabled economy.

The approach also promised significant gains without requiring the administration to expend the political capital that would have been needed to obtain legislative revisions of major regulatory statutes. As a result, the administration was free to use its political resources to push for the budget and tax bills and for some defense initiatives, such as the sale of AWACs planes to the Saudis. A number of observers have suggested that this deferral of legislative action was a critical mistake; they contend that some of the administration's most valued regulatory changes could have been appended to the tax and budget bills that moved quickly through Congress in the spring of 1981.

The low visibility of the regulatory process (compared with the legislative process), the skeletal substantive and procedural guidelines that constrain agency action, and the comparatively few participants meant that outcomes could be better controlled. Administrative action also permitted management of the timing of regulatory actions. In contrast, in the legislative process, the revision or repeal of major regulatory statutes would have to "play" to a wider constituency—one more likely to be influenced by the national media. Moreover, repeal or revision of the basic regulatory laws would require the promulgation of implementing administrative regulations before they could take effect.

The new administration had few illusions about the complexity of obtaining statutory change or about its eventual necessity. As David Stockman observed early in 1981:

> On a second front, both temporary and permanent statutory revision will be needed. . . . [A] fundamental legislative policy reform package to be considered after the 100 day period will have to be developed. This would primarily involve the insertion of mandatory cost-benefit, cost-effectiveness, and comparative risk analysis into the basic enabling acts—Clean Air and Water, Safe Drinking Water, TOSCA (the Toxic Substances Control Act), RCRA (the Resource Conservation and Recovery Act), OSHA (the Occupational Safety and Health Act), etc. Without these statutory changes, administrative rulemaking revisions in many cases will be subject to successful court challenge.[1]

Not only have legislative proposals of the kind contemplated not been forthcoming, but no general campaign materialized during the first two and a half years to alter administrative regulations so that they embodied the systematically applied, neutral, regulatory reform principles that Stockman and other advocates of more traditional regulatory reform recommended.

Stockman's fears that regulatory changes would be invalidated by the courts proved prescient, for a number of the most publicized rule revisions have been struck down in whole or in part by the federal judiciary. In some instances proposed rescissions and changes were found to have run afoul of controlling statutes. In other instances, policy changes violated the Administrative Procedure Act or clearly relevant federal court decisions. In sum, the agencies and their White House overseers often pressed philosophical claims without taking sufficient care to meet technical and procedural requirements.

The greatest disappointment of the regulatory relief program, however, was its failure to come up with a workable legislative reform package. Why was legislative reform so important? First, much of the social legislation enacted during the 1960s and 1970s tended to be highly prescriptive. For example, the Education of All Handicapped Children Act set out in the kind of detail typically reserved for administrative regulations extensive procedural safeguards to be provided disabled children and their parents. This statutory prescriptiveness stood directly in the path of significant administrative reform.

Second, as we noted in chapter 4, much of the legislation enacted during this reform period expressly prohibited just the kind of risk assessment and cost-effectiveness analysis Stockman described. Marginal changes in regulatory policy could skirt these prohibitions, but substantive reversals would require new legislation.

Third, where statutory standards were expressed in broad terms and congressional intent remained vague, the courts were often forced to provide specifics—many of which extended the rights and protections of underlying statutes along lines opposed by the administration. As a result, changes in administrative regulation ran head-on into established judicial precedent.

Fourth, legislative action is, by nature, more enduring than administrative change. Hence, legislative reform was more valuable to regulated firms because it theoretically enabled them to plan further ahead than would be the case with administrative change.

As this chapter demonstrates, however, not all substantive regulatory reform was dependent on legislative change. When a broad statutory mandate existed and a technically credible record had been developed, sweeping regulatory changes could be accomplished by administrative means. Administration-backed revision of the Davis-Bacon Act relating to wages in the construction industry and the deregulation of the radio industry (both of which are discussed later in this chapter) illustrate this point effectively.

Recognizing the value of legislative change did not make it any easier to obtain—particularly in the area of social regulation. As we noted in chapter 4, prior administrations' success in pressing their legislative agendas stemmed from thoroughly developed evidence of the feasibility of deregulation, effective executive branch advocacy, and continuous effort across administrations.

During the first half of Reagan's first term, agency officials did little to develop a strong empirical case for significant statutory reform of social regulation. Moreover, most Reagan appointees to major regulatory posts were not knowledgeable and popular spokesmen for the administration's reform goals.

Although no consensus had developed for social deregulation as it had for economic deregulation, overregulation in general had come to be widely viewed as a major problem. That view enjoyed wide support in Congress, as evidenced by the deep, congressionally approved cuts in regulatory agency budgets. And unlike Jimmy Carter's supporters, Ronald Reagan's constituency did not appear to be concerned about the entitlements and protections provided by social regulation. Because many of the most controversial regulatory statutes were due for reauthorization early in his presidency, Reagan appeared to have inherited a very promising opportunity for significant statutory reform. As becomes clear, that opportunity was largely missed.

The balance of this chapter (1) provides a brief overview of the direction and nature of the rule-making efforts conducted by the agencies; (2) explores a number of major rule-making changes attempted by the administration, as well as the political and legal challenges mounted against the changes; (3) surveys the administration's legislative efforts; and (4) draws some conclusions about the effectiveness of the administration's efforts to alter regulatory standards.

The Administrative Agenda

As we suggested in chapters 6 and 7, the White House (i.e., the Task Force on Regulatory Relief, the president's staff, and the Office of Management and Budget) played a crucial role in formulating and orchestrating the regulatory relief campaign. First, all proposed regulation would have to flow through the executive office not once but twice before promulgation. Second, the task force had, to a significant degree, set the relief agenda by choosing 119 of the "most questionable" proposed or existing regulations for agency review. Third, the White House-directed regulatory appointments and budget cuts had, in effect, notified bureaucrats about the kind of regulatory activities that would be acceptable to the new team. In the final analysis, however, the revision or repeal of regulatory standards would fall to the administrative agencies.

The administrative approach to regulatory relief involved four types of activities: repeal of existing and proposed regulations; revision of existing and proposed regulations; governmentwide reduction in new regulations; and promulgation of new regulations designed to minimize compliance costs.

After two years, one of the most notable results of the relief effort was an overall decline in the number of new regulations issued by the agencies. The final report of the Task Force on Regulatory Relief issued in August 1983 noted that both the number of pages in the *Federal Register* and the number of published rules dropped by more than one-fourth and proposed regulations dropped by nearly one-third, when compared with the record of the Carter administration. (We should caution, however, that the number of pages in the *Federal Register* can, and has at various times, been modified by changes in typeface or page size, elimination of blank pages, and, most important, changes in the detail used to describe proposed regulations. Moreover, agencies have substantial discretion regarding what they choose to publish in the *Federal Register*.) The report further noted that these quantitative measures understated the change in regulatory policy, as "many new regulations during the last two years have revised or eliminated rules that were on the books when President Reagan took office."[2]

Another indicator of the overall direction of regulatory activity during the Reagan administration is annual growth of the Washington legal establishment, which had averaged 10 percent during the Carter administration. A June 1983 survey by the *Legal Times* found that staffs at the city's twenty-five largest law firms grew by only 1.8 percent during FY 1982.[3] Moreover, for the first time since the *Legal Times* had begun its survey, the journal found that out-of-town law firms deciding to close their offices outnumbered those opening new offices. Although the economic impacts of the recession and a growing willingness among corporations to turn legal work over to their own law departments partially account for these results, a decline in regulatory activity is also responsible.

As new rule-making activity slowed, the agencies became involved in reviewing targeted regulations, identifying existing regulations for review and revision, and promulgating those new regulations which were required by law or circumstances.

Within this context, most of the completed regulatory actions completed during the first two years of the administration, fell within one or more of five substantive areas: intergovernmental regulations and grant reform; disposition of natural resources; pollution abatement; health and safety; and federal paperwork. Regulations that tightened or loosened restrictions under federal grant programs have, for the purposes of this analysis, been grouped under the first category.

In the following pages we describe major types of generic actions that have dominated the Reagan administration's administrative agenda using, where appropriate, the regulatory changes proposed in the "auto package" as illustrations. (Table 6 of chapter 6 sets out the nature and disposition of the principal regulatory actions originally included in the package.)

Rescission and Delay of Pending Regulations

To illustrate the types of administrative actions taken by the agencies in delivering regulatory relief, let us look at the contents of the Reagan administration's auto package. (We do so not because the package resembles efforts to alter regulatory standards taken by other agencies, but rather because the package clearly represents the single most ambitious coordinated initiative undertaken so far by the Reagan administration.) The summary of the deregulatory actions taken by the Environmental Protection Agency (EPA) and the National Highway Traffic Safety Administration (NHTSA), shown in table 6, reveals that a high proportion of agency actions involved a simple delay or rescission of pending regulatory standards. In fact, virtually all the regulatory actions taken by NHTSA listed were repeals or suspensions of Carter regulations.

A significant number of the other actions taken in the regulatory relief campaign, particularly during its first year, involved similar delays or rescissions of proposed or, in some instances, existing regulations. This is not surprising, given the complexity and length of the informal rule-making process. Accordingly, many of the successes the Reagan administration claimed at midterm constituted essentially negative actions that appeared to have simpler procedural and technical requirements than did the promulgation of new or revised regulatory standards.[4] (As we noted earlier, most of the "midnight" regulations proposed by Carter and temporarily frozen by Reagan eventually went forward unchanged.)

The negative agenda of delays and rescissions was appealing for two related reasons: First, it was overtly deregulatory by nature and more useful as a political symbol designed for popular consumption than were rule modifications, which often raised complex, technical issues regarding costs and benefits for the nonspecialist. Second, it appeared that rescissions could be summarily accomplished, since agency and administration officials evidently believed that, as a matter of law, revocation of administrative rules fell squarely within an agency's discretion. As Abner Mikva stated in his decision invalidating the administration's revocation of the passive restraint standard: "It is only in the rarest and most compelling circumstances that courts overturn an agency's 'expert' determination not to pursue a particular problem or policy at a given time."[5] Our discussion of the passive restraint case later in this chapter notes that the administration clearly overestimated the extent to which administrative actions—even those that withdraw an agency from an area of endeavor—remained within its discretion.

Revision of Regulatory Standards

When simple delays or revocations could not produce the result desired in the auto package, either EPA or NHTSA was forced to wade in and rewrite existing or proposed regulations. A review of proposed changes reveals that in all instances regulations were rewritten in a manner that (1) was fundamentally deregulatory and (2) provided some immediate regulatory relief to industry. Furthermore, combinations of individual actions occasionally provided compound relief for some of industry's most acutely felt regulatory ills. For example, EPA not only satisfied the industry's interest in obtaining fleet averaging for diesel emission of particulates (which are suspected of causing health problems), but it also delayed industry's compliance dates for the light-duty diesel particulate standard from 1985 to 1987. In addition, the agency waived the nitrogen oxide emissions standards for 1981-, 1982-, 1983-, and 1984-model-year light-duty vehicles, which included eighteen different classes of diesel engines. Thus, instead of trading off more flexible compliance procedures against higher or sustained health standards, the administration offered the industry multiple relaxed standards as well as more liberal compliance requirements.

The Reagan administration's auto package included only a few of the innovative regulatory techniques that had developed a constituency among regulatory reformers (see chapter 5) and that, among other things, call for a greater use of incentives and market-based regulatory solutions. The paucity of such techniques in the package may not be surprising given their inherent technical and political complexity and the relatively short time period in which the administration would have to produce results.

One important innovative technique in the auto package was the endorsement of fleet averaging for particulates emitted by diesel vehicles. The controls imposed on diesel emissions raise a policy dilemma. Although diesel-powered cars emit thirty to one hundred times as many particulates per mile as do gasoline-powered cars, diesel-powered cars provide fuel savings of 25 to 30 percent over gasoline-powered cars, emit substantially lower volumes of hydrocarbon and carbon monoxide emissions, and have proved significantly safer in accidents (because diesel fuel is less volatile than gasoline).

Fleet averaging, which is akin to the bubble concept applied to stationary sources, resembles in some ways the regulatory technique of performance standards. Under the averaging strategy, which was originally advanced during the Carter administration,[6] emission limits are applied to the various diesel engine classes rather than to each vehicle manufactured. Emission averages (which take into consideration the number of vehicles manufactured with each class of engine) are then set below the applicable particulate standards.[7] The objective of this approach is to give manufacturers some flexibility in designing control systems for the range of engine families they produce.

Another innovative regulatory technique in the administration's auto package was the use of a voluntary self-certifying standard. Heavy reliance on self-certification can be found throughout EPA's revision of its emissions testing standards—most notably in the agency's willingness to allow the industry to certify vehicles as meeting high-altitude emissions standards. Of course, determining whether a particular use of voluntary standards or the granting of self-certification authority constitutes simple deregulation or the adoption of an innovative, market-based solution can be a close call, as it is here.

Although regulatory innovations are not well represented in the auto package, the administration has taken a few steps to introduce them elsewhere in their drafts of existing or proposed regulations. Three notable examples—each of which is examined elsewhere in this book—are EPA's emissions trading statement (chapter 10), the Office of Surface Mining's broad reliance on performance rather than design standards in its modification of rules under the Surface Mining Act (chapter 10), and EPA's lead phasedown regulation, which allows refiners to trade the right to use lead in gasoline on a nationwide basis (chapter 6).

Drafting of "New" Rules

Another area of agency standard-setting activity (one for which the auto package does not provide useful guidance) is the drafting of "new" regulations. In this area as elsewhere, the administration's conscious efforts to limit the burden imposed by the proposed rules are plainly evident.

For example, under implementing regulations drafted by EPA during the Reagan administration, federal monies in the Superfund (a program to clean up existing hazardous waste sites that have been abandoned or are no longer in commercial operation) can be released only for the cleanup of sites that appear on the National Contingency Plan. The National Contingency Plan is a listing compiled over the past several years, of several hundred sites, that are considered to pose the most pressing health problems. Critics of the rule inside EPA say that it was written in a way that artificially limits federal intervention in national cleanups to sites on the list, and these may or may not at any particular time pose the greatest health problems. Furthermore, critics maintain that the Comprehensive Environmental Response, Compensation and Liability Act (CERCLA) contains no language to dictate that use of Superfund monies be restricted in this manner.

In other instances when the administration has had an opportunity to "write on a clean slate," it has responded in a more conventional, but similarly restrained, manner. One journal has noted that FDA's regulations on tamper-resistant packaging of over-the-counter drugs (which were hurriedly promulgated in the wake of the Tylenol scare) might not have passed OMB's cost-benefit test.[8] The journal acknowledges, however, that federal regulations were necessary to preempt the issuance of widely divergent regulations by localities across the country. The journal also noted approvingly that the rule explicitly does not aim to provide absolute safety and that it is set out as a performance rather than a design standard.

Economic Deregulation: Progress Continues at the Independent Agencies

The administration has gone to great pains to trumpet many of the questionable successes of its social deregulation campaign, but its efforts in the sphere of economic regulation drew less attention—at least through the first years of Reagan's term. As was discussed in chapter 4, much of the progress in this area was achieved by building on the efforts of Presidents Ford and Carter.

With the principal exception of trucking, where Reagan's appointee as Interstate Commerce Commission (ICC) chairman was initially reluctant to use the authority granted him by the Motor Carrier Reform Act of 1980 as aggressively as some in the administration might have liked, deregulation in surface and air transporation has been proceeding rapidly. The Civil Aeronautics Board is moving toward its scheduled demise at the end of 1984, shedding authority on the way. The ICC, through a series of rule makings and policy statements, has come close to deregulating the railroad industry, arguably moving even beyond the intent of the 1980 Staggers Act (court tests of these actions are now pending). And both pricing and entry in trucking have been substantially relaxed, putting strong pressure on established carriers to improve the efficiency of their operations and on the Teamsters' union to accept significant concessions in wages and work rules.

In the area of energy, the president kept his campaign promise and in his first day in office ended controls over domestic crude oil prices and retailing margins. Various regulations designed to control the choice of fuel by industry or to mandate energy efficiency standards for new commercial and residential buildings and for major home appliances have been suspended.

The deregulation of the broadcasting industry begun under Carter has also continued as a number of Carter initiatives were endorsed by Reagan's appointees to the Federal Communications Commission (FCC). In particular, broadcast licenses have been made less vulnerable to challenge—a shift that was itself contested and largely upheld. (This subject is discussed later in this chapter.) Efforts by the federal government to impose "public interest" obligations on broadcasters through specifying the general content of programming (for example, by limiting the number of minutes of commercials that can be aired per hour, or by urging an increase in the amount of children's programming) have been set aside in deference to the operation of the free market. Although the administration has pressed these deregulation initiatives quite forcefully, the Federal Communications Commission under Reagan has given lower priority to Carter administration efforts to increase the amount of competition in broadcasting by increasing the number of VHF television channels.

In the area of antitrust policy, the government's twin enforcement agencies, the Justice Department and the Federal Trade Commission, each issued new guidelines setting out their merger policies. A scholarly critique of the new guidelines found that in general they were somewhat less restrictive than the 1977 guidelines but that "the characteristics of a particular merger will determine whether and to what extent the new guidelines are less stringent than the old."[9] This analysis of the new guidelines found that (1) small firms will find it easier to make acquisitions in markets that are not highly concentrated; (2) large firms will perceive little change in acquiring firms; and (3) mergers will become more difficult regardless of the size of the firms involved in markets in the lower end of the concentrated range.

Deregulation by Statute: Modest Proposals

The high level of activity that characterized administration efforts to rescind or revise administrative regulations was not evident in the legislative area. One of the earliest published critiques of the Reagan administration's regulatory relief campaign noted the conspicuous absence of a clear legislative agenda.[10] Indeed, by spring 1983, with the debacle at EPA still fresh in the memories of the Congress and the electorate, the campaign's legislative program was widely acknowledged to have fallen into almost total disarray. The administration seemed to have spent relatively little political capital to obtain legislative reform, and in view of the growing political resistance to a number of the administration's proposed changes, sustaining a low profile seemed to be the best strategy—particularly in the critical area of environmental regulation.

Overall, the Reagan administration, like the Ford and Carter administrations, has made greater progress pushing its economic than its social deregulatory agenda in Congress. During Reagan's first two and one-half years in office, two significant deregulatory bills cleared Congress, one calling for the deregulation of the intercity bus industry, the other freeing thrift institutions from federal constraints that had limited their ability to compete with other financial institutions.

Legislation relaxing federal rules governing the intercity bus industry was on the agenda of both the Reagan administration and Congress to continue deregulation of surface transportation. With enactment of the Bus Regulatory Reform Act of 1982, intercity buses became the fourth major sector of the transportation industry to be deregulated in four years. The bill's overriding goals were to allow passenger carriers to enter new markets and to drop service in unprofitable ones with relative ease.

In the area of banking, while the primary goal of the 1982 Garn-St. Germain Depository Institutions Act was to provide savings and loan institutions and mutual savings banks with a means of competing with money market funds, a number of the principal strategies employed were deregulatory in nature. For example, by authorizing the creation of new deposit accounts not subject to interest rate ceilings, the act accelerated interest rate deregulation. The act also eased some restrictions on mergers between banks and thrift institutions and mergers between institutions in different states.

The administration's most significant legislative accomplishments outside the sphere of economic deregulation have come in intergovernmental relations and grant reform. The changes generally served three purposes: First, they enhanced discretion of state and local governments in the use of grant funds and promoted the goals of the president's New Federalism campaign. Second, the enhanced discretion has been used strategically to help justify reductions in federal grants in aid. And third, rule changes could be held out as victories for the regulatory relief effort. In fact, one of the administration's best publicized regulatory "hit lists" pertained exclusively to regulations affecting state and local governments.

Legislative achievements pertaining to intergovernmental relations and grant reform came in two areas—the collapsing of fifty-eight categorical grant programs into nine block grants and the simplification of the rules and regulations governing the construction grants program under the Clean Water Act. The legislation consolidating categorical grant programs into a set of block grants was not advanced in independent statutory form, but was folded into the massive 1981 Omnibus Reconciliation Act. Moreover, key policy changes were not advanced by the legislation per se, but were contained in the skeletal implementing regulations subsequently promulgated. Thus, legislative actions provided federal agencies with a congressionally sanctioned opportunity to eliminate those federal regulations that had operated as unpopular conditions of assistance.

In the area of construction grants, legislation enacted in December 1981 expanded the types of processes that could meet federal secondary treatment standards and stated that courts should acknowledge reduced federal funding levels when municipalities fail to comply with federal standards. Changes in the law also reduced the maximum federal contribution to individual projects from 75 percent to 55 percent of total costs, constrained the use of federal grant funds likely to be employed to stimulate future community growth, and delayed community receipt of federal planning funds.

Still, the real story of the administration's first two years remains the legislative changes that never received much high-level White House attention. Whether Congress could have been persuaded to pass legislation that substantially altered regulatory statutes will never be known. In some instances legislation that the administration valued highly—even bills falling generally within the sphere of economic deregulation—were relayed to Congress at an agonizingly slow pace. An example is the administration's proposed bill calling for further deregulation of natural gas, which was debated internally for two years before being sent to Capitol Hill.

During Reagan's first two and a half years in office, the area of greatest disappointment to administration supporters was, of course, environmental reform. There, the administration's inability to influence congressional action led in the short run to two different outcomes. First, legislation that might earlier have been influenced by administration preferences was written in a manner that departed from early administration positions. For example, markups in late spring 1983 for the reauthorization of the Resource Conservation and Recovery Act (one of two major federal vehicles for controlling hazardous waste) would have specified strict and comparatively short deadlines for EPA to process permits and promulgate stringent new regulations.[11] A bill reported to the floor in May 1983 set an eighteen-month deadline for the agency to promulgate rules bringing all toxic waste generators responsible for monthly disposal of more than 100 kilograms under the statute's regulations and permit program;[12] the law in force at the time applied only to generators disposing of more the 1,000 kilograms per month. Moreover, some agency personnel question whether the strict deadlines prescribed by the proposed bill would make the kind of reviews and assessments by OMB and EPA required by Executive Order 12291 effectively impossible. Clearly the changes were instigated by the widespread belief, in Congress and elsewhere, that EPA had not been enforcing the law.

In other instances, a number of environmental laws reauthorized during the 97th Congress's second session did not bear the administration's imprint. For example, the three-year reauthorization of the 1973 Endangered Species Act overrode the administration's preference for a one-year extension. The revision also codified in the act heretofore administrative interpretations that the administration had earlier tried to reverse. Similarly, Congress's reauthorization of the Federal Insecticide, Fungicide, and Rodenticide Act overrode the administration's attempts to restrict public access to information on the health and safety effects of pesticides.

Even before the Reagan administration's influence over environmental legislation sharply declined, many observers had been puzzled by the administration's limited involvement in the area. Take, for example, the Clean Air Act, which many scholars thought raised the most important regulatory issues on the administration's agenda. Since the act was due to be reauthorized in 1981, it posed the first and best opportunity for a critical legislative win. But the administration submitted a broad and somewhat vague statement of eleven principles an amended air act should reflect and then generally remained remote from the long-running congressional debate over the act's reauthorization.

The administration did develop and submit its own bill for consideration when the Clean Water Act came up for reauthorization. Environmental advocates were very unhappy with the fourteen changes proposed, but some commentators were surprised that the bill was not more far-reaching. Among other things, the changes would have—

- Granted a four-year delay from the 1984 deadline for industries to install the "best available technology" to treat industrial toxic wastes;
- Permitted EPA to waive toxic pretreatment requirements for industries discharging into publicly owned municipal sewage treatment plants if the plants could demonstrate that local water quality standards would continue to be upheld;
- Extended the maximum term for discharge permits from five to ten years;
- Exempted the nation's 2 million dams from specific clean water requirements;
- Deleted the requirement that mandatory national standards be established for the pretreatment of industrial toxic wastes by municipal treatment plants;
- Authorized the Clean Water Act's first felony provision, allowing EPA to seek criminal penalties of up to $50,000 a day for companies

and imprisonment for up to two years for individuals who "knowingly" violate the act;

- Granted the EPA the authority to assess civil penalties of up to $10,000 a day to a limit of $75,000. (At the time the changes were proposed, only courts had the power to set such penalties.)

Although many observers considered the proposed changes to be relatively modest, by spring 1983 there had been further retreat. Specifically, the administration had made it known that it would no longer press for elimination of the requirement that a national standard be developed for pretreating industrial toxic wastes[13] and that it would no longer seek waivers for its best available technology requirements. Administration proposals still appeared highly politicized and driven by a few strong special interest groups. One official quoted in the *National Journal* stated, "The agency's proposals reflected little analysis. Many of them had no support on the Hill or among this staff. Except for the penalties provision, they merely amounted to a loosening up of the act."[14]

Congressional response to the administration bill was cool at best; it had become apparent that administration influence over the legislative process—at least in the environmental area—had declined substantially. Moreover, environmental spokesmen who had taken a defensive position at the outset of the new administration, hoping to minimize their statutory and administrative losses, began to assume a more uncompromising stance regarding renewal of the nation's environmental laws.

Although the administration's legislative influence may have revived with the appointment of William Ruckelshaus, that development stems in part from expectations that Ruckelshaus would redirect the administration's environmental policy. For example, prior to Ruckelshaus' appointment, the EPA had recommended changes in the Clean Water Act that would allow the agency to waive toxic pretreatment requirements for industries discharging into publicly owned municipal sewage treatment plants if the plants could demonstrate that local water quality standards would be upheld. Ruckelshaus' concerns over the administration and technical difficulty of developing and implementing standards for granting the waivers prompted the Senate Subcommittee on Environmental Pollution to remove a proposed waiver provision from its draft revision of the Clean Water Act. Obtaining the waiver had been an important goal of the administration and EPA's former leadership.[15]

Another area in which the administration's influence may be declining is administrative reform. From the outset the administration had wanted the key provisions of E.O. 12291 pertaining to cost-benefit analysis and presidential oversight codified into law. The effort had received a substantial boost when the Senate passed—by a vote of 94 to 0—S.1080, which incorporated many of the administration's reforms. The bill's momentum was slowed, if not reversed, by the scandal at EPA and its fallout for the OMB oversight process. The shift was evidenced by several proposed House bills whose sponsors were clearly reacting to the secrecy that purportedly shrouds OMB's role in regulatory decision making. To illustrate, one controversial proposed provision, section 624 of H.R. 2327, states, "The Director (of OMB) may not participate in any way in deciding what regulatory action, if any, the agency will take in any rulemaking proceeding." If enacted, the bill would, in the words of Christopher DeMuth (the current administrator of OMB's Office of Information and Regulatory Affairs), "preclude effective executive oversight by cutting back sharply on existing statutory authorities as well as the review procedures President Reagan currently relies upon."[16]

Reversing Regulatory Relief: Political and Procedural Defeats

When a number of former Reagan administration regulatory principals and long-time observers of the regulatory process gathered at a conference sponsored by the Urban Institute in summer 1983, the consensus was that the administration's legislative agenda remained almost wholly unrealized. Although more participants conceded that the flow of federal regulations had ebbed, they also agreed that the critically important effort to roll back existing regulations had suffered a number of major political and legal defeats.

These losses were significant for several reasons. First, they struck down a number of the administration's most sought-after regulatory reforms. As a result, several key regulations that the administration had tried to eliminate remained in place and on firmer legal ground than ever. Furthermore, the much-ballyhooed cost savings that these changes were supposed to have generated had been lost; indeed, compliance costs may have increased as a result of delays. Now, not only had the fate of targeted regulations grown uncertain, but legal precedent emerging from successful challenges left the validity of other administration actions increasingly in doubt. Finally, repeated losses suggested that ideological motives had overridden procedural and technical concerns.

The administration's political errors in a way resembled all political misjudgments: In some instances, agency officials underestimated the extent to which proposed changes would be opposed by interest groups, Congress, and the media. In other instances, officials overstated the benefits likely to flow from proposed changes and found that their proposals did not have strong support—even among the regulated community.

One area in which agency officials underestimated opposition to proposed rule changes was the provision of public services to the disabled. Problems began with the administration's efforts in the summer of 1982 to revise key provisions of the Education Department's regulations implementing the Education of All Handicapped Children's Act. The proposals ran into a hailstorm of criticism from Congress, the media, interested parents, and educators and were withdrawn.

Chastened, the administration became reluctant to advance final regulations setting accessibility standards for the disabled. In July 1981 the administration had published interim regulations relieving transit operators of the responsibility for undertaking all but some vaguely defined "special efforts" to make their systems accessible. The Department of Transportation had issued these interim accessibility regulations in response to a decision by the U.S. Court of Appeals in *American Public Transit Association* v. *Lewis*[17] which invalidated the Carter administration's rules requiring that public transportation systems be made "fully accessible" to the handicapped. The Carter rules, which would have required major capital expenditures for most fixed rail and bus systems, were unpopular among city officials (as well as with a number of Carter's economic advisers) and had been designated early as key targets by the task force.

The court's opinion in *APTA* v. *Lewis* formally returned the regulations to the Department of Transportation so that some statutory basis could be found to justify them beyond the law relied on at trial (section 504 of the Rehabilitation Act of 1973).[18] Its work largely done for it, the administration simply announced the withdrawal of the rules and promulgated interim regulations in their place. The interim rules vested far greater discretion with local transit systems and led some cities to substantially limit the transportation services provided the disabled.[19] Not surprisingly, the new interim rules proved controversial, and the administration decided to delay promulgating final regulations on the issue. Congress then countered the administration's stalling tactics in December 1982 by amending the Federal Public Transportation Act of that year to require publication of a final regulation within 180 days.[20] In early September 1983, the administration proposed new regulations that represented a clear compromise between the "anything goes" special efforts rules and the "full accessibility" regulations of the Carter administration.

The controversy within the administration over OSHA's cotton dust standards provides a contrasting illustration of the White House's overestimation of support for its proposed regulatory changes. At issue were standards issued by OSHA calling for the use of individual respirators and installation of plantwide engineering controls by March 1983 to protect textile workers from the effects of exposure to cotton dust: byssinosis, or brown-lung disease (see chapter 3). In early 1981 the Task Force on Regulatory Relief targeted the standards for review, but in June 1981, after hearing a challenge to the rule's validity by the textile industry, the Supreme Court handed down a decision upholding OSHA's standards and limiting the use of cost-benefit analysis to measure their validity.

In the meantime, OSHA officials found that they could not justify changing the rules to accommodate OMB preferences for standards that would eliminate engineering controls. First, 80 percent of the mills and facilities covered by the requirement had already spent more than $140 million to install the required equipment. Second, plant operators were reported to be finding that the controls were increasing productivity and improving employee relations, so little industry support remained for revising the regulations. Finally, OSHA officials claimed that introduction of the controls appeared to have substantially reduced the number of brown-lung cases among textile workers. As a result, OMB efforts to force the Labor Department to change the standards were defeated.[21]

Weighing Regulatory Relief: The Courts Step In

Predicting the level of political support or opposition a given policy is likely to elicit is, of course, an uncertain art. Far more fixed and knowable, however, is the degree to which regulatory policy changes are likely to be upheld as rational and within the discretion of the promulgating agency. There, a substantial body of administrative law and procedure could serve as a useful guide to agencies interested in redirecting regulatory policies.

In this section we review the challenges—some successful, some not—to five of the administration's attempts to deregulate by means of administrative rule makings. We believe that the challenged actions can be viewed as touchstones for the success of the regulatory relief program and its methods. Each represents an area of social or economic regulatory policy that had been scrutinized and debated for some time; each promised major savings for regulated entities, turned on philosophical preferences, and had been highly publicized by the administration's regulatory relief team.

The rule changes and challenges are: rescission of the passive-restraint standard by the National Highway Traffic Safety Administration (NHTSA); rescission of liquor-labeling standards by the Department of the Treasury; the attempt by EPA to redefine the term "stationary source" under the Clean Air Act; alteration by the Department of Labor of its long-standing Davis-Bacon regulations (designed to protect employees on federal construction projects by guaranteeing them a minimum wage based on local prevailing wage rates); and deregulation of the commercial radio industry by the Federal

Communications Commission (FCC). All but the FCC action represented attempts to roll back social regulation. All had a direct impact on private industry, and two—the Davis-Bacon and Clean Air Act revisions—also had implications for state and local governments. In none of the five challenges were all the Reagan administration's actions completely upheld, although in the Davis-Bacon and FCC cases, most of the administration's deregulatory agenda was sustained.

Revision of the Passive-Restraint Standard

At the time the Reagan administration took office, the American auto industry was experiencing a severe slump in sales, high unemployment, and an eroding share of the total market. Among the administration's first regulatory actions was the presentation of its auto package. The package proposed to rescind a number of long-pending rules and existing rules, some of which (such as the passive-restraint standard) applied to future model years. The rules, which addressed emission control, safety, fuel economy, and consumer objectives, reflected the full spectrum of federal policy initiatives directed at the auto industry over the past fifteen years. Total capital cost savings provided to industry were estimated at $1.3 billion over five years. Reagan officials claimed that consumers, in turn, would save $8 billion over the same period.

NHTSA's most controversial safety-related action was rescission of the agency's passive-restraint standard—a standard that had been under development since 1967. Passive restraints (the use of automatic seat belts or air bags) had long been a controversial political issue. Not only had NHTSA twice adopted regulations calling for mandatory restraints, but agency actions had been formally reviewed and implicitly approved by Congress in 1977 and again in 1980. NHTSA officials had estimated that passive restraints could prevent 12,000 deaths and more than 100,000 serious injuries a year, and would provide annual savings of $4.23 billion in insurance premiums. Information from Nationwide Mutual Insurance Companies indicated that annual premiums would fall $32.50 per car if the entire U.S. auto fleet eventually were equipped with restraints. Cost-benefit analyses prepared by a consultant to the insurance industry (Professor William Nordhaus of Yale University, a former member of the Council of Economic Advisers), which found the proposed standard to be clearly cost-effective.

Reagan's officials were unconvinced and began a multistage operation to rescind the standard. They rationalized their action on the grounds that auto makers had chosen to rely on detachable, passive belts rather than nondetachable passive belts or air bags as their preferred means of complying with federal rules. Because the belts could be detached, they would be defeatable, and NHTSA officials assumed that owner usage would be low. Thus, the installation cost of the restraints would not be offset by estimated benefits.

Although it is hard to prove on the basis of the rule-making record, ideological concerns may have played a role in the agency's decision. Many people regarded either air bags or mandatory seat-belt usage as an unwanted, paternalistic intrusion by the government into the daily lives of its citizens. The administration preferred to rely on a major educational effort to enhance voluntary belt usage, on grounds that such an approach was less likely to fuel a public opinion backlash which might "cause significant long run harm to the safety program."[22]

Almost immediately, the State Farm Mutual Insurance Company and the National Association of Independent Insurers challenged the rescission of the standard. The case was argued on March 1, 1982, and on June 1, the U.S. Court of Appeals for the D.C. Circuit issued its opinion invalidating the rescission. The decision, written by Judge Abner Mikva, found NHTSA's action to be a "paradigm of arbitrary and capricious action." The court found that NHTSA had failed to demonstrate its central premise: that belt use would remain low. Beyond that, the agency's decision to rescind the passive-restraint standard rather than to assess the workability of other safety-promoting alternatives constituted a failure to carry out the purposes of the agency's legislative mandate.

In late June 1983, the U.S. Supreme Court announced that it would uphold the D.C. Court of Appeals' decision that rescission of NHTSA's passive-restraint standard was "arbitrary and capricious."[23] Justice White's opinion spoke not only to the matter of passive restraints but also to the procedures that administrative agencies were required to use in rescinding an existing regulation. After sixteen years and more than sixty notices of proposed rule makings, hearings, amendments, and court cases that the decision to mandate passive restraints on new cars would finally be settled.

The issue before the Supreme Court was whether rescission of an administrative regulation was analogous to an agency's decision not to act, and therefore wholly within its discretion. The repeal of the passive-restraint standard, which had been promulgated in accordance with the Motor Vehicle Safety Act, ran counter to the establishment of that principle. A key provision of that act expressly states that the procedural and judicial review provisions of the Administrative Procedure Act "shall apply to all orders establishing, amending, or *revoking* a Federal motor vehicle safety standard"[24] and, as the Court states, "suggests no difference in the scope of judicial review depending upon the nature of the agency's action."[25] (emphasis added)

Rather than relying narrowly on the language of the Motor Vehicle Safety Act, the Court went on to state the principle more broadly:

> Revocation constitutes a reversal of the agency's former views as to the proper course. A settled course of behavior embodies the agency's informed judgment that, by pursuing that course, it will carry out the policies committed to it by Congress. There is, then, at least a presumption that those policies will be carried out best if the settled rule is adhered to. . . . Accordingly, an agency changing its course by rescinding a rule is obligated to supply a reasoned analysis for the change beyond that which is required when an agency does not act in the first instance.[26]

The court then found NHTSA's revocation to have been arbitrary and capricious for two reasons. The first was that NHTSA had dismissed the passive-restraint standard without considering whether it should be revised to require that air bags rather than passive belts be installed. Air bags, the court noted, represented a "technological alternative within the ambit of the existing regulations."[27] Thus, a simple finding that the benefits of detachable belts would not offset presumed costs did not support the regulation's withdrawal. Accordingly, "at the very least this alternative way of achieving the objectives of the Act should have been addressed and adequate reason given for its abandonment."

A second reason for finding the agency's action to have been arbitrary was that it inadequately explained the dismissal of the use of automatic seat belts. Justice White held that NHTSA had failed to take account of critical differences between the operation of detachable automatic belts and manual belts currently in use. White noted that the force of inertia (which NHTSA appeared to consider very important) would work in favor of and not against the use of passive belts.[28]

The decision marked a major setback for the regulatory relief campaign. Not only had one of the most visible elements of the auto package been struck down, but the court, rather than relying on narrow statutory language which the agency had ignored, had gone on to clearly delineate general standards for the repeal of existing regulations.

Rescission of the Liquor-Labeling Regulations

A less significant but even more clear-cut case of an inadequately explained rescission involved the administration's summary repeal of regulations calling for labeling of alcoholic beverages. The rules at issue were promulgated in 1980, six years after they had first been proposed. Their purpose was to inform consumers, especially those with allergies, of the contents of alcoholic beverages. Under the rules, producers, bottlers, or importers could either list the beverage's ingredients on the label or elect to make an ingredient list available to purchasers. To comply with the requirements, labels would have to inform purchasers of the availability of such an ingredient list and provide a full address where one could be obtained. Rule changes permitting producers to provide ingredient lists on request had been promulgated in response to industry suggestions for mitigating regulatory costs.

Those changes did not, however, satisfy new appointees at the Treasury Department's Bureau of Alcohol, Tobacco, and Firearms, who rescinded the labeling rule in May 1981 with the publication of a one-page notice in the *Federal Register* (Vol. 46, p. 24962, 1981). The notice claimed that the cost of the regulations to consumers and to the industry would outweigh their benefits and were thus at odds with the department's mandate under E.O. 12291.

Judge John Pratt, of the U.S. District Court for the District of Columbia, responding to a suit by the Center for Science in the Public Interest, rejected that analysis. Concluding that the department had wholly failed to explain why it had reversed its prior decision that the rules were cost-beneficial and necessary to protect the health and welfare of consumers, Judge Pratt noted:

> The Department's initial decision to issue the regulations was the result of research and careful consideration. . . . It was predicated on an impressive factual record, which documented the range of costs to industry and the savings in health costs to consumers.[29]

He found that the department's failure to assess the marginal costs of the regulation—particularly the address label option—had rendered the rescission arbitrary and capricious. Treasury's failure to meet its burden of proof and to provide a reasoned explanation for its action led the court to hold that the agency had failed to comply with its statutory mandate under the Federal Alcohol Administration Act, as well as the substantive and procedural requirements of the Administration Procedure Act.

Redefining of "Stationary Source"

The administration suffered another major legal setback when an effort to rescind and revise a key provision of EPA's regulations implementing the 1977 Clean Air Act Amendments was struck down by the U.S. Court of Appeals for the District of Columbia in *Natural Resources Defense Council v. Gorsuch* (685 F.2d 718) on May 31, 1983. The Supreme Court subsequently granted the government's petition to hear the case. No decision had been issued at the time of this writing.

At issue in *NRDC* v. *Gorsuch* was the validity of EPA's proposed redefinition of the term *source* as it is applied in the Clean Air Act provisions
that set new source review standards for areas in which air quality fails to
meet federal standards ("nonattainment" areas).[30] The Reagan administration's redefinition of the term was intended to achieve three related goals: to
simplify the act's administration, to broaden application of the "bubble
concept"[31] to nonattainment areas, and to enhance the flexibility of states in
administering the Clean Air Act. Accordingly, EPA's rules redefining source
were eventually appended to the administration's highly publicized regulatory
relief package for state and local governments.

Under regulations promulgated in August 1980, the term *stationary source*
was defined differently for entities regulated under the 1977 Act's nonattainment and prevention of significant deterioration (PSD) programs. Under the
former, *source* was defined as both a plant and an individual piece of equipment (a smokestack, for example). The definition applied under the PSD
program does not include individual pieces of equipment. Rather, all pollutant-
emitting activities are accounted for only on an aggregated, plantwide basis.

The effects of this dual definition were to bring more units under review
within the nonattainment program and to subject all significant changes in an
individual plant's emissions sources to permit requirements and to certain
minimum technology standards. An additional practical effect of the dual
definition was to prohibit extension of the bubble concept to the nonattainment
program. In contrast, the design of the PSD program implicitly encouraged
a broader application of the bubble concept.

In October 1981, the Reagan administration rescinded the 1980 rules
setting out the dual definition of *source*. The new rules extended the definition
formerly applied to the PSD program to both the PSD and nonattainment
programs, effectively extending the bubble concept to new sources within
nonattainment areas.

Despite an acknowledged statutory silence, the U.S. Court of Appeals
invalidated EPA's action, relying primarily on recent judicial decisions that
determined the scope of the bubble concept's application.[32] The court found
that those decisions had drawn clear distinctions in the purpose and structure
of the nonattainment and the PSD programs that impelled the use of differing
regulations. Drawing on the decisions reached in two important cases, the
court held that the bubble concept, and thus the dual definition of source,
was inappropriate for sources regulated under the nonattainment program
where the principal legislative purpose was to "*improve* air quality." However, use of the bubble concept was perfectly consistent with the principal
legislative objectives of the PSD program—to *preserve* air quality. As in the
passive-restraint and liquor-labeling cases, EPA had failed to provide con-

vincing evidence that the existing regulatory scheme had failed to meet its legislative objective. In addition, the court remained unpersuaded by the government's arguments regarding its intent to advance the statutory goal of providing states with increased flexibility. Holding that improving air quality in nonattainment regions was the act's principal purpose, the court concluded: "Offering flexibility to the states may be a method of attaining that objective, but it is not an independent goal of the nonattainment scheme."

In *NRDC* v. *Gorsuch*, the evidence of agency technical and procedural carelessness is less strong. First, the plantwide definition of source adopted by EPA in 1981 did not originate with the Reagan administration. In fact the same definition had been proposed by EPA as late as 1979 and was only later reversed with the agency's promulgation of its August 7, 1980, regulations. Furthermore, it could be argued that the case for judicial deference to agency action is relatively strong here, where there is no clear, controlling statutory language or legislative history. Still this complete reversal of agency policy within a seven-month period, coupled with a failure to cleanly distinguish or circumvent the controlling case of *American Smelting and Refining Company* v. *EPA*, may have made the court's reversal of EPA's rule more predictable than many EPA officials suspected.

Revision of the Regulations Implementing the Davis-Bacon Act

The Department of Labor's regulations implementing the Davis-Bacon Act have been in place since the law's enactment during the Depression. The law was designed to stop contractors from taking advantage of widespread unemployment by hiring workers from distant areas for substandard wages and importing them to the construction site. Davis-Bacon has been the subject of long and spirited debate, with the law's opponents contending that it is an anachronism that artificially inflates the total costs of federally supported construction projects. More recently, the law has come under the attack of state and local officials compelled to pay prevailing wages on capital projects partially supported by federal funds. The task force targeted the rule for review and publicized its revision as a prominent element of its regulatory relief package for state and local governments.

In May 1982, the Department of Labor proposed new rules that substantially weakened five key provisions of the act's implementing regulations. Three of the new provisions would have changed the government's method for determining the local prevailing wage. They would have—

- Abandoned the "30 percent rule," which set the local prevailing wage at a level received by 30 percent of local workers, where a majority

of a class of workers are not paid the same rate. The new rule would
have employed a weighted average in setting rates paid in a district.

- Eliminated other federally supported construction projects from consideration when setting local prevailing wage standards.
- Excluded from consideration wages paid in metropolitan areas when calculating prevailing wage rates in rural areas. Prior regulations permitted this practice when no comparable projects had been undertaken in the immediate area of the proposed construction and where the nearest similar project was located in an urbanized area.

The proposed rules would also have:

- Abandoned the currently mandated practice of setting prevailing wage rates for narrowly defined, specialized classes of laborers and mechanics in favor of a scheme that would permit a substantial increase in the use of semiskilled "helpers." This expanded use of lower wages and lower skilled workers would have been accomplished by redefining "helpers" as a class of "mechanics or laborers" and by permitting their substitution for 40 percent of the total workers in a particular classification.
- No longer required submission of a contractor's weekly payroll, substituting instead a simple statement of compliance with federal standards.

The changes were viewed as a direct challenge by organized labor, which
responded by filing suit to enjoin the new rules' application. In *Building and
Construction Trades Department, AFL/CIO* v. *Donovan*, the U.S. District
Court for the District of Columbia granted the request, suspending and eventually halting all but the revised 30 percent rule from going into effect. The
court observed:

> For forty-seven years, through the administrations of eight presidents and fifteen
> Secretaries of Labor of many political and ideological persuasions, those interpretations and regulations stood without substantive alteration. During that
> period none of the administrators effected the kinds of fundamental changes
> that are brought about by the regulations adopted two months ago; instead, the
> various Secretaries of Labor continue to interpret and enforce the laws precisely
> in accordance with the original understanding.[33]

The D.C. Court of Appeals reversed a number of the lower court's
holdings, finding each of the three prevailing wage-related regulations as well
as the proposed liberalized use of semiskilled helpers to be securely within
the agency's discretion. Only provisions releasing contractors from part of
their reporting burden and a portion of the liberalized "helper" regulation

were struck down. In all, the case marked a significant court victory for the regulatory relief campaign.

Why did the outcome of this case differ from the outcome of the other proposed rule changes taken up in this section? The major difference derived primarily from the court's interpretation of the discretion that the Davis-Bacon Act granted the Department of Labor. With regard to the 30 percent rule, the court stated: "In brief, the statute delegates to the Secretary, in the broadest terms imaginable, the authority to determine which wages are prevailing." Noting that the statute empowered the secretary to adopt "regulations with legislative effect," the court upheld each of the three prevailing wage proposals. In reaching its conclusion, the court discounted the weight to be afforded prior administrative practices, pointing out that they had not been so consistently implemented as had been claimed. Indeed, the Carter administration itself had attempted to have urban counties excluded from rural wage determinations.

The court found no statutory language prohibiting expanded use of helpers and indeed found that, in many cases, prevailing wages paid in an area reflected greater use of helpers than had been authorized under the Davis-Bacon Act. Thus, the court concluded that the proposed regulation was "an entirely logical response to the problem of federal construction practice not reflecting the widespread, but not universal, practice of using helpers."[34]

In sum, then, the extraordinarily broad grant of authority provided the agency was largely responsible for sustaining the administration's efforts to revise these key regulations enjoyed. Also important, however, was the fact that although the administrative practices implementing the act may have been relatively consistent over the years, extensive data and well-considered theories arguing for substantial modification of key implementing regulations had also been developed. The restatement of these well-documented claims, coupled with the broad grant of authority, provided the Department of Labor with the rational basis it needed to sustain its proposed changes.

Deregulation of the Radio Industry

In May 1983, the U.S Court of Appeals for the District of Columbia announced that it would uphold most of the rule modifications proposed by the Federal Communications Commission (FCC) in its effort to deregulate the commercial radio industry. The changes that the FCC had originally advanced under the Carter administration were subsequently embraced by the Reagan administration and held out as an important initiative of the regulatory relief campaign.

Rule changes fell in four areas:

- Elimination of quantitative guidelines for public-interest programming (and hence reduced programming requirements);
- Elimination of formal procedures for ascertaining the nature of the issues facing the community served;
- Elimination of quantitative guidelines regarding the amount of commercial time broadcast (restrictions had previously been applied to airing more than eighteen minutes of commercials per hour);
- Elimination of the requirement that stations maintain program logs providing information on the content and nature of programs broadcast over the channel.

The court's opinion in *United Church of Christ* v. *FCC* upheld all but the FCC's lifting of the program log requirements. Without exploring the court's rationale for sustaining each of the specific changes falling in the areas just identified, we can point to two crucial reasons for the case's outcome. First, the agency's "Notice of Inquiry and Proposed Rulemaking, Deregulation of Radio" in 1979 had provided a detailed economic analysis of conditions in the radio industry and had set forth a number of alternatives for each proposed modification.[35] Subsequently, panel discussions and public participation workshops had been held across the nation, and more than 20,000 public comments had been received. Thus, the FCC was able to demonstrate that the number of stations had increased, the level of competitiveness had grown substantially, and the industry had been transformed into a more specialized source of entertainment and information. The FCC was then able to demonstrate that shifts in industry structure would support the proposed deregulating measures without forcing the agency to abandon its statutory mandate to "regulate in the public interest."[36]

A second factor influencing the case's outcome was the broad grant of discretion the FCC had under its governing act. This plus the empirical framework that had evolved over a four-year period were generally sufficient to override the court's concerns regarding the agency's departure from "prior policies and precedents."

Two other factors also appear to account for the broad grant of discretion accorded the FCC by the court. The first flows from the federal government's continuing control over the granting of broadcast licenses to applicants. In a number of instances the court found itself able to sanction the withdrawal or severe reduction of public-interest programming regulations because "the extent to which nonentertainment programming has traditionally been considered in the competitive process is not being changed in this rulemaking."[37] The second factor was the court's faith that the agency would continue to monitor and modify the deregulation experiment in the future. For example, in regard to its lifting of constraints on the quantity of commercial broadcast, the court wrote,

> The Commission may well find that market forces alone will not sufficiently limit over-commercialization. In that event, we trust the Commission will be true to its word and will revisit the area in a future rulemaking proceeding.

Still, while the court felt itself compelled to defer to the agency's use of the administrative rule-making process to accomplish its sweeping deregulation, it did so with "serious reservations." The author of this opinion, Judge J. Skelly Wright, concluded:

> In these proceedings the Commission has on its own undertaken to enact a significant deregulation of the radio industry. In so doing it has pushed hard against the inherent limitations and natural reading of the Communications Act. For the reasons stated above, we affirm most of the Commission's orders, remanding only those portions relating to program logs with instructions that the Commission undertake further inquiry in accordance with this opinion. However, we take this opportunity to note that Congress, and not the Commission, may be the more appropriate source of such significant deregulation. It was Congress, after all, that created and oversaw the evolution of the original regulatory scheme for radio and television licenses. It should thus be Congress, and not the unrepresentative bureaucracy and judiciary, that takes the lead in grossly amending that system, thereby providing the public with a greater voice in this important process. And yet, in the absence of more specific congressional direction, we cannot say that the Commission has overstepped either the bounds of its statutory authority or its administrative discretion in undertaking most of the deregulatory actions under review.[38]

Conclusion

As our analysis of challenges to a number of the administration's significant regulatory reforms suggests, rule-making actions taken by the administration were designed to dramatically alter if not reverse prior federal policy. As we demonstrate elsewhere in this chapter, those changes were undertaken without the benefit of complementary legislative changes. Thus, for the most part the administration used the rule-making process, not the legislative process to reverse rather than refine federal regulatory policy.

When administration-sponsored changes were able to weather subsequent legal challenges, those successes usually were attributable to a record of evidence or a theoretical argument to support a change in existing policy, or both. As the review of these five cases has shown, when such a record or such arguments were in place, they had been advanced by one or more of this administration's predecessors and essentially reflected a measure of continuity in governmental actions. A second critical factor in sustaining proposed changes was the existence of broad (usually long-standing) enabling statutes that vested the administering agency with a level of discretion not provided by newer, often more prescriptive laws.

When the administration did not have a solid informational and theoretical base upon which to build, it proceeded incautiously in promoting reversals of existing policies. In such cases extraordinary technical and procedural care was required for three reasons: (1) sharp reversals in policy direction—particularly if effected quickly—trigger intensive judicial review; (2) the courts, which are typically relatively deferential when it comes to administrative actions, need demonstrate no such deference when statutory interpretation is at issue, as is often the case with summary reversals of regulatory policy; and (3) rule changes that pertain to health issues (as the wine-labeling, passive-restraint, and emissions-trading regulations do) frequently trigger intense judicial scrutiny.

In retrospect, there was no reason for the whole of the administration's regulatory relief efforts regarding social regulation to take place in the adminstrative arena. The president came to power at a time when popular and congressional distaste for overregulation ran high and when a number of the nation's most important regulatory statutes were due for reauthorization. Through time, however, the companion strategies to legislative action—the appointments, budget cuts, centralization of oversight, and the freewheeling use of the administrative process—alienated the constituency for legislative reform of social regulation.

9

Enforcement

Legislative change requires congressional approval. Changing implementing regulations, as we have seen, is comparatively visible, is subject to OMB scrutiny, and is vulnerable to judicial review. Even most agency appointments and budget matters require congressional action. Enforcement of existing laws and regulations, however, appears to fall squarely within an administration's unhampered discretion. With rare exceptions, enforcement standards are rarely prescribed by regulation and even more rarely prescribed by statute.[1] Rather, enforcement strategies—determining which laws will be enforced, against whom, and how strictly—are typically incorporated in operating procedures set out in internal memoranda, in unpublished agency directives, or simply in the daily exercise of judgment by agency managers. Thus, these strategies are usually informally established and unsystematically applied.

Like regulatory oversight, enforcement performance is relatively hard to track, largely because it varies by agency and frequently by program. Furthermore, exactly what constitutes good enforcement performance is hard to define. The process of regulation has become so complex and the number of regulated entities so large that universal enforcement is clearly impractical. Agencies exercising what is known as "prosecutorial discretion," choose among possible enforcement targets, selecting appropriate penalties and remedies.

Even if universal enforcement were possible, it would probably not be desirable. As two scholars, Bardach and Kagan (whose work was cited earlier in chapter 5), observed in a recent book:

> Legalistic enforcement cannot encompass in formal, enforceable rules the sheer diversity of the causes of harm that arise in a large, technologically dynamic economy. The inspector who walks through a factory and faithfully enforces each regulation may not detect or do anything about more serious sources of risk that happen to lie outside the rulebook; at the same time he alienates the regulated enterprise and encourages noncooperative attitudes.[2]

The politics of enforcement is, then, quite complex. By its nature, enforcement (mechanistic practices, in particular) will appear unfair to regulated entities that are fundamentally law-abiding. Still, no enforcement program can identify "bad apples" and target its actions solely against them. As a result, the hassle and waste of inspections and other enforcement activities must be borne by a certain number of law-abiding entities whose resentment is often acutely felt by the acting agency.

At the same time, flexible enforcement practices, which are often more rational, are likely to appear arbitrary. Such flexible practices resemble the approach to law taken by Bardach and Kagan's "good policeman." That approach measures law enforcement performance by overall results rather than by the number of times that statutes or regulations are invoked. Accordingly, an effective inspector might in some instances attempt to get firms to take actions not required by regulation (when, for example, obvious hazards are not covered by law) but in other instances will not cite technical or trivial violations. This approach obviously vests an extraordinary degree of discretion in public officials, generates opportunities for bribery or favoritism, and provides agency critics with examples of overlooked violations.

Swings in an agency's political approach to enforcement from mechanistic to flexible strategies reflect what Bardach and Kagan referred to as the movement of the "regulatory ratchet." They observed that the basic movement of that ratchet is toward less and less flexibility and discretion. Why?

> The lesson for regulatory agencies is that they are vulnerable to powerful journalistic and political sanctions levied, at unpredictable intervals, against even the appearance of undue leniency. Further, their vulnerability is magnified because these alleged failings typically are described in the news media without the benefit of historical perspective, without a sense of the overall distribution of compliant and noncompliant firms in the regulated population, and without a feeling for what is really possible. The best defense. . . [is to] become rule-following policemen. Additional security is provided by maintaining statistics showing that the agency is conducting regular inspections, imposing high num-

bers of citations and fines, and mounting prosecutions often—with resulting pressures on inspectors to do what is necessary to keep those statistics at a high level. Thus legalistic enforcement tactics are likely to become and remain entrenched, not because of their useful offensive function of providing more deterrence, but because of their defensive function of showing that the agency has been acting in conformance with the law and has been as systematic and as tough as existing manpower and sanctions enable it to be.[3]

Developing a balanced approach to regulation is extremely difficult—even for an administration that seeks out regulators basically sympathetic to agency missions. When an administration is suspected of intentionally weakening regulatory protections, as has been true of the Reagan administration, obtaining support for enforcement from the public—and, in some instances, the regulated community—becomes almost impossible. On the one hand, the protected community comes to suspect that its interests are being traded off against competing governmental concerns (industrial productivity, for example). The firms against which enforcement actions are brought often believe themselves to have been unfairly singled out, leading to more intense resistance than might otherwise be the case. Thus it should be no surprise that enforcement is the area in which the Reagan administration's regulatory relief effort has come most conspicuously to grief.

The term *enforcement* is used here to mean efforts to determine compliance with federal standards and actions taken upon detection of noncompliance. Specific enforceable standards can be (1) federal laws and their implementing regulations; (2) conditions attached to the receipt of federal subsidies; and (3) conditions attached to permits issued by federal agencies.

Despite the fact that enforcement strategies are relatively fluid and fall largely within an agency's discretion, a number of factors dictate the minimum scale of such programs. One is simply the number and location of entities or sources (e.g., the number of polluting plants) or the extent of illegal activity (e.g., job-related discriminatory acts) to be regulated. A second is the historical level of activity in the regulated area and the expectations that have been engendered among the regulated and protected communities. A third factor, one that pertains to compliance programs involving a significant capital component, is the stage of program maturity. Initial inspections and enforcement actions based on the installation of appropriate equipment are easier and often less expensive than follow-up actions geared to determining the maintenance and performance of that equipment through time.

Looking across regulatory programs we can discern a number of recurring enforcement strategies in the Reagan administration. A representative list could include a general reduction in the dollar amount of civil penalties assessed; adoption of new and more exclusive screening criteria for identifying potential violators; unwillingness to test new legal or economic theories that might expand the existing classes of violators; reduced discretion for field enforcement personnel; willing reliance on state and local governments and trade and professional associations as substitutes for federal enforcers; adoption of a less threatening, more flexible posture toward regulated entities; and greater interest in pursuing violators of regulatory statutes whose actions may have established criminal liability.

In this chapter we survey the enforcement policies and practices of the Occupational Safety and Health Administration (OSHA) and the Securities and Exchange Commission (SEC), as well as the controversial efforts of the Environmental Protection Agency (EPA) regarding the disposal of hazardous waste. In each case, elements of the Reagan administration's enforcement strategies departed from those adopted by earlier administrations.

The Occupational Safety and Health Administration

One of the most systematic efforts to revamp an agency's enforcement strategy took place during 1981 and 1982 at OSHA. New policy directives issued by the agency's director, Thorne Auchter, reduced the number of establishments subject to routine inspections and limited the discretion of field personnel to issue certain types of citations.

Because of the vast number of workplaces in the nation (approximately 5 million) and the limited number of OSHA inspectors, some targeting of inspections has always been necessary. In the past, that targeting limited general schedule inspections to the categories of industry found to be more hazardous than the norm for all industries listed in the standard industrial classification scheme of the Bureau of Labor Statistics (BLS). Firms or workplaces that fell within this high-hazard class were subjected to regular, thorough inspections.

A highly controversial OSHA directive, issued in the summer of 1982, calls for workplaces that fall within this high-hazard range to be subject initially only to a simple examination of records. During that inspection, OSHA staff review the injury records of the specific workplace to determine whether the workplace falls below the BLS norm for all standard industrial categories.[4] Only if it does will a "walk through" inspection be conducted. Thus, the fact that a firm falls within a high-hazard industrial category is no longer sufficient reason for a full "programmed" inspection.[5]

As shown in table 10, this double screening process has not led to any

TABLE 10

MEASURES OF OSHA ENFORCEMENT ACTIVITY

	FY 1980	FY 1981	FY 1982	Change, FY 1980– FY 1982 (Percentage)
Inspections				
Establishment	63,363	57,241	52,783	− 17
Records	—	—	8,442	NA
General Schedule	33,320	36,135	34,134[a]	+ 2
General Schedule plus Records	33,320	36,135	42,576	+ 28
Complaint	16,093	13,448	6,761	− 58
Follow-up	11,664	5,427	1,567	− 87
Citations				
Initial Inspections with Citations (Percentage)	64	61	59	− 8
Total No. Citations	132,719[b]	111,859	97,136	− 27
Serious Citations	44,695	32,765	22,542	− 50
Willful Citations	1,238	662	113	− 91
Repeat Citations	3,541	2,255	1,253	− 65
Serious, Willful, Repeat Citations as a Percentage of Total	37	32	25	− 32
Penalties				
Total Penalties	$25,497,832	$13,498,004	$5,579,882	− 78
Failure-to-Abate Penalties	$2,007,324	$749,544	$173,532	− 91
Worker Complaints (No.)	26,823	22,978	13,864	− 48
Contested Cases (Percentage)	22	11	5	− 77

SOURCE: AFL-CIO Department of Occupational Safety and Health, March 1983.

    a. Includes 8,442 records inspections.

    b. More than one citation can result from a single inspection.

significant decline in the number of initial inspections, though establishments fell by 17 percent. General schedule inspections rose by 2 percent between fiscal year (FY) 1980 and FY 1982. However, when records inspections are added to general schedule inspections, the total rose by 28 percent.

That was not, however, the case with two prominent types of unprogrammed inspections—complaint inspections (down 58 percent) and follow-up inspections (down 87 percent). The drop in complaint-initiated inspections can be attributed in part to a policy—begun toward the end of the Carter administration and accelerated during the Reagan administration—to conduct inspections only when formal (i.e., written) complaints are received from employees. Other complaints elicit only a letter to a workplace's manager. OSHA personnel suggest that the recession and fears of unemployment may have chilled employees' willingness to submit complaints: worker complaints fell 48 percent in the two-year period.

Regarding follow-up inspections, OSHA is, in most instances, taking companies at their word that they will bring violations into compliance. Accordingly, follow-up inspections have fallen dramatically (down 87 percent), as have penalties for "failure to abate"—that is, failure to remedy detected violations. These fell 91 percent.

But despite the fact that the number of initial inspections remained high and that they were more precisely and exclusively targeted than ever on "bad apples," the number of citations issued and penalties collected have fallen off substantially. As table 10 indicates, the number of serious citations issued between 1980 and 1982 declined 50 percent, the number of willful citations issued declined 91 percent, and the number of repeat citations dropped 65 percent. This decline in repeat violations is partially explained by a recent OSHA order stating that violations over three years old would no longer be considered in identifying repeat violations.[6]

The 78 percent drop in the dollar amount of penalties assessed is a direct result of a new philosophy at OSHA that encourages a more cooperative stance regarding industry. Assistant Secretary Auchter repeatedly stated that he was less interested in collecting first-instance penalties than in remedying violations through settlements with company managers. The *Washington Post* quoted him as saying, "Our philosophy is one of safety and health and not one of crime and punishment."[7]

Critics of the administration's general approach to inspection contend that it offers industry a strong incentive to under-report disease and injury. According to the critics, the more narrowly drawn the class of firms subject to inspections, the greater will be the temptation for firms not identified as being within a high-hazard category to ignore OSHA's exacting and expensive regulations. Finally, critics note that the sharp decline in follow-up inspections and failure-to-abate penalties provides little incentive to detected violators to comply with agency orders.

OSHA's defenders argue that its more cooperative posture and more efficient management of resources, as well as changed worker priorities in a recessionary economy, combine to make for a more rational and flexible enforcement policy, noting that workplace injury rates have continued to fall.

Another important enforcement initiative undertaken by Auchter was a significant limiting of agency discretion in applying the "general duty clause" of the Occupational Safety and Health Act.[8] General duty clause citations have been invoked in the past to protect employees working under special circumstances for which no standard had been adopted. Reliance on the clause has increased through time, and, not surprisingly, its use has been frequently challenged. New standards issued in March 1982 set forth three strict guidelines for substantiating citations on the basis of the clause: The hazard must be "recognized" by industry employees, it must be a serious threat to worker health or safety, and there must be a feasible means to correct the problem.[9]

The mandate that particular hazards are not to be cited unless they have been "recognized" by industry employers or, in special circumstances, by "common sense" observation, is very controversial.[10] Employee recognition or documentation by the National Institute of Occupational Safety and Health (NIOSH) may now be used only as supplementary evidence to establish that a particular condition has been "recognized" as a hazard. According to union officials, OSHA's recent directive downgrades the role formerly played by firm employees and by NIOSH.

Finally, we should note that limitation of OSHA field officers' enforcement discretion (by restricting application of the general duty clause) is consistent with the performance criteria recently adopted for OSHA personnel. Those criteria evaluate field officers in part on the number of citations they issue that are later challenged in court. Data indicate that since these criteria were adopted, the number of contested cases has dropped 77 percent.

OSHA, then, has made four major changes in enforcement: (1) OSHA has added new, ostensibly neutral, criteria to existing screening procedures—criteria that will exempt a broad range of workplaces from programmed inspections. (2) OSHA has adopted a new policy that downplays the appropriateness of dollar penalties for noncomplying companies. (3) OSHA has demonstrated greater faith in corporate willingness to remedy cited violations, as evidenced in its unwillingness to conduct follow-up inspections and its reluctance to assess nonabatement penalties. (4) OSHA is demonstrating a strong interest in limiting certain types of discretionary authority formally enjoyed by agency field officers.

The Securities and Exchange Commission

While OSHA has refined the targeting of its enforcement efforts, the SEC has redirected certain aspects of its program. The most significant development in enforcement policy at the SEC has been a shift of emphasis away from actions to punish corporate misconduct and management fraud to regulating insider trading and market manipulation. Observers suggest that a related shift in the targets of enforcement actions has brought brokers, dealers, and their attorneys (or those directly engaged in market trading operations) front and center and permitted corporations and their officers to recede somewhat.

The SEC has announced that it will shy away from enforcement actions in cases involving failure to disclose conduct that does not have a "material economic impact on a corporation."[11] In other words, the SEC will generally refrain from taking legal action in cases where the adverse impact of illegal conduct by corporate management would not have been sufficient to influence voting or investment decisions. One rationale current SEC officials use for retreating from such action is the absence of law enforcement policy spelling out the types of unethical or illegal conduct that should be pursued.

Among the types of corporate behavior that might fall outside the "materiality" requirements are (1) illegal management action taken solely to advance corporate interests (as opposed to that which constitutes a breach of trust) and (2) illegal payments not material to corporate finances. In addition, the SEC has petitioned Congress to relieve the agency of the responsibility for enforcing the antibribery provisions of the Foreign Corrupt Practices Act.[12]

This diminished interest in enforcing corporate morality has been linked to the recent controversy over the SEC's decision not to bring an enforcement action against Citicorp, which had been accused of systematically circumventing foreign tax laws. SEC staff under former Enforcement Division Director Stanley Sporkin believed that Citicorp's failure to disclose its "parking" arrangements (shifting profits from foreign banking operations in high-tax countries to low-tax locations) constituted a violation of the securities laws. In January 1982, the SEC voted not to take enforcement actions against the bank, citing, among other things, the age of the case, the fact that the amounts involved were not material to Citicorp, and the lack of clarity in the law concerning disclosure of unadjudicated allegations.

Statistics issued by the SEC seem to confirm that although the enforcement emphasis has shifted since the final years of the Carter administration, the general level of enforcement activity appears to have been sustained. Table 11 indicates that despite a 12 percent reduction in staff years devoted to enforcement, the number of civil injunctive actions initiated during the

TABLE 11
NATIONWIDE ENFORCEMENT PROGRAM OF THE SECURITIES AND EXCHANGE COMMISSION,
COMPARATIVE STATISTICS FOR FISCAL YEARS 1980–1982

	FY 1980	FY 1981	Change, FY 1980– FY 1981 (Percentage)	FY 1982 9/30/82	Change, FY 1981– FY 1982 (Percentage)	Change, FY 1980– FY 1982 (Percentage)
Number of Commission Staff Years Devoted to Enforcement Activities During Period	649.6	610.2	−6	574.3	−6	−12
Civil Injunctive Actions Initiated During Period (Including Civil and Criminal Contempt)	106	119	+12	145	+22	+37
Administrative Proceedings Initiated During Period	70	72	+3	104	+44	+49
Total	176	191	+9	249	+30	+41
Investigations Opened During Period	322	303	−6	294	−3	−9
Investigations Closed During Period	394	481	+22	476	−1	+21
Investigations Pending at End of Period	1,099	921	−16	739	−20	−33

SOURCE: Securities and Exchange Commission, October 19, 1982.

period between FY 1980 and FY 1982 rose by 37 percent. Similarly, the number of administrative proceedings initiated during the period rose by 49 percent.

A change in remedies appears to have accompanied the agency's shift in regulatory targets. During the 1970s, the agency frequently sought ancillary as well as injunctive relief to remedy violations. Many remedies called for the formation of independent review committees to systematically examine corporate conduct and report their findings to the agency and the general public. This type of remedy appears to have fallen from favor at the SEC.

No systematic study of SEC enforcement activities has been undertaken to date. If we rely, then, on agency data and public statements, SEC enforcement activities appear to fall squarely within the bounds of prosecutorial discretion. Assuming the shift in enforcement emphasis does not violate a clear congressional mandate, given the high, sustained level of enforcement activity, it appears that such retargeting is plainly within the agency's prerogative.

Enforcement of Regulations for Disposal of Hazardous Wastes

Enforcement of regulations relating to the disposal of hazardous wastes is dictated by two legislative schemes—one set out by the Resource Conservation and Recovery Act, the other by Superfund (or the Comprehensive Response, Compensation, and Liability Act—CERCLA). As in a number of regulatory areas, enforcement actions in hazardous waste disposal cases fell off sharply between FY 1980 and FY 1982. One congressional committee reported that only seven federal cases were filed under the Resource Conservation and Recovery Act (RCRA) during 1981—and only three cases were filed by the end of FY 1982. Forty-three such actions had been filed in 1980.

Enforcement data for the Superfund program, which was signed into law in 1980, reveal that twenty legal actions had been filed at the time Anne Gorsuch took office in 1981. From January 1981 to September 30, 1982, sixteen pending RCRA cases had been amended to add Superfund counts. EPA had referred eleven of those sixteen to the Justice Department for enforcement—most on September 30, the last day of the fiscal year. In all, enforcement actions relating to hazardous waste disposal dropped sharply in 1981 but made modest, if unspectacular, gains in 1982.

This dramatic slowdown in agency enforcement efforts was effectively summarized by a former Justice Department official in April 1982, who testified before the House Subcommittee on Oversight and Investigations: "I resigned my job on January 4, 1982, because I had no work. The development of Department of Justice theories of liability under Superfund was completed and not one new hazardous waste enforcement case was initiated by EPA.''[13] That official, Anthony Roisman, had served as chief of the Justice Department's Land and Natural Resources Hazardous Waste Section and later as special litigator for hazardous wastes and Superfund. Roisman's responsibilities in those positions, which he held from October 1979 to January 1982, were to formulate theories of liability under the Superfund Act and to handle major new hazardous waste litigation initiated by EPA.

Roisman's case may have been a somewhat extreme example, but throughout the first two and a half years of the Reagan administration, systematic reductions were obvious in EPA's budget, its enforcement activity, and the severity of fines it levied against violators. This situation was typical of regulatory enforcement in all agencies during the Reagan administration. The enforcement—or the generally perceived lack of enforcement—of the nation's hazardous waste laws, however, threatened to scuttle the administration's regulatory relief efforts. At minimum, the controversy that erupted over EPA's handling of its hazardous waste enforcement duties has made settlements of ongoing and future waste disposal cases far more politically complicated than they would otherwise have been. Agency discretion has been substantially reduced, and whatever flexibility companies that were cited for waste violations might have once enjoyed has been eliminated.

The Resource Conservation and Recovery Act, enacted in 1976, was the first major federal effort to control hazardous waste disposal. Its structure resembles that of the other principal environmental acts of the 1970s in that it is forward looking, calls for the issuance of administratively set standards, establishes a permit program based on those standards, and provides penalties and injunctions for noncompliance. Under RCRA, firms generating, storing, treating, disposing of, or otherwise handling hazardous wastes must keep records and file periodic reports. Firms storing, treating, or disposing of such wastes must obtain operating permits from EPA or a federally authorized state agency.[14]

By contrast, Superfund is retrospective, its purpose being to clean up existing, inactive, waste disposal sites. Spurred by the Love Canal furor, the act works by establishing liability and apportioning costs among responsible parties.[15] The act imposes liability on four groups: present owners and operators of disposal facilities; owners at the time of disposal; persons or firms who arranged for disposal or treatment at a facility; and those who transported hazardous substances to a disposal site. Among the forms of action authorized by the statute are administrative orders and injunctive suits to force the cleanup of sites and suits for recoupment when the government undertakes the cleanup. Government cleanup efforts are financed with monies provided by the $1.6 billion Superfund.

The basic design of the Superfund statute, along with its unclear liability standards, provides officials with more administrative flexibility than do the more uniform environmental statutes enacted in the 1970s. That flexibility is evident in the variety of actions available to government officials, as well as in their discretionary authority to apportion liability and to determine the scope and nature of the cleanup undertaken at each site.

Whether this discretion was abused in targeting enforcement actions or negotiating settlements—the much-mentioned "sweetheart deals"—is now largely moot. Charges of mismanagement, collusion, perjury, conflict of interest, and political favoritism, as well as an ill-advised constitutional confrontation between the president and Congress, aroused public concern and led to the turnover in leadership at EPA described in earlier chapters.

Although much of the attention focused on EPA's hazardous waste program has been directed at the extracurricular activities of its former managers, a number of allegations directly relating to enforcement have surfaced. Congressional critics point to an EPA official's purposeful disclosure of the agency's negotiating strategy, in particular, its confidential settlement figure, to an industry representative.[16] Those critics also question EPA's action in assuring settling parties that they will not be liable for any further cleanup costs, even if the federal court hearing cases brought against nonsettling parties finds that some parties did not pay their fair share. In fact, Ohio's Environmental Protection Agency refused to sign part of EPA's settlement of Chem-Dyne's Hamilton, Ohio, dump for just that reason.[17]

The adequacy of the settlements negotiated by EPA has also been questioned. For example, under existing agreements, the agency will receive approximately $11 million from private companies to clean up the Seymour, Indiana, dump site; EPA originally estimated that $30 million would be needed to clean up the site.[18]

Congressional critics have contended that elements of EPA's past enforcement approach have been so tame as to appear, at best, naive. For example, in February 1982, EPA sent out more than 700 notices to firms responsible for dumping at the agency's targeted list of 115 priority sites. (The number of priority sites has subsequently been expanded to 418.) The letters advised the companies that they had the option of voluntarily cleaning up or being drawn into legal action. The director of enforcement at that time was quoted as saying, "I believe there may be many more companies—in addition to those that already have started to clean up on their own—which have simply been waiting to be contacted and told how the agency wants to proceed.''[19] Three months after the letters were mailed, EPA had received responses from only seven companies expressing a willingness to negotiate.[20]

The controversy at EPA has prompted a shift in enforcement policy. The agency has retreated from its willingness to settle with hazardous waste generators willing to pay their "fair share" of cleanup costs and now requires the full cost of cleanup from generators wishing to be released from all future liability at a site. Industry attorneys believe this policy will subvert the possibility of future settlements and result in extensive litigation. Such litigation is likely to produce long delays, require an extraordinary commitment of depleted enforcement personnel and resources, and lead to uncertain outcomes. It would do so, not only because the burden of proof needed to procure a favorable settlement is lower than that required to prevail at trial, but also because, at least in the case of Superfund, the litigation would proceed in largely uncharted waters.

EPA's enforcement of hazardous waste disposal regulations may not have been so exceptional as the recent public outcry would suggest—particularly when viewed in the context of the administration's decided preference for negotiation and voluntary compliance instead of litigation. Plainly the furor over EPA's enforcement of hazardous waste disposal rules stemmed from the EPA staff's insensitivity to the appearance of favoritism, discounting of the issue's political volatility, and to public suspicion aroused by assertions of executive privilege. Furthermore, by permitting Superfund's implementation to be tarnished by allegations of nonenforcement, the administration may have lost an excellent opportunity to take advantage of an uncharacteristically broad legislative grant of discretion in a manner that would rationalize regulation.

Enforcement Elsewhere.   The movement toward reduced enforcement activity has not been universal. In fields that have been subject to economic deregulation, enforcement—typically of the antitrust laws—was intended to ensure that the competition Congress envisaged did in fact take place.

For example, the transportation section of the Justice Department's Antitrust Division is currently spending 70 percent of its resources on antitrust investigations and litigation and about 30 percent on participation in regulatory proceedings; these figures represent a reversal of the section's allocation of resources before deregulation began. Indeed, the proportion of resources the section allocates to enforcement matters is unusually high compared with the proportion in other sections of the Antitrust Division.[21] The transportation section's activity is particularly notable when viewed in the context of antitrust enforcement activities elsewhere in the administration. The overall number of cases instituted by Justice's Antitrust Division is reported to have dropped

75 percent from the level during the Carter administration.[22] Similarly, as of January 1, 1983, the FTC's Bureau of Competition had filed only two new administrative complaints and had obtained civil penalties in only four proceedings. The latter figure is down from fifteen final or provisional orders obtained by the previous administration during the same amount of time.

Another area in which enforcement activity has increased is banking—as a result of the cumulative effects of a sour economy, deregulation, and high interest rates. It has been suggested that such enforcement may be of particular importance during a period of deregulation in "order to assure that the rules that remain are followed."[23]

Evaluating the Enforcement Strategy

Regulatory relief has not meant universal abandonment of enforcement. In areas such as transportation and banking, where significant economic deregulation has occurred, congressional intent appears to have been carried out by comparatively vigilant enforcement efforts. Because resources are always limited, regulatory officials must always set enforcement priorities, and one administration's priorities will not necessarily be another's.

As we have seen, enforcement activities within OSHA, the SEC, and EPA have shifted substantially since the Reagan administration took office in January 1981. Most enforcement activities that have not been significantly reduced have been redirected. The significance of that shift is underscored by the fact that routines at regulatory agencies generally change little from administration to administration. Indeed, as new issues have emerged, expansion has been the rule, retrenchment the exception.

Under the Reagan administration, however, resources devoted to enforcement have been cut almost across the board—even in areas where Congress has increased federal activity. Where resources have been comparatively undisturbed, new priorities have forced a realignment of agency dollars, people, and effort. Finally, in areas to which the administration has shown little commitment, enforcement efforts have been dropped or neglected.

Affirmative enforcement practices are both visible and subject to review, but decisions that lead to inaction are difficult to discern and rarely challenged. And when challenged, they are usually upheld as being within an agency's lawful discretion. But this is not always the case. In *Save Our Cumberland Mountains, Inc.* v. *James Watt*,[24] the U.S. District Court for the District of Columbia held that the Surface Mining Control and Reclamation Act of 1977 required the Secretary of the Interior to impose a mandatory minimum daily fine on mine owners who had been cited for violations of the act, failed to come into compliance, and subsequently been ordered to stop mining operations.[25] Hundreds of such mines were discovered to have been operating illegally for years, with minimum daily fines of $750 a day accruing throughout the period. Moreover, the owners of the mines had been routinely and improperly receiving permits to open and operate other mines. At the time of this writing, a major settlement was being negotiated that would force the Department of the Interior to penalize noncomplying owners a prescribed amount.

The *Cumberland Mountains* case suggests that under certain statutes, enforcement decisions do not fall wholly within the discretion of the administering agency. But legal constraints are relatively minor impediments to a relaxed enforcement strategy when compared with the political problems and constraints that a nonenforcement strategy can generate. If enforcement is to be relied upon as a de facto deregulation strategy, it must retain its credibility. Clearly the administration's management of EPA's enforcement mandate transgressed this political boundary of prosecutorial discretion.

How, then, should enforcement strategies that do not transgress these legal and political limits be evaluated? University of Chicago law professor Frank Easterbrook has suggested a number of legitimate rationales for choosing not to enforce the law. According to Easterbrook, changes in economic or legal theory—that is, new knowledge—may justify a redirection of enforcement policies. He also suggests that changes in enforcement policies may be justified as a means of reinterpreting otherwise vague legislative intent. Finally, Easterbrook implied that legitimately altered enforcement policies entail the substitution of new targets for old ones and generally do not simply sanction reduced activity. He wrote:

> For example, Congress does not just pass a rule; it also gives the Department of Justice a budget with which to enforce the rules. When the Antitrust Division stops filing prosecutions against manufacturers that suggest dealers' resale prices, it does not send its staff away to take knitting lessons. It puts the lawyers to work on other cases. A conscientious department keeps changing its enforcement decisions until it gets the most benefit it can out of them.[26]

Easterbrook also implied that a minimum sustained level of effort and resources may establish one characteristic of legitimately exercised prosecutorial discretion.

How do the Reagan administration's efforts comport with Easterbrook's guidelines? Taking the last criterion—sustained effort—first, we have noted in this chapter some instances in which the level of enforcement activity has exceeded that of former administrations. The two areas that stand out are the Department of Justice's antitrust activities in the transportation area and the efforts of federal banking regulatory agencies. Both fields have recently been the objects of important legislative deregulatory action.

In another finance-related area, SEC enforcers appear to have sustained relatively high productivity despite a 12 percent staff reduction. Some negative decisions—not to pursue activities with a nonmaterial impact on corporate finances—have been complemented by some positive ones—to aggressively pursue violations of securities marketing rules.

In general, however, enforcement appears to have dropped substantially. Most agencies or departments administering social regulation have experienced budget and staff cuts and have rapidly become converts to the merits of voluntary compliance. Decisions not to act, not to fine, not to reinspect—exemplified by the OSHA figures found in this chapter—appear to predominate. Old enforcement regimes do not appear to have been supplanted by new ones, but to have been pared back and reduced in scope or stringency.

As for Easterbrook's other criteria for shifting enforcement policies—"new learning" and a reinterpretation of undefined legal requirements—new learning accounts for relatively few shifts in enforcement policy, and only a few altered enforcement policies can be attributed to a redefining of vague legal mandates. OSHA's attempts to circumscribe enforcement efforts under the general duty clause draw on this latter rationale, as does the SEC's abandonment of efforts to force disclosure of corporate behavior with non-material impacts.

In sum, then, it appears that a number of the administration's enforcement changes could be characterized as falling within Easterbrook's formulation of the legitimate exercise of prosecutorial discretion. However, to the extent that those policy shifts lend themselves to being characterized as a broad retreat from the government's obligation to enforce the law, or the capture of law enforcement by ideology, they remain areas of political vulnerability for the administration.

10

Transferring Authority to the States

The 1982 Economic Report to the President by the Council of Economic Advisers states, "One important principle of this Administration is an increased reliance on State and local governments to carry out necessary governmental activities."[1]

The report later develops that theme as it applies to regulation:

Regulation should take place at the appropriate level of government. The primary economic reason for most regulation is the existence of external effects. The costs or tolerance of these external effects may vary among locations. Economic efficiency, therefore, calls for the degree and type of regulation to vary also. National standards tend to be too severe in some regions, while being too lax in others. Federal regulation should be limited to situations where the actions in one State have substantial external effects in other States, constitutional rights are involved, or interstate commerce would be significantly disrupted by differences in local regulations.[2]

The report's clear implication was that the intergovernmental assignment of regulatory responsibilities had not served the goals of economic efficiency. Thus it could be claimed that devolution—that is, transfer—of regulatory responsibilities to lower levels of government would serve both the political goals and the economic goals of the administration. Politically, devolution sustained the administration's efforts in reducing the reach of the federal government and enhancing state autonomy—essentially the goal of the short-lived New Federalism initiative. Economically, transfer of regulatory authority to state and local governments would promote the tailoring of regulations to local conditions—theoretically providing greater benefits at lower costs. Furthermore, the way in which authority was to be delegated would streamline regulatory processes involving multiple layers of government, saving time and money.

This chapter provides a discussion of the statutory and procedural background for the transfer of regulatory authority, the advantages and disadvantages of this transfer of authority as a regulatory strategy, and the four transfer techniques employed by the administration. These techniques are (1) accelerating the formal delegation of program authority to the states; (2) promulgating generic regulations; (3) reducing federal oversight of state regulatory activities; and (4) relaxing federal compliance standards.

Background

A growing number of health and safety laws—many in the environmental area—have been structured in a way that has provided the administration with an unusual opportunity to realize its regulatory federalism goals. Congress clearly intended these laws to be implemented by means of a formally negotiated, cooperative arrangement that would permit states to play a central role in program administration. Although the statutes differ in the specific responsibilities divided between states and the federal government, certain fundamental structural similarities can be discerned.

The basic design—sometimes referred to as "partial federal preemption" in the literature[3]—calls for the federal government to conduct necessary scientific research and to set minimum national standards. States are authorized to assume responsibility for all or much of program administration within their boundaries so long as they meet two conditions: the states' own implementing regulations must be at least as stringent as the federal government's, and the states must appear to have the resources and legal authority to carry out an acceptable program. Federal law and regulations, then, set a floor for state standards and performance but typically no ceiling regarding their stringency or the vigilance with which they are enforced.[4] Federal officials must review and approve all delegations of regulatory authority, and the federal regulatory agency retains authority to override individual state decisions. If, following delegation of authority, a state should utterly fail to adopt or enforce equivalent standards, the appropriate federal agency is authorized to apply federal rules. To help states carry out their responsibilities, the federal government typically provides substantial grants. For example, in fiscal year 1982 federal assistance to state environmental management programs totaled

$227.8 million and represented approximately half of all state expenditures in such programs.[5]

The value of this model of shared federal-state regulatory responsibilities within the federal system is clear. Delegation of federal authority preserves to some degree the regulatory sovereignty of the states, permitting them to serve as laboratories for innovation. In addition the arrangement is designed to promote efficiency in a number of ways. On one level, it does so by assigning to the federal government those tasks for which significant economies of scale may be achieved, such as training, research, and development. On a second, and more important level, this arrangement promotes efficiency by promoting national uniformity or preemption as needed. National uniformity may be desirable when state regulatory autonomy would burden interstate commerce, would expose citizens to widely varying health standards, would stimulate competition among states based on "minimum technology-based requirements," or would lead to parochial vetoes of projects involving important national interests, such as hazardous waste disposal. From a practical standpoint, it is extraordinarily cost-effective for the federal government to enlist state enforcement and administrative personnel, because their wages are often significantly lower than those of their federal counterparts.[6]

Furthermore, advocates of increased delegation of authority to the states contend that states have gone through a period of significant reform. As one prominent environmental lawyer has written, "Constitutions have been modernized, court systems streamlined, legislatures reorganized and professionally staffed, and governors' authority as chief executives strengthened. States have set up and staffed natural resource protection agencies with experienced and competent staffs." Indeed, staff size has increased tenfold over the past ten years, and education and salary levels have also risen.[7]

Although the merits of this incentive-based cooperative federalism scheme are clear—at least in theory—state officials have claimed that, in practice, little regulatory discretion has been given to the states and that their programs serve as little more than surrogate federal regional offices. The coercive nature of partial preemption is revealed by the highly detailed, prescriptive regulations that set minimum program standards for states. Congressionally authorized procedures give federal officials review or veto power, or both, over virtually all delegated state regulatory activities and decisions. Moreover, cumbersome procedures involving multiple layers of state and federal bureaucracies have slowed reviews and proved an irritant to both the states and regulated parties alike.

Advantages and Disadvantages of a Strategy of Delegation

Besides its philosophical appeal, delegation of regulatory authority to the states has proved a useful strategy to the Reagan administration, in part because of its political and procedural feasibility. The eventual transfer of federal authority to the states is contemplated by many of the health and safety statutes enacted during the 1970s. Thus the transfer of authority can be accomplished by means of administrative mechanisms, and the political vagaries of the legislative process can be avoided. Some policy changes can be made without even having to go through the administrative rule-making process. (For example, the Environmental Protection Agency's state implementation plan (SIP) review guidelines and new policy on emissions trading were not issued as administrative regulations.) Moreover, given the labyrinthine nature of intergovernmental relations, regulatory responsibilities can probably be reshuffled without attracting much attention or controversy.

Not only is delegation workable, it has a developed political constituency. A number of the administration's most important proposed changes—such as EPA's emissions-trading policy guidelines or the revision of regulations implementing the Surface Mining, Reclamation, and Enforcement Act of 1977—are founded on an existing technical and political base. Delegation of authority can be viewed as evolutionary, and thus quite different from more radical policy reversals proposed by administration regulatory reformers.[8] Further, while delegations of authority are by no means immune from legal challenge,[9] many have proved more durable than other regulatory relief actions (see chapter 8).

One important aspect of transferring regulatory authority is the practical permanence of delegation. This permanence owes less to the legal status of delegated programs than to the substantial political difficulties associated with revoking program authority. Actions that transfer federal regulatory authority to lower levels of government are, then, likely to be among the longest lived of all the Reagan administration's regulatory changes for two reasons: because they represent a continuation (albeit an accelerated one) of prior federal policies and because their undoing is politically impractical.

Viewed from the perspective of regulatory relief, delegation of regulatory responsibilities has posed some problems. In the first place there is no assurance that giving states increased regulatory responsibilities will lead to fewer inefficient rules. Powerful state-level firms might in some instances lobby for restrictive regulations in order to limit competition from out-of-state firms.[10] Interest groups might exert increased pressure at the state level for sustained or increased regulatory protections. For example, state regulation of nuclear power and nuclear waste disposal is often more stringent than federal regulation.[11]

Delegation has also raised fears that a profusion of state standards, whatever their relative stringency, would prove to be more troublesome and inefficient for many firms than uniformly imposed and enforced federal standards. This might be especially true for firms that sell and perform in national markets.

Finally, there is the issue of resources. Anne Gorsuch, the former administrator of the Environmental Protection Agency (the agency with the greatest number of transferable programs and responsibilities), announced soon after she was appointed that the agency would within the next four years "zero fund" state administrative efforts. Not surprisingly, this raised a furor among those state officials and environmental activists who saw delegation as a simple code for deregulation. The "zero funding" approach, like Ms. Burford's government career, was short lived. Delegation, then, could not be looked to for significant federal budget relief.

An Overview of Transfer Strategies

The Reagan administration has relied primarily on four strategies to enhance state regulatory authority in health and safety.[12] This section briefly describes these strategies and provides several examples of their use.

The first, and most obvious strategy has been to accelerate the formal delegation of program authority. In many cases, delegations proceed in phases, with states moving incrementally to full delegation status. (For example, program delegation under the Occupational Safety and Health Act (OSHA) follows this model.) To date, administration efforts to promote formal delegation have involved relaxing the conditions and standards that state programs must meet to qualify for program responsibility.

A second strategy for enhancing state discretion has been to promulgate generic regulations. Generic regulations authorize states to conduct predetermined "permitting" and enforcement actions without being subject to the level of federal scrutiny that such actions would otherwise trigger. Examples include EPA's emissions-trading policy and the Army Corps of Engineers' general permit guidelines issued under Section 404 of the Clean Water Act.

A third strategy for enhancing state regulatory authority has been to reduce federal oversight of state regulatory activities. A notable example is OSHA's removal of federal field inspectors in states with certified occupational safety and health programs. Another example is EPA's new approval procedures for "noncontroversial" alterations of state implementation plans under the Clean Air Act.

A fourth strategy for transferring responsibility has been to relax federally promulgated program standards. In order to qualify for delegation, a state must have program standards roughly equivalent to those adopted by the federal government. Therefore, relaxing requirements of all sorts can in effect ease eligibility requirements and should increase the states' administrative flexibility. Since federal rules only set a floor on regulatory stringency, states retain the option of maintaining older, more stringent standards. Because changes in specific program standards are motivated by a wide range of concerns—of which enhanced state discretion is only one—this "strategy" may be more conceptually problematic than the others.

The scope of discretion transferred by individual rule changes will, of course, vary depending on the nature of the waived mandate. For example, elimination of simple reporting requirements can have implications far beyond the preparation of a specified report to the kinds of data kept and the kinds of activities monitored.

The impact of relaxing federal standards varies with the timing of federal action. Standards altered after state programs are in place and that have weathered state legislative or administrative review are likely to have a much slower, trickle-down effect than are changes incorporated as state plans are developed.

Accelerating Formal Delegation of Program Authority to the States

In January 1983, a trade journal reported that since Ronald Reagan assumed office—

- The number of states authorized to carry out the Clean Air Act's prevention of significant deterioration program had increased from sixteen to twenty-six;
- Three additional states had assumed full responsibility for permitting under the Clean Water Act's national pollutant discharge elimination system, and six more states had taken on increased permitting roles;
- The Safe Drinking Water Act's underground injection control program had been delegated to the first four states, and full delegations to another twenty states were expected in the upcoming months.[13]

In addition, then EPA Administrator Anne Gorsuch boasted that delegation of the Clean Air Act's new source performance standards program had increased 38 percent nationwide since the Reagan administration took office, that delegation of the national emissions standards for hazardous air pollutants had increased 32 percent nationwide, and that delegated construction grant activities had increased 48 percent from January 1981 through October 1982.

Aggregated in this manner, these numbers raise a host of questions. First, no baseline data are provided. Second, the numbers fail to differentiate between interim authorizations and final delegations. Third, the numbers fail to account for program maturity.

EPA: The Resource Conservation and Recovery Act. To provide a better understanding of EPA's efforts to delegate regulatory authority over the course of the past two and one-half years, table 12 presents a detailed listing of jurisdictions granted interim authorization under Phases I and II of the Resource Conservation and Recovery Act (RCRA). The table indicates that, as of May 26, 1983, twenty-seven of the thirty-seven delegations of Phase I program authority had been completed during President Reagan's term in office. EPA staff point out, however, that the agency's first administrator under President Reagan, Anne Gorsuch, did not assume office until May 1981; at that time, almost 60 percent of all Phase I program delegations had been completed. Twelve of those approvals had taken place within a leaderless EPA after Reagan's inauguration. Increased delegations were, then, primarily a function of program maturity and career-staff activity, and less a function of the political preferences or bureaucratic prowess of administration officials. Regulations implementing RCRA were first promulgated in 1980, and delegation of RCRA program authorization was not possible until late fall 1980, when the Carter administration itself embarked on an effort to rapidly transfer responsibility to the states, granting Phase I authorization to nine states within three months. As the table indicates, Phase II authorizations have only recently begun. All ten authorizations were approved by Reagan administration officials during or after March 1982.

OSM: The Surface Mining, Reclamation, and Enforcement Act. Another agency in which the pace of program delegations has quickened is the Office of Surface Mining (OSM). According to documents provided by OSM (see table 13) twenty-five state programs have been granted either final or conditional approval under the Surface Mining, Reclamation, and Enforcement Act of 1977. Thirteen of the twenty-five state programs receiving such approval did so during the first two and one-half years of the Reagan administration. However, once again, aggregate program approvals tell only part of the delegation story; the imposition and removal of conditions to program delegation must be considered.

Under the Carter administration, programs receiving both "final" and "conditional" approvals were heavily freighted with conditions that states

TABLE 12

JURISDICTIONS GRANTED INTERIM AUTHORIZATION
UNDER PHASE I AND PHASE II OF RCRA

Jurisdiction	Date Authorized	*Federal Register Page Number*
Phase I		
Arkansas	November 18, 1980	76144
Utah	December 12, 1980	81757
North Dakota	December 12, 1980	81758[a]
North Carolina	December 18, 1980	83229
Louisiana	December 19, 1980	83498
Texas	December 24, 1980	85016
Mississippi	January 7, 1981	1727
Oklahoma	January 14, 1981	3207
Vermont	January 15, 1981	3517
Iowa	January 30, 1981	9948
Georgia	February 3, 1981	10487
Alabama	February 25, 1981	14088
Delaware	February 25, 1981	14009
Massachusetts	February 25, 1981	14010
South Carolina	February 25, 1981	14012
Montana	February 26, 1981	14123[b]
	February 17, 1982	6831
Maine	March 18, 1981	17194
Kentucky	April 1, 1981	19819
Pennsylvania	May 26, 1981	28161
Rhode Island	May 29, 1981	28850
California	June 4, 1981	29938
Maryland	July 8, 1981	35259
Oregon	July 16, 1981	36844
Tennessee	July 16, 1981	36846
Kansas	September 21, 1981	46576
New Hampshire	November 3, 1981	54544
Virginia	November 3, 1981	54545
Wisconsin	January 15, 1982	2314
Connecticut	April 21, 1982	17055
Nebraska	May 14, 1982	20773
Illinois	May 17, 1982	21043
Florida	May 19, 1982	19698[c]
Arizona	August 18, 1982	35967
Indiana	August 18, 1982	35970
Puerto Rico	October 14, 1982	45880

TABLE 12 (*continued*)

Jurisdiction		Date Authorized	Federal Register Page Number
New Jersey		February 2, 1983	4661
Phase II			
Guam		May 16, 1983	21953
Texas	(A & B)	March 23, 1982	12347
North Carolina	(A & B)	March 26, 1982	12366
Arkansas	(A & B)	April 19, 1982	16625
Georgia	(A & B)	May 21, 1982	22096
Mississippi	(A & B)	August 31, 1982	38323
	(C)	April 26, 1983	18814
South Carolina	(A & B)	November 3, 1982	49842
Oklahoma	(A & B)	December 13, 1982	55680
California	(A)	January 11, 1983	1197[d]
Kentucky	(A & B)	January 28, 1983	3983
New Hampshire	(A & B)	March 31, 1983	13430

SOURCE: Environmental Protection Agency.

  a. North Dakota received partial Phase I Interim Authorization on December 12, 1980.

  b. Montana was granted partial Phase I Interim Authorization on February 26, 1981. Complete Phase I Interim Authorization was granted on February 17, 1982.

  c. Appeared in *Federal Register* on May 7.

  d. State is not authorized to control storage/treatment in surface impoundments.

would have to satisfy to obtain or retain full program authority. Not only has the Reagan administration attached far fewer conditions to its delegations, it has since waived or otherwise removed virtually all the conditions imposed by the Carter administration (see table 13).

Two developments helped contribute to this accelerated devolution of program authority to the states. First, the administration successfully recast what is termed the "state window rule." In so doing, OSM officials changed the standard for evaluating state programs from one requiring that they be "no less stringent than federal rules" to one requiring that they be "no less effective than federal rules." The U.S. District Court for the District of Columbia upheld the new standard in *Sierra Club* v. *Watt* (D.D.C. No. 81-3157, 18 ERC 1565) issued on September 17, 1982. This broad performance standard gave OSM review officers greater flexibility when comparing federal and state programs and has marginally increased total approvals.

TABLE 13
DELEGATIONS UNDER THE SURFACE MINING ACT

State	Status	Date Secretarial Decision Published	Comments
Alabama	Cond. Approval	May 20, 1982	
Alaska	Full Approval	March 23, 1983	Effective May 2, 1983
Arizona			Federal program proposed October 5, 1982; proposal withdrawn December 1982
Arkansas	Full Approval	November 21, 1980	4 conditions removed January 22, 1982
California			Federal program proposed July 28, 1982; final program postponed until further notice
Colorado	Cond. Approval	December 15, 1980	35 of 45 conditions removed December 16, 1982
Georgia	Federal Program	August 19, 1982	Effective September 20, 1982
Idaho			Federal program proposed July 12, 1982; final program to be promulgated April 1983
Illinois	Cond. Approval	June 1, 1982	
Indiana	Cond. Approval	July 26, 1982	Effective July 29, 1982 Of 9 conditions, 0.2 of a condition removed December 17, 1982; 6.9 conditions removed March 4, 1983
Iowa	Full Approval	January 21, 1981	Effective April 10, 1981 2 of 3 conditions removed May 26, 1982; 1 condition removed September 7, 1982
Kansas	Full Approval	January 21, 1981	6 conditions removed April 14, 1983
Kentucky	Cond. Approval	May 18, 1982	3 of 12 conditions removed January 4, 1983

TABLE 13 (*continued*)

State	Status	Date Secretarial Decision Published	Comments
Louisiana	Full Approval	October 10, 1980	
Maryland	Full Approval	December 1, 1980	34 conditions removed February 18, 1982
Massachusetts	Federal Coal Exploration Program	April 28, 1982	Full federal program proposed April 1, 1983
Michigan	Federal Program	October 22, 1982	
Mississippi	Full Approval	September 4, 1980	
Missouri	Full Approval	November 21, 1980	2 of 3 conditions removed May 11, 1982; 1 condition removed January 17, 1983
Montana	Full Approval	April 1, 1980	6 conditions removed February 11, 1982
Nebraska			Federal program proposed December 22, 1982; proposal withdrawn February 1983
Nevada			Federal program proposed July 27, 1982; proposal withdrawn February 1983
New Mexico	Cond. Approval	December 31, 1980	3 of 12 conditions removed May 27, 1982; 4 conditions removed October 26, 1982
North Carolina			Federal program proposed March 2, 1983
North Dakota	Cond. Approval	December 15, 1980	10 of 13 conditions removed February 9, 1983
Ohio	Cond. Approval	August 10, 1982	Effective August 16, 1982 1 of 11 conditions removed January 17, 1983
Oklahoma	Cond. Approval	January 19, 1981	

TABLE 13 (*continued*)

DELEGATIONS UNDER THE SURFACE MINING ACT

State	Status	Date Secretarial Decision Published	Comments
Oregon	Federal Program	November 3, 1982	
Pennsylvania	Cond. Approval	July 30, 1982	Effective July 31, 1982
Rhode Island	Federal Coal Exploration Program	April 28, 1982	Full federal program proposed December 22, 1982; final program to be promulgated July 15, 1983
South Dakota			Federal program proposed August 10, 1982; final program to be promulgated April 1983
Tennessee	Cond. Approval	August 10, 1982	
Texas	Full Approval	February 27, 1980	1 condition removed June 18, 1980
Utah	Full Approval	January 21, 1981	7 of 13 conditions removed June 22, 1982; 4 conditions removed December 13, 1982; 2 conditions removed March 7, 1983
Virginia	Cond. Approval	December 15, 1981	1 of 19 conditions removed July 21, 1982; 16 conditions removed December 13, 1982
Washington			Federal program proposed June 21, 1982; interim final program published February 24, 1983
West Virginia	Cond. Approval	January 21, 1981	Of 35 conditions, 0.2 of a condition removed September 10, 1982; 8 conditions removed March 1, 1983
Wyoming	Cond. Approval	November 26, 1980	4 of 7 conditions removed February 18, 1982; 1 condition removed September 27, 1982

Second, the accelerated rate of delegation is partially due to program maturity, as was the case with the Resource Conservation and Recovery Act. Most of the recent delegations have been in the eastern coal-mining states, which had lagged their western counterparts.

OSHA: The Occupational Safety and Health Act. OSHA has one of the most complex and rigidly prescribed of all partial preemption programs. Four steps to full, formal delegation are prescribed by the Occupational Safety and Health Act. First, a state must develop a comprehensive plan that demonstrates that state enforcement of occupational safety and health standards will be "at least as effective" as federal enforcement. Then, during the plan's developmental phase, OSHA may negotiate an "operational status agreement" if the agency believes the state is capable of enforcing minimum designated standards. Under an operational status agreement, federal enforcement actions that duplicate state efforts are suspended.

When OSHA has concluded that the required legal, administrative, and regulatory elements of a state plan are acceptable, the agency may formally certify that the state has the capacity to operate effectively. Such certification is an essential preliminary to final approval. After certification, OSHA continues to monitor a state plan closely for at least a year in order to determine whether the program is being implemented effectively. If the agency so decides and if the program has been in operation for at least three years, OSHA may grant final approval. At that time, federal enforcement authority ceases for those occupational safety and health standards that are included in the state's program—with the caveat that authority to monitor the program always remains an important responsibility of federal OSHA.

To date, no state program has been granted final approval—largely because of judicially imposed requirements, labeled "benchmarks," that states must meet to be eligible for delegation of final program responsibility. This does not mean, however, that the Reagan administration has not been effectively accelerating the transfer of regulatory authority to the states. Since the Reagan administration took office, three of fifty-five eligible states and jurisdictions have progressed to the point at which they are on the verge of being granted final program responsibility;[14] eight have been certified, and ten have signed operational status agreements with the agency.

In addition, administration efforts to revise court-designated standards for the delegation of program authority under OSHA may prove to have particularly significant long-term impacts on the transfer of authority among governments. In 1978, the U.S. Court of Appeals for the District of Columbia held in *AFL-CIO* v. *Marshall* (570 F.2d 1030 [D.C. Cir. 1978]) that OSHA was obligated to establish benchmarks for state-plan staffing levels that would reflect "a fully effective enforcement effort." As developed subsequently by OSHA, the new benchmarks would have required, among other things, a sharp increase in state staffing levels, adding an estimated 305 safety personnel and 1,351 health personnel to state program staffs.[15]

Aided by congressional action,[16] the administration has proposed to revise administratively these staffing standards. The revision calls for approval standards to be set at levels in effect prior to the Court of Appeals decision in 1978. It also specifies that state staffing levels need be no higher than current federal staffing levels.[17]

Summary. Looking across program areas, it is quite clear that the Reagan administration has accelerated the pace of program delegations of authority. Although in some instances prior efforts by former administrations and program maturity have been responsible for a significant proportion of new delegations, in others the Reagan administration has played an important role in restructuring the rules under which eligibility determinations are made. OSM's revision of the state window rule and OSHA's efforts to redefine judicially designated benchmarks for determining state program adequacy are good examples of affirmative, structural changes.

One related finding is that despite proclaimed budgetary fears, a large number of states apparently remain interested in assuming further regulatory responsibilities. Thus, at least to date, the lure of regulatory sovereignty has proved stronger than fears of substantial federal budget reduction—at least for a significant number of states.[18]

Promulgating Generic Regulations

A second, even less conspicuous, approach to enhancing state regulatory discretion has been the promulgation of generic regulations. Generic rules typically return to state control a designated group of transactions formerly subject to case-by-case federal review and approval. In order for states to assume this new authority, they are usually required to adopt regulations that conform to broad decision principles set out as federal policy. States are then free to set and implement policy subject only to federal oversight and audit responsibilities. This approach offers states, the federal government, and regulated industries a means of conserving resources and mitigating uncertainty because proposed actions become subject to one, rather than two, levels of government review.

EPA: Emissions Trading. The administration's most publicized adoption of a generic approach to standard setting has been its emissions-trading statement promulgated in April 1982.[19] Rather than requiring that firms meet uniform emissions limits, emissions trading allows sources to adopt alternative compliance strategies that would achieve the same or greater reductions in polluting emissions than control strategies that would otherwise be required.

EPA's published statement consolidated a number of closely related, market-based, pollution-abatement reforms, including bubbles, offsets, netting, and emission-reduction banking.[20] The reforms were intended to make extra pollution control profitable "by letting firms trade inexpensive reductions created at one emission point and time for expensive regulatory requirements on other points at different times, under controlled conditions to assure air quality and enforceability."[21]

Prior to the adoption of EPA's trading rules in April 1982, applications for permits that involved emissions trading could only be approved if state implementation plans were revised. The revision triggered a lengthy and often cumbersome process of public notice, comment, and review at both the state and federal levels. Under the new generic rules, many trades will be exempt from the SIP revision process and direct case-by-case federal review, although they will remain subject to federal audit and possible override. Trades that do not fall within the general rules may still be approved, but they must be submitted to the same complex administrative process that all such trades once had to clear. (As the following section indicates, however, that process has been simplified and expedited for proposed "noncontroversial" amendments to state implementation plans.)

As noted in chapter 8, emissions trading has been one of the few innovative regulatory techniques embraced by the Reagan administration, and in some ways it appears to have been one of the administration's more successful relief initiatives. As of the end of 1982, 179 bubbles had been approved or proposed or were under development. (This total includes bubbles proposed under state generic trading rules and those advanced as SIP amendments in states that had not adopted generic regulations. See table 14 for a list of approved and proposed Pennsylvania bubbles and their projected cost savings.) At that time EPA had approved seven generic bubble rules allowing New Jersey, Massachusetts, Connecticut, North Carolina, Oregon, and Pennsylvania to approve large numbers of bubble applications without prior federal review. EPA had also proposed to approve three other generic bubble rules, and twelve other states and localities were actively developing rules.[22] However, that success has been offset by a successful challenge to the extension of EPA's netting policy to sources located within nonattainment areas. The

TABLE 14

BUBBLE ADOPTIONS IN PENNSYLVANIA AS OF DECEMBER 30, 1982

Bubble	Industry Category	Source of Emission Credit	Cost Savings
3M Bristol, Pa.	tape manufacture	change in process	$3 million capital or $1.2 million/yr. operating expense
Andre's Greenhouse	greenhouse	switch in fuel	$250,000/yr. operating expense
Shenango Allegheny, Pa.	steel	change in control	$4 million capital
Proposed Approvals			
U.S. Steel Fairless Hills, Pa.	steel	change in control	$27 million capital
U.S. Steel Allegheny Co., Pa.	steel	reduced operation	$10,000/day
Scott Paper Co. Chester, Pa.	papermill	switch in fuel	$220,000/yr.
Arbogast & Bastion Allentown, Pa.	meat packing	switch in fuel	$100,000/yr.
J. H. Thompson Kennett Square, Pa.	greenhouse	switch in fuel	$100,000/yr.
Bethlehem Steel Bethlehem, Pa.	steel	change in control	$10 million capital

SOURCE: The Environmental Protection Agency, Office of Regulatory Reform.

decision by the U.S. Court of Appeals in *NRDC* v. *Gorsuch* was described at some length in chapter 8.[23]

The administration's emissions-trading initiatives differ from many other elements of the regulatory relief effort, as EPA's efforts represent a continuation of prior federal regulatory policies rather than a departure from them. As Michael Levin notes in his useful history of the bubble, proposals for its development date back to 1972.[24] Over time, a strong constituency formed supporting the innovation—first among EPA's professional staff, then among key government officials outside the agency, and finally with the development of the generic rule principle) among state and local officials. Years of careful, diligent groundwork by agency career staff, along with the development of a workable implementing mechanism, clearly contributed to the success of this element of the president's regulatory federalism campaign.

The Army Corps of Engineers. Another example of the Reagan administration's reliance on generic regulations is the Army Corps of Engineers' issuance of general permits under the Clean Water Act's Section 404. This section prohibits the discharge of any pollutant, including dredged materials or fill, into the waters of the United States. Those "waters" have been defined to include 80 percent of the nation's wetlands. Section 404(e) authorizes the issuance of general permits on a state, regional, or national basis for categories of activity that are "similar in nature" and "will cause only minimal adverse environmental impacts." Thus, activities covered by general permits would typically be monitored only by state or local governments and would be essentially exempt from federal review.[25]

The Corps' most significant initiative in this area was announced on July 22, 1982, when it issued interim final regulations setting out twenty-seven nationwide permits.[26] From 1977 to 1982 only seven such nationwide permits had been issued. The Corps' action had been spurred by recommendations from the President's Task Force on Regulatory Relief directing the agency to provide increased incentives and simplified procedures for state assumption of the 404 program.[27]

Six of the twenty-seven nationwide permits proved to be particularly controversial and were subsequently challenged in court. The two that received the most attention were proposals to exempt from federal review discharges into rivers, streams, and wetlands located above headwaters and discharges into isolated water bodies. The implications of these innocent-sounding exemptions were vast. To illustrate, EPA's Region III estimated that under the proposed nationwide permits the percentage of wetlands in Pennsylvania's Pocono Mountains covered by general permits and outside federal review would increase from 3 percent to 60 percent.[28] Senator John Chafee claimed that the new permits would remove or reduce regulation of dredge and fill activities in 1 to 2 million acres of lakes and adjacent wetlands in Minnesota, Michigan, and Wisconsin alone. To all appearances, the permits eliminated federal enforcement over thousands of acres of wetlands, were clearly deregulatory in purpose, and represented a sharp break from prior federal policy. No wonder they generated substantial controversy.

In an interesting reversal of willing state acceptance of federal generic regulations and reduced federal oversight, Wisconsin, followed by twelve other states, informed the Army Corps of Engineers that it would exercise its prerogative to deny certification for a number of the most controversial general permits. That is, state officials essentially rejected the Corps' attempt to shift its enforcement responsibilities to Wisconsin. As a result the Corps was forced to retain jurisdiction and to review on a case-by-case basis all permits in the two contested critical areas—headwaters and isolated water bodies.

Despite the fact that Wisconsin and the Corps eventually negotiated a mutually satisfactory settlement, the political manipulation of the 404 general permit mechanisms by the Corps appeared to have undermined its devolution objectives. In the wake of the thirteen-state rebellion and the strong legal challenge filed by environmental groups, the Corps retreated from its two most controversial reforms. A notice published in the *Federal Register* on May 12, 1983 stated that the agency was willing to reconsider the wisdom of its proposal in each area.

Summary. The use of generic rules to grant states authority to oversee emissions trading presents an interesting contrast to the approach taken by the Army Corps of Engineers in trying to shed its enforcement responsibilities. Generic rules for emissions trading were developed after extensive consensus building within the federal government, the states, and, to some extent, the community of public interest groups. The rules represented a continuation of federal policy—indeed they made the proposed reforms workable for many state governments. In contrast, the rules and permits proposed by the Corps represented a clear departure in federal policy. Their promulgation did not have the support of key federal agencies. Both EPA and U.S. Fish and Wildlife Service officials had gone on record objecting to the proposed permits. State support was also clearly lacking, as the state denials of certification indicate, and the public-interest community was plainly angry—ultimately sixteen co-plaintiffs sued the Corps. Viewed from a number of perspectives, the proposed rules resembled an unwanted abandonment of federal responsibility more than a careful legal and political effort to transfer authority to the states and to eliminate troublesome regulatory delays and costs.

The use of generic rules documented in this brief section raises two arguments for continued federal oversight. First, when regulations (such as those relating to emissions trading) require that states perform sophisticated technological permitting and enforcement activities, federal checks should be sustained—at least until state capacity has been demonstrated. Second, exempting predesignated classes of activities from scrutiny by using mechanisms such as generic rules always creates a temptation to misclassify proposed actions. Some federal oversight will remain necessary to ensure that proposals likely to have significant environmental impacts are not being misinterpreted in order to receive relatively unexamined, expedited treatment.

Reducing Federal Oversight of State Regulatory Activities

In contrast to the formal delegation of regulatory authority and the development of generic rules, diminished federal oversight of state actions does not affect the structure of federal-state relations. And, although reduced oversight may enhance state authority, that result is likely to be a secondary or derived effect of federal policy.

Clearly, reduced federal review of state or local actions can take many forms. It can mean an accelerated, relatively uncritical review of submissions prior to program delegation. It can also mean less second-guessing of state-drawn permits, decisions to prosecute or not to prosecute, settlements, fines, staffing patterns, and resource commitments. Indeed, reduced federal review embraces all those occasions upon which the federal government can choose to abide by or override state environmental decisions.

The Occupational Safety and Health Administration. One of the first actions of the Reagan administration sent a strong signal that the new team intended to reduce federal oversight of state program performance. That action was OSHA's announcement that it was going to withdraw a proposed revocation of Indiana's occupational safety and health plan.[29] The revocation had been proposed by the Carter administration the week before Ronald Reagan's inauguration[30] and marked the culmination of efforts begun by the Indiana and national AFL-CIO in 1977. The union contended that the state had (1) failed to hire a sufficient number of qualified industrial hygienists, (2) failed to identify and cite a substantial number of hazards in the workplace, and (3) proposed penalties for violations that were substantially lower than those imposed by federal OSHA for the same violations.[31]

The revocation was withdrawn for two reasons. First, OSHA officials claimed that the state's health program had improved substantially. A review of OSHA's evaluation report on the Indiana program for the year ending June 1982 showed that the number of hygienists had risen from three to thirteen (including three federal inspectors working under contract). Still, less than 4 percent of the state's total inspections were in the health area, compared with more than 17 percent for federal OSHA. Furthermore, the number of health inspections concluded in fiscal year 1981 was 50 percent lower than the total number conducted in 1977.[32] Second, the administration claimed that the evidence upon which the planned revocation was based had grown stale. Subsequent legal action taken by the union proved futile, and the rescission remained in place.

Following its action in Indiana, OSHA proceeded to remove all federal compliance officers from states that had signed operational agreements with the agency. This reduction in federal monitors was accompanied by a halving of federal staff assigned to monitoring state plans. OSHA officials claim that the development of a field information system (the integrated management information system) for state performance data would provide a more effective means of monitoring state programs. As yet it remains unclear whether the quality of data fed into the system will be continuously evaluated, and thus whether the system will be an effective substitute for field monitoring.

The Office of Surface Mining.   The Office of Surface Mining also appears to have adopted a "hands off" approach toward state enforcement. However, as a result of a settlement agreement in *National Wildlife Federation* v. *Watt* (Civil Action No. 82-0320), the agency was forced to reexamine its deference to states when state officials fail to enforce the law. A new OSM policy announced in March 1983 declared that federal inspectors are to issue violation notices to mine operators when states have been notified of a violation's existence and have failed to take appropriate action or show cause within ten days.[33] Internal data developed by OSM underscore the policy's relevance. One recent OSM report found that Kentucky state inspectors were at least three times more likely to write a violation when accompanied by federal inspectors than when acting alone.[34]

EPA: State Implementation Plans.   One key to federal oversight during the Reagan administration has been EPA's successful efforts to reduce the backlog of state implementation plans awaiting agency review.[35] From January 1981 through October 1982, pending SIP revisions dropped 97 percent, from 643 to 20.

Previously, the SIP revision process had required that all changes in SIPs, no matter how minor or routine, receive both state and federal approval. At each level the revision had to satisfy notice and comment rule-making procedures. Moreover, federal approvals typically went through a two-stage process: Proposed revisions were promulgated first as proposed rules and later as final rules.

Encountering massive backlogs upon assuming office, the current administration made three procedural changes in the management of the SIP program.[36] First, minor proposed changes are now permitted to go directly to final federal review. If any comments are received during the mandated review period, then the revisions are rescinded and submitted to the full, two-stage review process. Second, to the extent possible, state and federal review of proposed SIP revisions are to be conducted concurrently rather than consecutively. This practice permits federal officials to "front load" their suggestions and recommendations and is intended to avoid having to return rejected, fully developed plans to the states for further revision, with all the procedural consequences that revision entails. Third, if no comments are received after a proposed SIP revision has been published in the *Federal Register*, then full responsibility for approving the revision is assigned to the appropriate regional office and no review is undertaken at EPA headquarters.

While better management practices are clearly partially responsible for EPA's accelerated reviews, agency staffers also concede that state plans are now given greater deference than they were in the past.[37]

One example of the relatively uncritical deference accorded some proposed SIP revisions emerged in Texas. There, the Monsanto Company proposed a "bubble" for its Texas City and Chocolate Bayou chemical plants that would require a revision of Texas's SIP. (The proposed bubble could not be approved under any state-adopted generic emissions-trading rule.) In brief, Monsanto's proposal would have allowed the company to reduce emissions controls on eighteen specified chemical storage tanks thanks to certain offsetting emissions-reduction credits to which the company claimed it was entitled. The Texas Air Control Board approved the proposal, and EPA indicated that it intended to do the same.[38]

A challenge to the proposed bubble, however, raised serious questions regarding both the plan's merits and the advisability of relaxed EPA oversight. Attorneys for the National Resources Defense Council (NRDC) have contended that in calculating the amount of offsetting credits to which it was entitled, Monsanto (1) overstated by 100 percent the emissions credit due by relying on figures that reflected *potential* rather than *actual* annual emissions of the source responsible for generating emissions credits[39] and (2) improperly took credit for emissions from a plant that had been closed in 1980 and was in the process of being torn down.[40]

If NRDC's claims are proved correct, then it could be concluded that, at least in relatively complex areas such as emissions trading, systematic federal scrutiny of locally developed calculations should probably be retained—at least until states demonstrate technical competence. Indeed, proponents of the bubble concept worry that the potential benefits of emissions trading will be subverted if a series of unexamined, "tainted" trades are brought to public officials' attention before the value of this innovative regulatory strategy has been demonstrated.

Despite the administration's clear interest in delegating federal regulatory responsibility, political pressures have occasionally undermined deference to state authority. For example, just before the change in leadership at EPA in spring 1983, an agency directive was issued ordering EPA's regional staff to take enforcement actions against sources not in compliance with emission regulations—even if those sources were operating under local district variances.[41] The policy was put in effect in all states, even those like California, which for years had been administering more stringent regulatory programs than those of the federal government. In California variances were usually granted only for compelling reasons. Critics of the enforcement efforts contended that the efforts were driven by a simple interest in increasing politically sensitive enforcement numbers—not by an interest in deterring violators in a meaningful way. Furthermore, this willingness to override state and local decisions appeared to breach administration promises for a new cooperative federalism. However, as one EPA official stated, "When you're bleeding to death politically, state partnerships go by the board."

Summary. Oversight can provide opportunities for important procedural reforms—as the administration's restructuring of the SIP review process indicates. In addition federal supervision of state regulatory activities is an area that falls securely within the legal bounds of a responsible agency's administrative discretion. However, as demonstrated by the successful challenge to the Office of Surface Mining's deference to state nonenforcement policies, that discretion is not limitless. Further, as EPA's rapid turnabout on air-pollution enforcement suggests, relaxed oversight, perhaps to an even greater extent than other administrative strategies, is vulnerable to shifting political winds.

Relaxing Federal Compliance Standards

The fourth category of administrative action that effectively enhances state regulatory authority is the relaxation, elimination, or modification of federally promulgated program standards. Such efforts enhance state authority in a number of ways. When regulatory standards are reduced or made less stringent, states gain the option of keeping old rules or adopting new, more lenient regulations. A fuller discussion of the general strategy of reducing compliance standards has been set out in chapter 8.

An interesting and straightforward means of delegating enforcement authority through standard setting is the adoption of performance rather than design standards.[42] Perhaps the most publicized and systematic administration effort to switch from design to performance standards has been the Office of Surface Mining's revision of its 1979 regulations implementing the Surface Mining Control and Reclamation Act. Suggestions that the regulations governing the mining industry should endorse performance rather than design standards originated with reports by the Carter administration's Regulatory Council and the National Academy of Science's National Research Council.[43]

Although the proposals did not receive much attention during the final months of the Carter administration, they found a receptive audience within the Office of Surface Mining and at the Task Force for Regulatory Relief after Ronald Reagan's election. The Reagan administration's rationale for relying on performance standards (and their relationship to its regulatory federalism goals) is suggested by the following paragraph from the environmental impact statement analyzing the effect of proposed OSM rule changes:

> The current design regulations tend . . . to create a relatively inflexible national set of regulations. Because the acceptability of State regulations is based on the permanent program regulations, this approach allows the Federal Government to maintain stringent control over State programs. Although this results in facilities and structures that meet national standards, it also results locally in some facilities and structures being underdesigned while others are overdesigned. . . .
>
> The draft final regulations, on the other hand, emphasize performance standards and general goals. The regulations are more adaptable to variations in climate, geology, topography, and other physical conditions. This technique of regulation maximizes State control of the specifics of each State's regulatory program (often referred to as State primacy) at the expense of national uniformity of State regulations.[44]

One potential disadvantage of shifting from design to performance standards is candidly addressed in OSM's environmental impact statement: "This approach requires greater technical sophistication on the part of State and Federal employees to interpret and apply such regulations on a mine-by-mine basis, and by the public in perceiving if compliance occurs."[45] Critics of the proposed regulations concur, but conclude that enhanced flexibility will inevitably lead to less effective standards for safety and environmental protection. Noting that reliance on performance standards makes compliance determination more difficult, these critics contend that the change will require greater technical expertise and a greater commitment of resources than most state programs can afford. Moreover, they argue that compliance under performance standards is typically measured retrospectively—after improvements have been constructed, when their modification is more expensive and more complicated politically.[46]

The adoption of performance standards may provide regulated entities with an opportunity to adopt more cost-effective design and engineering strategies, and will certainly vest state agencies with increased discretion. However, that discretion is likely to make good-faith state efforts substantially more complicated for two reasons: First, states may be required to perform detailed engineering analyses in order to determine whether proposed designs will satisfy performance criteria. Second, negotiations between operators and state bureaucrats are likely to grow more frequent and protracted, and continued monitoring of sites to determine compliance with performance standards will become increasingly important. Both raise real cost concerns. High attrition levels at OSM field offices[47] and widespread funding and staffing difficulties within state agencies[48] raise questions about the general institutional capacity at all government levels to adopt the kind of sophisticated techniques required to implement performance standards.

Summary

The focus of this chapter has been Reagan administration actions that have, with a few exceptions, enhanced state authority and promoted harmonious federal-state relations. That is not to say, however, that intergovernmental relations under the Reagan administration have not been strained on occasion. Despite the rhetoric of the New Federalism campaign, when administration priorities have clashed with state preferences, state interests have often been overridden.

Even for an administration with a strong states' rights bias, sorting out appropriate regulatory roles poses complex legal and economic questions. In some instances, federal preemption of a regulatory field will be necessary to conform to constitutionally based prohibitions on state actions burdening interstate commerce. In other instances the scale economies offered by federal preemption provide industries and their spokesmen with convincing evidence for the adoption of uniform federal standards.

The economies associated with uniform federal regulation became quite clear to the nation's chemical industry in the wake of the Reagan administration's rescission of pending Carter administration regulations setting standards for the labeling of toxic chemicals in the workplace. The administration based the rescission (ironically) on the grounds that the area was more suitable to state than federal regulation. At the time the rules were revoked—February 1981—five states had their own chemical labeling statutes—often referred to as worker or community right to know statutes. However, soon after the administration's action, the nation's unions, led by the AFL-CIO, began an intensive lobbying campaign at the state level for legislation covering the politically volatile issue. By winter of 1983 fourteen states had enacted statutes whose stringency and scope of coverage varied widely.

In March 1982 the Occupational Safety and Health Administration reentered the fray with new proposed regulations that applied only to manufacturing industries but that appeared to preempt state regulations whose coverage was significantly broader. Neither the states, which had enacted their own statutes, nor labor was at all pleased with the rules (which were made final in November 1983).[49] Litigation over the administration's assertion of preemption as well as other aspects of the rules appeared certain.

Another example of Reagan administration willingness to override state preferences resulted from efforts to defuse trucking industry opposition to the administration's bill imposing a 5¢ per gallon tax on gasoline. In order to offset industry opposition, the administration proposed to increase the national standards for width, length, and weight of trucks allowed on interstate highways and to permit trucks to haul two semitrailers.[50] States that refused to comply would be denied federal highway assistance. The new policies went into effect in April 1983 and met with outright state defiance. The governor of Connecticut signed an emergency order directing state police to set up checkpoints along state highways to enforce the state's existing ban on the larger trucks. Almost immediately thereafter New Jersey, Vermont, Massachusetts, Maryland, Georgia, and Virginia pledged that they too would defy the federal edict.

To assume then, that the administration's actions equaled its rhetorical commitment to state sovereignty would be incorrect. As the chemical labeling and truck-size rules demonstrate, some political trade-offs and economic objectives would clearly outweigh state interests.

Administration efforts to shift regulatory authority to the states did, however, result in a number of significant regulatory reforms. Among the most notable described in this chapter are EPA's revised SIP review regulations, that agency's generic emissions-trading policy, OSM's recast state window rule, and OSHA's attempts to redefine the "benchmarks" state programs must meet to qualify for full delegation. Each reform would to some extent trade the safeguard of comparatively intense multiagency review for more efficient, streamlined procedures that vest states with greater decision-making authority.

The Reagan administration had in effect inherited a number of the more significant and successful efforts to transfer regulatory authority to the states. In several instances accelerated delegations of regulatory authority have been the result of legislatively designed program structure, program maturity, and the efforts of career agency staff. Administration initiatives represented a continuation of, rather than a departure from, prior federal policy and were evolutionary, not revolutionary.

The Reagan administration has in general appeared committed to its efforts to remove the federal government from the critical, interventionist role it had assumed in the past. However, even in the area of sorting out federal and state regulatory rules, the administration has had mixed success in obtaining significant structural reform. Plainly, its legislative agenda has gone unfulfilled; the president's inability to get a revised Clean Air Act restructuring the complex mix of federal, state, and local roles under the SIP and permit programs is an obvious example. To the extent that substantial changes have been implemented, they have been achieved by means of administrative action—the rapid approval of state SIPs, the promulgation of nationwide wetlands permits, the issuance of general emissions-trading regulations, and the delegation of federal programs to the states. And when these efforts appear to have been inconsistent with the intent of Congress, they have been vulnerable to court challenge. The D.C. Court of Appeals significantly limited the application of EPA's emissions-trading guidelines, and the National Wildlife Federation has strongly challenged the Army Corps of Engineers' nationwide permits.

Still, in many instances the transfer of program authority to the states by delegation and other mechanisms is likely to prove difficult to undo and may prove to be one of the more lasting actions of the Reagan administration. Without legislative changes, however, substantial room for federal oversight and intervention remains—and delegated authority could, at least in theory, be rescinded by future administrations. Moreover, transferring enforcement authority for existing programs to the states without changing the underlying rules will not dramatically alter the regulated community's legal obligations. Although the probability that noncompliance will be detected may drop somewhat, causing some "bad actors" to recalculate the costs of noncompliance, potential liabilities will basically remain unchanged—not a reliable prescription for changing long-term corporate strategies.

Another key issue, besides the long-term structural significance of the Reagan administration's regulatory federalism campaign, is the funding of state programs. William Eichbaum a Maryland environmental official, has written,

> The federal dollar has become an absolutely essential ingredient in the development of state environmental protection efforts. The magnitude of that contribution is especially significant when one considers that over the last decade state funds going into these programs have remained generally the same or even grown smaller on a proportional basis. . . . In effect, the growth in size and associated responsibility of these programs during the past "decade of the environment" has been almost entirely supported by the infusion of new federal dollars. . . . The sad fact is that environmental protection has not been able to compete for state funds and state regulators have been able to assume expanded responsibility only through the availability of federal funds.[51]

Severe cuts in federal funding—particularly those previously proposed by the Reagan administration in state environmental programs—when coupled with reductions in EPA funding and competing fiscal pressures at the state level, not only may have chilled future delegations, but may have led to a substantial reduction in aggregate enforcement capacity. The administration's zero-funding option would have wreaked havoc on the states' and nation's capability for environmental law enforcement.

However, given the strong political support enjoyed by proponents of environmental protection, the prospects for the zero-funding option are dim. Even the proposed 20 percent reduction in state grant funds for fiscal year 1983 proved unacceptable to Congress, which reinstated most of the proposed sites. Moreover, the House of Representatives has recently voted to reinstate federal funding for state environmental programs at pre-Reagan levels.[52] Although it seems unlikely in the current economic environment that there will be generally increased spending for enforcement of health and safety regulations, future losses are likely to be real, but marginal.

Given this political-economic scenario, what is likely to happen in the continued devolution of federal authority to the states? One commentator has written,

> In sum, for each environmental regulatory program, each state makes a specific, independent decision whether to undertake responsibility for the program, and the decision is essentially independent of its decision with respect to other programs.[53]

A myriad of factors will determine a state's inclination to accept or pursue delegation, just as a myriad of factors will determine the relative success of delegated programs. Factors such as a state's political history, its fiscal health, the economic value of the regulated resource to the state, the nature of the industry that the state regulates and the type of industry that the state would like to attract, the flexibility of the state's judicial and administrative systems, and the responsiveness of the state's federal regional office will all combine to determine the results of enhanced authority at the individual state level.

At this early stage in the Reagan administration's devolution of regulatory authority, it appears that the success of its efforts may have been subverted to some degree by its budgetary rhetoric. A jurisdiction that might have accepted some delegations of authority may, like Ohio, prove reluctant if program administration would impose incremental costs that exceed the state's economic capacity or fall outside its political interests. In addition, if the administration appears to act unilaterally to rid the federal government of formerly shared regulatory responsibilities without facing up to the real political and economic problems that could result, strong state resistance is likely to ensue—as it did with the Corps' proposed Section 404 changes.

Finally, viewed from the perspective of corporate planners, the transfer of regulatory authority to subnational levels of government may revive the enduring problems associated with trading less stringent regulations for less regulatory uniformity. Firms in a position to benefit from uniform national rules by standardizing service or product lines may lose that advantage if a general trend to balkanized regulation emerges.

The conventional wisdom holds that states are rushing in to fill the role formerly played by the federal government, but convincing evidence regarding a broad, general trend in this direction has yet to emerge. There are, of course, discrete areas in which states have been particularly active, the most obvious being the handling and disposal of hazardous and toxic substances.[54] For example, the National Agricultural Chemical Association announced in 1982 that state legislatures would consider 1,000 pesticide-related bills in 1983—400 more than in 1981.[55] But even given the delegation of regulatory authority undertaken by the federal government over the past two years, states in aggregate have not assumed the activist role that the federal government is thought to have abandoned. Indeed, rather than supplanting federal regulatory authority, many states have mimicked federal regulatory relief efforts.[56] In areas other than hazardous waste and toxic substances, it appears that, in general, corporate fears regarding the emergence of "fifty little EPAs" may have been exaggerated.

11

Assessing Reagan's Regulatory Relief Program

In the preceding five chapters we have traced the major elements of the Reagan administration's regulatory relief program. In this chapter we assess what the program did and did not accomplish.

As has been true of so many discussions in this book, economic and social regulation must be considered separately. As far as economic regulation is concerned, the administration was able to maintain, and in some cases even increase, the momentum inherited from its predecessors. This is not to say that all economic regulation has been ended; in this respect, the hopes of some of the administration's supporters have been dashed.[1] But the general easing of economic regulation that began under Ford and gained speed under Carter has continued.

Assessing the administration's accomplishments with regard to social regulation is much more complicated. The administration claims that it has wrought significant changes, including "the institutionalization—for the first time—of a credible, effective, and even-handed executive oversight mechanism, centered in OMB, for the review and coordination of new regulations." It asserts savings from "administrative and regulatory changes" totaling "more than \$150 billion over the next decade for investment, research and development, increased productivity, and new jobs . . . without jeopardizing the environment, job or consumer safety, or other regulatory goals." Finally, the administration also argues that "just as important as the cost savings generated from these reviews [have been] Administrative decisions to maintain or improve certain regulatory requirements."[2]

We are skeptical of these assertions, and this chapter lays out the basis for this skepticism. Previous chapters have already suggested that the regulatory review process has not been operating as effectively or evenhandedly as the administration maintains. The idea that the cost savings resulting from the program are anywhere close to the levels claimed or that they have been achieved with absolutely no reductions in benefits is also open to serious challenge. Finally, the administration's newfound interest in claiming credit for certain *increases* in regulatory protection appears to be motivated primarily by its desire as the 1984 election approaches to diminish the outcry that its earlier antiregulatory stand generated. It does not seem to reflect any substantial change in approach.

Regulatory cost burdens may have been reduced somewhat, and this reduction may have offset some of the adverse impact on productivity previously attributable to regulation. Moreover, there is some evidence that businesses expect future regulatory costs to be reduced, and this expectation may increase their willingness to invest. The first section of this chapter reviews the evidence on the regulatory relief program's economic impact and attempts to disentangle the effects of the Reagan program from those of the programs of Reagan's predecessors and from the effects of the back-to-back recessions of 1980 and 1981–1982.

But the regulatory relief program's impact has not been only economic. One of its original purposes was to help generate the political momentum necessary to secure the enactment of the president's tax and budget legislation. The second section of this chapter explores both the program's success in doing this and the longer-term (and, we believe, strongly adverse) political consequences of this short-run success.

The final section of this chapter examines the implications of the Reagan regulatory relief program for the future of regulatory reform. Chapter 5 described the consensus that something was amiss with social regulation and the various remedies that were being put forward by late 1980. The Reagan administration's decisions to title its program "regulatory relief," to staff it at the highest levels with people chosen largely for their ideology rather than their knowledge of the programs they were to administer or their managerial competence, and to pursue primarily an administrative rather than a legislative approach have now been substantially reversed. The legacy of the first two and one-half years is likely to make it extremely hard for the administration to obtain serious consideration of legislative changes significantly broadening the discretion given administrators of social regulatory programs, to make increased use of less intrusive, more flexible regulatory techniques, or to scale back some of the absolutist goals embodied in certain parts of current legislation. Such legislative changes might have been possible had the administration chosen to pursue a different set of strategies, but only at a sacrifice of the short-term favorable political impact that appears to have weighed so heavily in its initial calculations.

Measures of the Program's Economic Impact

Several sources of evidence confirm that the administration is justified in claiming a measure of economic success for its regulatory relief program—although the success is not nearly so sweeping as the claims suggest. The program appears to have succeeded modestly in reducing expenditures for regulatory compliance and thus in improving productivity. Finally, business does appear to have become convinced that future regulatory burdens will also be reduced—the "shock" to expectations that the administration was seeking. The twofold analytical problem is to determine how large and durable these results are likely to be and to distinguish the impact of the Reagan program from that of the regulatory reform programs of the Ford and Carter administrations.

Reduction in Outlays for Regulatory Compliance: The Administration's Claims

There are several ways in which the regulatory cost relief produced by the program can be measured. The first is to rely on the claims made by the administration itself. As noted in earlier chapters, in August 1981, 1982, and 1983 the President's Task Force on Regulatory Relief published progress reports in which attained and projected cost savings resulting from the regulatory relief program were totaled. Table 15, drawn from the task force's final report, sets out the administration's tally of regulatory cost savings achieved through August 1983. This final report claimed investment (or one-time savings) of between $15.2 billion and $17.2 billion and annually recurring savings of between $13.5 billion and $13.9 billion.[3] The administration calculated ten-year cumulative savings by multiplying the latter figure by ten and adding the former figure. The resulting figure of approximately $150 billion in cumulative savings included $110 billion that were said to have resulted from the "modification or rescission of unnecessary existing regulation." The remaining $42 billion were said to represent "increased income to the consumer . . . generated by the removal of interest rate ceilings during the term of the Administration, particularly as a result of the passage

TABLE 15

MAJOR COST SAVINGS OF COMPLETED REGULATORY REFORMS

	Investment or One-time (in millions of $)	Annually Recurring (in millions of $)
Architectural and Transportation Barriers Compliance Board		
Minimum Guidelines	—	250
Department of Agriculture		
Mechanically Processed (Species) Product	—	500
National School Lunch Program	—	117
WIC Program Recordkeeping	—	30
Special Milk Program Paperwork	—	28
Model Food Stamp Form	—	5
Corps of Engineers		
Section 404 of the Clean Water Act	—	1,000
Department of Education		
Bilingual Education Regulations	900–2,950	70–155
Education Consolidation and Improvement Act	—	2
Department of Energy		
Residential Conservation Service Program	—	100–150
Coal Conversion	—	100
Appliance Efficiency Standards	—	30–60
Building Compliance Form	—	20
Department of Health and Human Services		
Medicare-Medicaid Form	—	100
Regulations Implementing Block Grants	—	52
Patient Package Inserts	—	20
Department of Housing and Urban Development		
Direct Endorsement	—	11–15
Environmental Policies	—	5
Community Development	—	3
Modernization of Public Housing Projects	—	2
Department of the Interior		
Phase I Reform Effort	—	10
Federal Coal Management	—	3
Department of Labor		
Equal Pension Benefits for Men and Women	—	1,500
Prevailing Wage: Davis-Bacon	—	585
Suspension of Pension Benefit Restrictions	—	200–300
OSHA Hearing Conservation Rules	—	81

TABLE 15 (*continued*)

	Investment or One-time (in millions of $)	Annually Recurring (in millions of $)
Department of Labor (continued)		
ESA Salary Tests for Overtime	—	55
Occupational Exposure to Lead	—	50
OSHA Respirator Fit Testing for Lead	—	6
Department of Transportation		
Passive Restraints—Rescission	400	1,000
Passive Restraints—Delay	135	—
Highway 402 Program Paperwork	—	680
Bumper Standard	—	300
Driver's Log	—	164
Low Tire Pressure Warning	—	130
Railroad Power Brake Rules	—	100
Multipiece Rims	300	75
Field of Direct View—Cars	160	25
Marine Vessel Construction Standards	368	17
Speedometers and Odometers	—	12
Blue Signal Protection and Hours of Service	—	12
Uniform Tire Quality Grading Standards	—	10
Theft Protection	—	10
Marine Vessel Documentation	—	5
Pipeline Retention of Radiographic Film	—	3
Hydraulic Brakes	—	2
Limited Quantity Radioactive Materials	—	1
Plastic Pipeline Mechanical Joint Couplings	—	1
Section 504 of the Rehabilitation Act	2,200	—
Tank Truck Specification Relief	80	—
Coast Guard Complementary Navigation Systems	24	—
Department of the Treasury		
IRS Simplified Tax Forms	—	650
Alcoholic Beverages Paperwork	—	5
ERISA Form 5500 and 5500C Paperwork	—	2
Depository Institutions Deregulation (OCC, FRB, FDIUC, FHLBB)		
Incremental Interest to Depositors	6,200	3,600
Equal Employment Opportunity Commission		
EEO-1 Paperwork	—	3
EEO-4 Paperwork	—	2
EEO-5 Paperwork	—	2

TABLE 15 *(continued)*

MAJOR COST SAVINGS OF COMPLETED REGULATORY REFORMS

	Investment or One-time *(in millions of $)*	Annually Recurring *(in millions of $)*
Environmental Protection Agency		
Onboard Technology for Control of HC Emissions	103	240
1984 High Altitude Requirement	—	200
Diesel Particulate Emissions Averaging	—	50–111
BCT Effluent Guidelines	1,100	80
Truck Mounted Solid Waste Compactors	—	33
Iron and Steel Effluent Guidelines	580	30
Dual Definition of Source	1,300	—
Emissions Trading Policy	1,000	—
Noise Emission Limits for Trucks	130	—
Standards for Paint Shops	75	
General Motors Offset Remedy for NOx	38	—
Acceptable Quality Level for Assembly Line Testing of Trucks	31	—
Steel Stretchout Agreements	10	—
Selective Enforcement Audit for Heavy Truck Engines	9	—
Motor Vehicle Certification	5	—
Assembly Line Test Orders	1	—
Self-Certification for Vehicles Sold at High Altitudes	1	—
Federal Communications Commission		
Maritime Radio Station Logs	—	21
Ham Radio Operator Logs	—	3
Mobile Radio Service Paperwork	—	1
Federal Energy Regulatory Commission		
Power Plants Paperwork	—	1
National Credit Union Administration		
Recordkeeping Requirements	—	670
Securities and Exchange Commission		
Integration Program	—	350
Regulation D	—	50
Office of Management and Budget		
Circular A-95	—	50
TOTAL	15,150–17,200	13,525–13,855

SOURCE: *Reagan Administration Regulatory Achievements*, Presidential Task Force on Regulatory Relief, August 11, 1983.

of the financial deregulation bill of 1982.''[4] In addition, the administration asserted that regulation-related paperwork had been reduced by approximately 300 million person-hours per year.[5]

It is not new for high-level executive branch officials (up to and including presidents of the United States) to make sweeping assertions about regulation's costs and to claim that their administration is going to do (or has done) something to reduce these costs. Rhetorical excess is an ancient American political tradition. Yet the claims made by the Reagan administration in August 1983 stand out as among the most sweeping. They are certainly among the most painstakingly documented. But are they valid?

To evaluate these claims, let us return to the framework for assessing regulatory costs developed in chapter 2. In that chapter we distinguished *costs*, which include alteration in the use of real resources, from *transfers*, which merely involve the shifting of resources from one group in society to another.[6]

Counting Transfers as Cost Savings. How do the published cost-savings claims of the Reagan administration fare when viewed in the light of this critical distinction? Not very well, it turns out. The claimed savings include a substantial body of transfers. The clearest example is the $42 billion in increased interest income to consumers as a result of financial deregulation. (Let us leave aside the question of whether it is even appropriate to credit the Reagan administration with this "savings," given the history of deregulation of financial institutions. As the reader will recall, the process was well under way when Reagan took office.) This higher interest paid to consumers presumably is offset by higher interest banks charged borrowers— unless the administration is willing to claim that all the higher interest came out of banks' profits. To be sure, a credible case can be made that holding interest rates artificially low misallocated credit and that this misallocation saddled the economy with real resource losses. But the statement from the Federal Home Loan Bank Board (FHLBB) documenting the task force's claim makes clear that the asserted savings are *not* based on an estimate of these real resource costs.[7] Furthermore, the FHLBB statement makes it clear that no attempt has been made to estimate the degree to which the payment of higher interest to depositors has led financial institutions to curtail the amount of nonprice competition they once engaged in. In short, the number cited by the task force may even substantially overstate the magnitude of the *transfers* involved.[8]

A second example of a transfer is $1.5 billion the administration claims was "saved" annually because the Supreme Court did not apply its *Norris*[9] decision retroactively. *Norris* ruled illegal pension plans that paid unequal pension benefits to men and women (hence the rationale for listing this item in Table 15 as "equal pension benefits for men and women.") The Supreme Court decided only to apply *Norris* prospectively—this had been urged on the court by the Justice Department in its brief. Had it not chosen to do this, the Department of Labor, acting under the provisions of the Employee Retirement Income Security Act (ERISA), would have been forced to promulgate regulations putting the retroactivity requirement into effect. According to the Labor Department, the first-year cost of such a retroactivity provision would have been approximately $1.5 billion, hence the claimed savings.

Ignoring the extremely tendentious nature of the claim that this "savings" is attributable in any way to the administration's regulatory relief program, it should be clear that what is involved is a transfer, not a saving in real resource cost. Although the initial incidence of a decision to require retroactive pension adjustments would have fallen on employers, one can assume that, as with changes in interest rates, the "costs" would have been quickly passed on. In effect, women would have benefited at the expense of men.

These two items total $57 billion of the Reagan administration's claimed $150 billion in cost savings. But they by no means exhaust the list of examples in which transfers are counted as savings in real resource costs.

Consider the claimed $300 million in annual savings from the bumper standard rescission. Under prodding from the auto industry, the Reagan administration in May of 1982 reduced the required performance level for car bumpers from five miles per hour to 2½ miles per hour. Not all auto makers chose to weaken their bumpers, but purchasers of cars from those that did immediately reported higher repair bills. Insurance companies raised rates on otherwise identical cars equipped with the weaker bumpers.[10] Thus, though the bumper rule making did lead to certain real changes in the use of resources, it also involved an important element of transfer. It is clearly incorrect to label the entire $300 million in annual compliance costs for the auto industry as "savings."

Another example of a claimed savings that embodies a substantial element of transfer (in this case, between industries) and that actually may have led to higher overall costs is the postponement of emissions standards for auto industry paint shops by the Environmental Protection Agency (EPA). The Carter administration refused to include this postponement in its 1980 auto package on the grounds that, on balance, it would have imposed significantly greater costs on other industries than it would have saved the auto industry. The Reagan administration granted the industry its request that the regulation be postponed.[11] If, as the administration claimed in its August 1983 report, no environmental benefits were lost as a result of the delay, then the additional cost that other industries were required to bear should be included as an offset.

(Recall that failure to impose the requirement on the auto paint shops caused the geographic areas in which they were located to be out of compliance with the Clean Air Act. Bringing these areas into compliance in the presence of the delay would have required equivalent emissions reductions by other sources.) But if these additional costs were not imposed, then environmental benefits were clearly forgone, undermining the administration's assertion to the contrary.

To summarize, where changes in regulations represent merely shifts in income among groups in society or reflect a reallocation of resource use with some groups bearing lower costs and other groups bearing higher costs, crediting the total reduction in regulatory expenditures as a "cost saving" is clearly illegitimate. If the transaction includes nothing but an income transfer, then *no* savings in resource cost occur. Where the transaction involves a change in resource use, only the *net change* in burden counts as a saving— provided, of course, that the net result of the changes is included to reduce the use of real resources devoted to regulatory compliance. If the change involves a net *increase* in resource use—as the paint shop regulation deferral and the bumper rescission each may have—then it should be recorded as a cost *increase*.

Claiming Credit for Rescinding Regulations That Were Unlikely Ever to Have Been Implemented.   The examples cited thus far refer to changes in regulations actually in force that were made by the Reagan administration. (That is, the change in the bumper standard was a change from an already existing regulation.) But the administration's estimates of cost savings can also be faulted on the grounds that they include "savings" from rescissions of regulations that had only been proposed—sometimes very tentatively— by the outgoing Carter administration. There is no evidence that the Carter administration, had it been reelected, would have permitted these regulations to go forward with their initial stringency—and costs—if indeed they had been permitted to go forward at all. Three good examples are the National Highway Traffic Safety Administration's withdrawal of the advanced (i.e., highly tentative) notice of proposed rule making for regulations requiring low tire pressure warnings (claimed savings of $130 million annually), NHTSA's withdrawal of proposed regulations banning multipiece tire rims (claimed one-time savings of $300 million and annual savings of $75 million), and EPA's withdrawal of proposed regulations for onboard control of hydrocarbon emissions (claimed one-time savings of $103 million and annual savings of $240 million).

The Reagan administration is not the first to claim savings as a result of actions that were never likely to have been taken anyway. As observed in chapter 6, the entire Carter auto package was just this sort of empty box. But in determining the likely economic impact of the cost savings claimed by the Reagan regulatory relief program, we must discount such rhetorical excesses.

Claiming Credit for Savings Connected With Regulations Ordered Reinstated by the Courts.   A third problem with the task force's list is that it includes savings from changes in regulations that courts have ordered reversed. The clearest example is the $400 million in one-time costs and $1 billion in annual costs resulting from rescission of the standard for passive restraints in automobiles.[12] (A further consideration is that credible economic analyses show that imposition of the standard would have generated substantial benefits. Not even the administration claims that the standard would have been totally ineffective.) Other regulations are under court challenge. For example, the "Dual Definition" regulations (regulations redefining what constitutes a pollution "source" in areas of the country not meeting national ambient air quality standards, which purportedly saved $1.3 billion) have been overturned by the District of Columbia Court of Appeals.

Employing a Double Accounting Standard for Regulations Added and Regulations Deleted.   Perhaps most curiously, the administration notes that the figures in the August 1983 report do not include the costs of regulations *added* during its term of office—regulations that it acknowledges will impose costs amounting to "billions [of dollars] over the next ten years." Why are these regulations omitted? Because "the administration is confident . . . that the benefits of these rules exceed their costs."[13] If the administration is correct about the cost-benefit relationship of these regulations, then indeed they do not impose a "cost" but they result in a net savings to the economy.[14] But this is the only place in the report where this particular accounting standard is employed. Moreover, it rests only on assertion. No evidence is supplied to support it. However, had such a standard been applied with respect to the "savings" claims made by the administration, many of those claims might not have been reportable as such.

Possible Underestimations of Savings.   In some respects, however, the estimates may be low. That is certainly the view of the administration, which has publicly claimed that the cost savings it has reported "substantially understate the total expected economic impact of [its] regulatory relief efforts" since "the figures include only those rules and only those costs that could be quantified with reasonable accuracy."[15] In the task force's August 1982 progress report, which provides more complete regulation-by-regulation detail than the report published in August 1983, explicit savings figures, in terms of either dollars or hours of paperwork, are provided for only twenty-seven of the fifty-one reforms listed as having been completed by that date. The administration also asserts that where savings estimates have been provided, they are "conservative."[16]

A more questionable assertion in the August 1983 report is that there is no need to readjust the cost figures to account for benefits forgone since "the changes have not sacrificed any values protected by the relevant statutes."[17] This is clearly untrue, for example, for the reported "savings" attributable to the bumper standards, for the delay in reduction for auto industry paint shop hydrocarbon emissions (to the extent that other standards were not relaxed), and for the passive-restraint delay.

A more serious undercounting issue concerns the general absence from the administration's list of real resource savings due to economic deregulation. As noted, the only instance in which "benefits" attributable to economic deregulation are included (and then incorrectly) is the "increased income to the consumer . . . generated by the removal of interest rate ceilings." When dealing with the savings due to economic deregulation it is difficult to apportion responsibility between the Reagan administration and past administrations. But there can be no doubt that the resource savings due to economic deregulation have been significant.

Reduction in Outlays for Regulatory Compliance: Commerce Department Survey Data

The validity of the administration's claim to have reduced regulatory burdens significantly can also be tested by examining data collected by the Commerce Department showing expenditures by various sectors of the economy for pollution control. Pollution control is certainly not the only element of social regulation generating substantial costs, but it is one of the most significant.[18] It also is the one area in which reasonably consistent data have been collected. Some caution needs to be exercised in attributing current cost savings to current regulatory changes, because current expenditures often reflect past regulatory requirements. Yet if the Reagan administration has really reduced regulatory burdens substantially, the results should be showing up in business outlays for pollution abatement.

The most recent comprehensive data available are contained in an article in the February 1983 issue of *Survey of Current Business*.[19] This article reported newly revised estimates of real expenditures on pollution abatement and control by the business sector and by the economy as a whole for the years 1972 through 1981. Table 16 confirms that real spending did decline

TABLE 16

REAL Expenditures on Pollution Abatement and Control: 1972–1981
(*Millions of 1972 Dollars*)

		Expenditures by Business			
Year	Total Expenditures[a]	Total	On Capital Account	On Current Account	Private R&D Expenditures
1972	18,434	10,960	5,399	5,561	519
1973	20,603	12,330	6,435	5,895	575
1974	21,307	12,372	6,200	6,172	512
1975	23,008	13,057	6,662	6,395	461
1976	24,325	13,789	6,762	7,027	501
1977	24,800	14,315	6,760	7,555	562
1978	26,330	15,011	6,758	8,253	604
1979	26,936	15,651	6,992	8,658	654
1980	26,730	15,582	6,815	8,767	621
1981	26,407	15,480	6,510	8,970	604
1981 vs. 1980 (%)	− 1.2	− 0.6	− 4.7	+ 2.3	− 2.8

SOURCE: *Survey of Current Business*, February 1983, pp. 16–17.

    a. Includes expenditures by business, consumers, and governmental units.

during 1981. Of course, the table shows that it also declined in 1980, the last year of the Carter administration.

These results could reflect the impact of the anemic performance of the economy since 1979, which has cut both industrial output and investment, as well as the maturation of some programs controlling air and water pollution. However, a comparison of the 1980 and 1981 figures with the data for 1974 and 1975, when the economy also went through a sharp recession, cautions against attributing all the recent decline to underlying economic conditions. In 1974 pollution-control expenditures by business on capital account and private pollution-related research and development did decline in real terms. But overall spending, both by business and in the economy as a whole, still increased. During 1980 and 1981, total spending, spending by business, spending by business on capital account, and private research and development spending all fell. Only spending by business on current account continued to rise. Underlying detail shows that this rise is accounted for almost entirely by the increasing cost to business of operating cars and trucks equipped with pollution-control devices.[20]

Data from a separate Commerce Department series show expenditures by business on new plant and equipment devoted to pollution abatement. They exclude expenditures by business for pollution-abatement devices on purchased cars and trucks. That is, they reflect investments made in process improvements (about 30 percent of the total) and "end of pipe" controls (the remaining 70 percent) to eliminate air and water pollution, and to dispose of solid wastes in establishments engaged in manufacturing and distribution. The series includes 1982 actual and 1983 intended investments.

According to this series, between 1980 and 1982, new plant and equipment expenditures by total U.S. nonfarm business for pollution abatement fell by 8 percent in current dollars and by 22 percent in constant dollars.[21] For 1983, planned investment was scheduled to fall another 5 to 7 percent in constant dollars.

Again, the recession might be suspected of having had something to do with this decline. Indeed, planned investment overall by nonfarm business in 1983 was 3.1 percent below the 1981 current-dollar level—but still 5.1 percent above the 1980 level (also in current dollars).

To correct for the influence of the recession, and also to explore how the share of pollution-control expenditures in total business investment has changed as a result of the Reagan regulatory relief program, figure 2 plots pollution-abatement expenditures as a percentage of total new plant and equip-

FIGURE 2

POLLUTION-ABATEMENT EXPENDITURES AS A PERCENTAGE OF TOTAL EXPENDITURES ON NEW PLANT AND EQUIPMENT, TOTAL U.S. NONFARM BUSINESS, 1973–1983

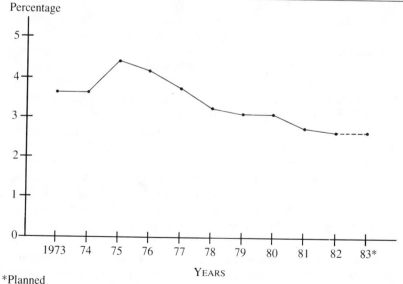

Percentage

YEARS

*Planned

SOURCE: *Survey of Current Business*, June 1981, pp 20–21; June 1982, p. 18; June 1983, p. 25.

ment expenditures for total U.S. nonfarm business. In 1983 this number is down considerably from its peak of 4.4 percent in 1975. Indeed, it has been lower during the years of the Reagan administration than during any period in which these data have been collected. But the trend was also downward throughout most of the Carter administration. Indeed, during the first three Carter years the share of business plant and equipment expenditure accounted for by pollution control fell more than twice as much as it did during the first three Reagan years.

Figure 3 plots this same percentage figure for several important major industries: chemicals, paper, petroleum, nonferrous metals, iron and steel, and electric utilities. Two facts stand out. First, in certain cases, pollution-abatement expenditures have constituted an extremely significant share of total industry investment. Reductions in such investment could be expected to "free" substantial amounts of capital for "productive" investment. Second, in almost every case, the decline in this share of investment accounted for by pollution control predates the Reagan administration. Only in the case of electric utilities is the peak as late as 1980. This pattern of timing suggests that the maturing of certain environmental programs may be extremely important in explaining the ratio's recent decline. Certainly there is no evidence that the Reagan program constitutes the sharp break from the past that the administration claims.

Impact on Productivity

If regulatory costs have been reduced, has there been a resulting favorable impact on productivity? Given the lags and the underlying complexity of the relationships involved, it probably is still too early to give a definitive answer. But one provocative finding is contained in a paper presented by two economists at a June 1983 Urban Institute conference.[22] Gregory Christiansen and Robert Haveman were asked to assume that the administration estimates of August 1982 concerning cost savings attributable to the regulatory relief program were accurate and to calculate the impact that these cost savings would have on productivity. They fully recognized the speculative nature of this exercise and the difficulties in specifying the necessary relationships.

Christainsen and Haveman added annualized values of one-time capital savings to annual operating cost savings to produce their estimate of total factor cost savings attributable to the administration's 1981–1982 efforts—between $7.2 and $9.9 billion dollars. Using a growth-accounting approach (which translates these factor cost savings into dollar-for-dollar reductions in business factor costs) and taking the average level of total factor productivity in 1980 as a base, they concluded that the regulatory savings claimed by the

FIGURE 3

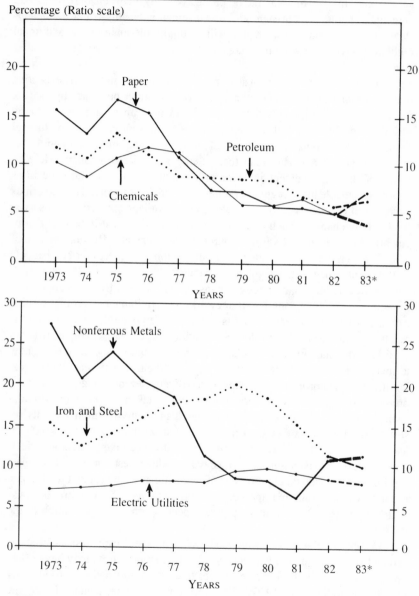

POLLUTION-ABATEMENT EXPENDITURES BY INDUSTRY

*Planned

SOURCE: U.S. Department of Commerce, Bureau of Economic Analysis.

task force, if fully realized (taking into account no productivity-reducing effects of the loss of regulatory benefits), would have increased the economy's annual growth rate of total factor productivity by between 0.16 and 0.22 percentage point. As Christainsen and Haveman note, this is not a "steady-state" change. That is, the change will gradually dissipate unless additional regulatory savings of a similar magnitude continue to be generated year after year.

Christainsen and Haveman attempted to partition the savings by executive branch agencies using agency-by-agency savings figures published by the task force. They concluded that about half the savings can be accounted for by actions taken by EPA and the Department of Transportation. An additional 10 percent is attributable to actions taken by the Department of Labor.

Christainsen and Haveman then attempted to derive econometric estimates of the improvement in labor productivity for the nonfarm business sector attributable to the regulatory relief program. This involved using various measures of regulatory activity (as well as other variables) to explain observed productivity changes. Such a methodology permits, at least in theory, distinguishing the influence of various nonregulatory elements affecting the rate of labor productivity growth (such as the recession and energy price changes) from the influence of the regulatory changes.

However, this methodology is considerably more difficult to apply than the simple growth-accounting framework. Determining the proper specification for the econometric model is not completely straightforward, and the results are quite sensitive to the specification chosen. For example, it is not clear how the magnitude of regulatory activity should be specified (i.e., how to measure the level of regulatory "output" and changes in that level), what lag structure is appropriate (i.e., how much of any current changes in observed productivity is due to regulatory reform actions taken by previous administrations), or how to treat regulatory-related productivity improvements resulting from actions other than those reported by the task force (which, at least in the August 1982 report, limited itself to executive branch agencies). Nevertheless, Christiansen and Haveman produced estimates with at least semirespectable statistical properties. These estimates suggest that the Reagan regulatory relief program improved labor productivity in the nonfarm business sector by up to 0.22 percentage point, depending on the specification of the model.

Combining the results from these two methods of estimation, Christiansen and Haveman judged that post-1980 deregulation efforts may have offset up to roughly half the adverse effects that regulation had on productivity growth throughout the 1970s. This result is not inconsequential, but the relatively modest importance of regulation in the overall productivity slow-down should be kept in mind (see chapter 2).

Impact on Expectations

We noted in chapter 2 that a major goal of the Reagan regulatory relief effort was to shock expectations. That is, cost reductions were to be important not only for the actual relief they generated but also for what they signaled to business about *future* regulatory burdens. As the following discussion will clarify, much of the program's early activity, especially its packaging of groups of important regulations for review and its publicizing of aggregate cost savings, is best understood as being intended primarily to produce this expectational shock. This may even be true of the vice president's August 1983 announcement that the program had "accomplished its basic mission" and that the task force was being terminated as an active institution.[23]

How well did the program succeed in altering the expectations of business about future regulatory burdens? Since economists are not able to measure expectations very well, answering this question is hard. One source of information is the survey data published by the Commerce Department on new plant and equipment expenditures on pollution abatement by business. These data include not only estimates of actual expenditures made during the survey year but also planned expenditures for the coming year. Table 17 shows both planned and actual expenditures for all years for which there are data—1974 through 1983 (the 1983 data include only planned expenditures). As is generally true in business, planned and actual expenditures often diverge. But the trend in planned expenditures is generally upward until 1981, after which time it declines sharply. The survey for 1982 planned spending was, of course, taken near the end of 1981, the first year that the Reagan regulatory program was in place.

Actual spending in 1981 turned out to be somewhat less than had been anticipated in 1980 when the survey was taken. Also, actual spending declined in 1981 for the first time. Nevertheless, in late 1981 (when the survey of planned spending for 1982 was taken), business indicated that it expected 1982 pollution-control spending to be higher than actually experienced in 1981. This finding is consistent with the forecast of economists who dispute the extreme "rational expectations" viewpoint and hold instead that expectations change only slowly and in response to observed changes in actual events.

As table 17 shows, business substantially overestimated its actual 1982 spending on new plant and equipment devoted to pollution control. This is

TABLE 17

PLANNED AND ACTUAL NEW PLANT AND EQUIPMENT EXPENDITURES ON POLLUTION
ABATEMENT: TOTAL U.S. NONFARM BUSINESS, 1974–1983
(*Billions of Current Dollars*)

Year	Planned	Actual	Ratio of Planned to Actual
1974	6.87	5.70	1.27
1975	6.70	6.97	0.96
1976	7.61	7.23	1.05
1977	7.99	7.34	1.09
1978	7.87	7.58	1.04
1979	8.18	8.42	0.97
1980	9.64	9.20	1.05
1981	10.00	8.93	1.12
1982	9.37	8.49	1.10
1983	8.26	NA	NA

SOURCE: *Survey of Current Business*, June 1983, p. 25. Information on planned expenditures is
gathered during November and December prior to the year for which it is shown and
is adjusted by the Commerce Department to exclude "systematic bias." Data on planned
expenditures for 1974 through 1980 were derived by multiplying the ratio of planned
to actual expenditures for those years by the actual expenditures reported by the Department of Commerce.

perhaps why the planned spending for 1983 is below actual 1982 levels—
the first such decline.

Sorting out the impact of regulatory changes from the impact of the
recent back-to-back recessions and the sharp decline in inflation (both of
which would also tend to cause planned expenditures to decrease) is probably
impossible. Nevertheless, it is appropriate to attribute *some* of the change in
planned pollution-control spending to the "expectations shock" produced by
the Reagan regulatory relief effort. But the massive expectations shock that
the program's designers had once hoped for did not occur; expectations adjusted only gradually in response to observed events.

Indeed, in its planning, business gives no sign of believing—contrary
to the charges of some environmentalists—that the pollution-control laws are
about to be swept off the books or that enforcement of existing laws has been
totally suspended. Planned expenditures have indeed fallen, but the roughly
$8.3 billion in planned 1983 spending still represents a major outlay.

How has the controversy generated by the regulatory relief program
affected the expectations of business regarding future levels of regulatory
compliance? Increasingly, fear has been expressed of a "regulatory backlash." Stories such as the *Business Week* article published in May 1983, "A
Bipartisan Swing Back to More Regulation,"[24] and concerns about the cost

consequences of increased regulatory activity at the state level in the face of federal regulatory inaction[25] must be affecting businesses' expectations about the durability of any relief produced by the Reagan regulatory relief program.

A concrete case is the change in attitude shown by the automobile industry. Perhaps better than any other group of regulatory actions the Reagan administration took, the auto package reflected the kind of significant breakthrough the administration hoped to achieve in paring back regulation in a major industry. The administration masterfully assembled, published, and pushed through major elements of this package—an achievement that seemed especially impressive when contrasted with the Carter administration's earlier struggles. The auto industry appears to have been pleased. Betsy Ancker-Johnson, General Motors' vice president for environmental affairs, is quoted as having originally lauded the Reagan package, stating that the difference between the Reagan administration's attitude toward auto regulation and that of Carter's was "like the difference between night and day."[26] Surely the announcement of the package yielded an important expectations dividend—and probably not only in the auto industry.

Important elements of the Reagan auto package have subsequently come unwrapped. Some of the promised changes in regulations never were made. Others—most important, the standard for passive restraints—have been overturned by the courts. Still others are now in limbo. Indeed, as table 6 in chapter 6 showed, as of August 1983, a significant portion of the $1.6 billion in projected industry savings and $5.8 billion in projected savings to the public fell in the "uncertain" category.

Relations between the regulatory agencies and the auto industry have recently become less amicable. General Motors was angered by NHTSA's December 1982 request that GM reconsider its refusal to recall its X-cars to correct a braking problem at an estimated cost of $170 million to the company—and by NHTSA's August 1983 decision to file suit against GM in this matter. Little wonder that the *National Journal's* recent review of the results of the auto package found GM's Ancker-Johnson in a less than euphoric mood, complaining about "butting heads" with unyielding regulators and minimizing the value to the industry of the relief package.[27]

In a paper prepared for the Urban Institute conference mentioned earlier, Robert Leone examined the impact of Reagan administration actions (including the regulatory changes) on the auto industry. Specifically, he examined the overall impact on the auto firms' "strategic focus"—the extent to which they can concentrate on factors other than regulation in making decisions on matters such as product design and market positioning.[28] Leone concluded that the manner in which the regulatory changes were undertaken (in particular, the uncertainty generated by their vulnerability to court challenge) plus the tendency of the administration to react to political criticism of its regulatory relief effort by "toughening up" at EPA and NHTSA (thereby underscoring the reversibility of administrative actions even without court challenges) have seriously undercut any hopes that the industry might once have had of being able to act "deregulated." Consequently, in both the auto industry and industries that might have tended to base their assessment of the performance of regulatory relief on the auto example, a significant proportion of any favorable "expectations shock" the program might once have generated has by now probably been dissipated.

The Regulatory Relief Program's Political Impact

During the early months of the Reagan administration's term in office, the regulatory relief program was clearly an important political plus for the administration, but that was the only time when this was so. After those first few heady months, the program increasingly became a political albatross, with its damage to the administration peaking during the spring of 1983 as revelations of misconduct at EPA dominated the news reports. The administration moved to contain this political damage by making wholesale changes in regulatory personnel, toning down its antiregulation excesses, and, finally, "declaring victory" and formally terminating the regulatory relief program itself. Concern with reducing regulatory burdens would nominally remain a goal of the administration, but henceforth it would be clothed in the more traditional guise of regulatory reform.

This outcome certainly cannot be the one sought by the officials who designed and launched the program with such fanfare in January 1981. They may have expected certain setbacks, but they cannot be pleased with the eventual political failure of their effort—a failure that has created significant barriers to the eventual reform of social regulation.

What went wrong? We have already suggested that the broad outlines of the eventual outcome ought to have been obvious to the designers of the program even before it was launched. And indeed there is evidence that at least some problems were anticipated. In his "Dunkirk" memo, David Stockman clearly spelled out the dangers inherent in pursuing a strategy that relied primarily on administrative actions rather than legislative change. But the administration apparently did not anticipate the general level of public outrage that the program would generate. It was only in mid-1983 that an administration official, William Ruckelshaus, would admit in a press interview that the administration had "confused" the public's wish to improve the way in which government protects the environment and public health with the administration's own desire to change the goals. Ruckelshaus declared, "We cannot deregulate in this area."[29] Of course, since Ruckelshaus was not one of those who had misread the public, the admission was easy for him to make.

The mention of the impossibility of deregulation in the area of environmental protection suggests another fundamental miscalculation that the administration made—extrapolating from the experience of economic deregulation. An example of this extrapolation is to be found in an article by Christopher DeMuth in the January/February 1982 issue of *Regulation*. In defending the administration's initial approach to regulatory reform, DeMuth argued:

> The history of deregulation is that administrative reform is a necessary prerequisite to statutory reform. Before Congress itself will act, external changes are required to dislodge accumulated interests in the status quo and to assure the doubtful of the economy's ability to continue functioning in the absence of federal controls. . . . If we are to achieve major statutory reform in the last two years of President Reagan's first term, we must first build a solid foundation of administrative deregulation. . . .[30]

DeMuth's history is correct, but his extrapolation from it is not. The strategy of putting dedicated deregulators into agencies such as the ICC and CAB—persons who showed themselves willing to deregulate through administrative action, even going so far as to invite the courts to slap them down—led not to a backlash against their actions but to a rush by Congress to confirm these actions legislatively, if only to limit the degree to which this discretion could be used. This strategy worked only because the impression by that time was widespread that economic regulation had failed as a strategy of social control of business. Deregulation was therefore an appropriate alternative.

In contrast, the failure of social regulation to achieve its stated goals was generally perceived not as a reflection of any fundamental flaw with either the goals or the regulatory techniques employed but as a failure of will. Various administrations just had not tried hard enough to make social regulation work. Trying harder, not scaling back programs, was seen as the generally acceptable solution. In such an environment, appointing administrators who were openly hostile to social regulation's goals and who, whether fairly or not, were perceived as prepared to do everything in their power to make certain that social regulation *did not* work could hardly be expected to call forth cries for a scaling back of social regulatory programs.

The use of the economic deregulation analogy not only betrays the fundamental misreading of the public's mood that Ruckelshaus referred to but also reflects a misunderstanding of the kind of change in social regulation that *ever* is likely to occur. There never was a serious possibility that Congress would have been willing to consider the outright repeal of statutes such as the Clean Air Act, Clean Water Act, and Occupational Health and Safety Act. At most, Congress might have been persuaded to ease the requirements of these statutes in ways that increased the flexibility permitted in their administration. But a necessary concomitant to a grant of greater administrative discretion would have been a high degree of trust that the acts would indeed have been administered with competence and an eye toward achieving their objectives—that any increased flexibility would be used to reduce unnecessary burdens without abandoning the acts' underlying goals.

Viewed in this way, administrative deregulation might reasonably have been seen as a necessary prerequisite to statutory reform. But a program of administrative deregulation would have had to have proceeded from a very different premise—a premise that accepted the underlying legitimacy of social regulation and that was dedicated to making it work. This was not a premise that the Reagan administration accepted.

The various elements of the Reagan regulatory relief strategy that played so well politically during the first few months of the administration—the freeze on effective dates for rules, the regulatory hit lists, the appointment of politically attuned rather than professionally competent administrators, the targeted budget cuts and personnel actions, the meetings with business groups to the virtual exclusion of any other interested parties—all tended to undermine the perception that the Reagan administration could be counted on to use in a responsible way any additional discretion it might be granted. Indeed, the opposite impression was created. Congress was put in a mood to tighten, not loosen, the ''regulatory ratchet'' and to scrutinize every action of administration regulatory officials.

This failure to appreciate the critical distinction between economic deregulation and reform of social regulation contributed to a second miscalculation: the failure of the administration to appreciate the damage that untalented appointees to high-level posts in social regulatory agencies could do to the attainment of the regulatory cost reductions the administration was seeking.

The administrators of agencies such as EPA, NHTSA, and OSHA were deliberately chosen not for their expertise in the areas in which they would be working but for their willingness to support the president's regulatory goals. Far from being willing to use and trust the lawyers and other professional staffs they inherited, most of the new administrators, as well as those running the White House oversight operation, viewed these holdovers as the principal obstruction to their goals. To be sure, this suspicion was in some cases justified. But it helped hamstring several of Reagan's appointees as they attempted to move beyond promises to generate the modifications of rules and regulations on which the longer-term success of the program depended. Appointees neither familiar with the programs they were to administer nor willing to rely on the career staffs in their agencies proved unable to use effectively the discretion they *did* have to modify or eliminate rules and regulations. They quickly ran afoul of the complexities of the administrative process, thereby opening up their decisions to judicial reversal. They proved unable to defend their actions before Congress, where detailed knowledge of complex programs commands respect. And they lacked sensitivity to the public's fears and concerns relating to the various hazards, real and imagined, that they were charged with controlling.

The importance of expertise can be seen by comparing the record of someone like Raymond Peck or Anne Burford with that of William Baxter, the former head of the Justice Department's Antitrust Division. Baxter was dedicated to major changes in antitrust enforcement, but he was also an extremely skilled and knowledgeable antitrust lawyer. He made the changes he desired and generated substantial controversy in the process. But Baxter's actions were not reversed in court. Also, as discussed in chapter 7, the deregulation of radio by a deregulation-minded Federal Communications Commission (FCC) was upheld—though by a clearly reluctant court—on the grounds that the proper administrative procedures had been followed and that the FCC had not exceeded its discretion. Even James Watt, the politically controversial Secretary of the Interior, achieved a relatively good record of administrative deregulation. Watt knew the programs of the Interior Department, having served in several positions there during the Nixon administration. Thus his proposed changes to existing surface mining regulations proceeded in a comparatively slow and procedurally regular manner. In fact, Watt's primary problem was not with the courts but with Congress and the public at large, where his outspoken opposition to environmental programs kept him constantly in trouble.

The third miscalculation of the designers of the Reagan regulatory relief program was to pay insufficient attention to the perceptions generated by the processes they developed for reviewing and revising regulations. As is true of many parts of the program, these processes appear to have been designed primarily to create the impression among the business community that the regulatory tide was being rolled back. However, the processes also helped to reinforce the belief that Reagan administration officials were paying excessive attention to the wishes of business and were interested not in legitimate regulatory relief but in eliminating social regulatory programs, regardless of their merits.

The backlash that the operation of these review processes generated in Congress is similar to the one that earlier had been generated by the operation of the Nixon administration's Quality of Life Review. Congress's dissatisfaction with the earlier process had caused it to insert language into the 1977 Clean Air Act Amendments that was intended to undercut the operation of White House oversight activities. Quieting this suspicion, and even then only partially, had required the efforts of two subsequent administrations.

In mid-1983, when the House Judiciary Committee held hearings on administration-backed omnibus regulatory reform legislation, attention focused not on how the oversight process could be best enacted into law but on the controversy generated by the activities of the Office of Management and Budget (OMB) under Executive Order 12291. The principal legislative vehicle, H.R. 2327, contained several provisions explicitly designed to limit OMB's influence over the rulemaking process. For example, one provision prohibited agencies from sending the president (and therefore presumably OMB) regulatory analyses before they were made public. Another removed from OMB the authority to issue guidelines for agency regulatory agendas. A third explicitly prohibited the director of OMB from "participat[ing] in any way in deciding what action, if any, [an] agency will take in any rulemaking proceeding."

The Reagan administration failed to realize that a crucial element in generating and sustaining the perception of a good-faith administration of social regulation is an open and relatively transparent process of regulatory decision making, including regulatory oversight as exercised by the White House. Although attention to process can be overdone, insufficient attention to process, both its actual operation and the perception of the operation by important groups in society, can be fatal to efforts to convince Congress and the courts to grant the increased discretion necessary to produce genuine and lasting regulatory relief. Indeed, a regulatory decision-making process that is (or merely appears to be) biased to favor any one interest group (especially the entities supposedly being regulated) invites Congress and the courts to further constrain existing administrative discretion and to engage increasingly in second-guessing individual administrative actions. Given the nature of the issues involved, the potential for arbitrary decisions and abuse of discretion is so inherently great in social regulation that faith in the fairness of the decision-making process is an absolute prerequisite to increased regulatory flexibility.

Thus, the regulatory relief program was damaged by the failure to recognize the significance of the subtle yet important distinction between economic and social regulation, by the decision to emphasize the program's short-term political payoff even at the expense of not laying the foundation for longer-term results, and by the failure to appreciate the importance of external perceptions of the fairness and openness of the oversight process.

These hardly could have seemed crucial issues to people who viewed themselves as embarked on a moral crusade to save the nation from the perils of excessive regulation and to pull the country back from the brink of the greatest economic catastrophe since the Great Depression. Yet they caused that crusade to backfire and, in the process, significantly set back the cause of regulatory reform.

The Regulatory Relief Program's Impact on the Future of Regulatory Reform

During the summer of 1983, the Reagan administration declared that legislative change, both substantive and procedural, was to become from that point on "the prime focus of the regulatory reform effort."[31] Indeed, the vice president cited the shift in focus from administrative to legislative actions as one reason for ending the Task Force on Regulatory Relief. The final task force report listed the administration's legislative priorities in the area of regulation. With the single exception of omnibus regulatory reform legislation, the examples fall into the category of economic deregulation—natural gas deregulation, additional deregulation of financial institutions, oil pipeline deregulation, and repeal of an obscure statute known as the Public Utility Holding Company Act.[32]

The absence from this list of any major initiatives in the area of social regulation was disappointing, especially to conservatives. In January 1983, the House Republican Research Committee's Task Force on Congressional and Regulatory Reform had urged such a legislative program directed at social regulation.[33] And in April 1983, Murray Weidenbaum, having by then returned to his academic post at Washington University, published a pamphlet titled "The Next Step in Regulatory Reform: Updating the Statutes."[34]

The administration's decision in August 1983 not to commit the president to an ambitious legislative agenda of social deregulation probably reflected less a disagreement over the merits of such a program than a political judgement that the time was not ripe for such an initiative. Whether the president and his advisers recognized the extent to which their own earlier decisions and actions had contributed to this inhospitable climate is unknown.

But suppose this assessment is incorrect. Or suppose that the administration's regulatory "midcourse correction" undertaken in 1983 were to succeed much faster than seems possible in making people forget the administration's earlier antiregulation stance. What proposals for social regulatory legislation might then emerge?

The fact is that no coherent set of principles upon which to base such legislation now exists. Recall the range of prescriptions for solving the problems associated with social regulation described in chapter 5. Most of the suggested solutions involved legislation of some form. But only in the case of the libertarian prescription was the nature of the necessary legislation clear—pass statutes abolishing many, if not all, of the social regulatory agencies and turn over either to the market or to other mechanisms for social control (such as the civil liability system) the functions these agencies have been attempting to perform. If it was not clear in late 1980, it certainly was clear by 1983 that there was no serious public support for this type of legislation.

A second kind of legislative change that was mentioned in chapter 5 was directed at what regulatory reformers see as conspicuous symbols of regulatory excess—the Delaney Amendment, the prohibition in the Clean Air Act and the OSHA statute against the consideration of costs, and the "fishable/swimmable" provisions of the Clean Water Act, among others.

But the characteristics that make these statutory provisions appear so ludicrous to regulatory reformers enhance their symbolic value to the supporters of regulation. Moreover, in practice these provisions do not really impede cost-effective regulation all that much. As OSHA has found, if agency heads really want to examine systematically the benefits and costs of regulations, they can find a way to do so.[35] Moreover, proponents of modifying agency statutes to *force* a cost-benefit balancing on agencies such as OSHA should recall the limited value that such a provision had in leading to better decisions in Corps of Engineers' water projects.

Attacking social regulation's major symbols does not appear to be either necessary or especially appealing politically. Perhaps one day when this nation has developed an effective system of social regulation, these symbols will lose their value and be permitted to disappear quietly.

If neither of these two legislative targets seems appealing, where should attention be directed? One important area may be legislation that would permit implementation of economists' proposals to employ markets and marketlike mechanisms instead of "command-and-control" regulation. This legislation might require a major restructuring of social regulatory statutes—not to eliminate their value as symbols but to permit their underlying goals to be more effectively accomplished.

The problem is that no one now knows what such legislation would look like. Economists have not yet met the challenge of specifying where and how their proposals could be implemented in sufficient detail to permit legislative changes to be drawn up. Neither have economists seriously addressed the ethical and political objections that have been raised to the use of marketlike mechanisms.[36] Finally, questions of how to handle the distributional effects of regulation have received scarcely any attention. Therefore, as of now, proposals for "marketable permits" and "emissions taxes" are interesting theoretical curiosities more than serious reform candidates.

If these proposals ever are to become more than curiosities, agencies such as EPA will have to mount a serious effort to operationalize the concepts. The necessary research will never be undertaken by the academic community. Instead, EPA and other agencies seeking to advance the use of marketlike systems of regulation will have to emulate the example of the Department of Transportation (DOT) under the Ford and Carter administrations. As described in chapter 4, DOT sponsored the research that addressed the nuts and bolts questions that made deregulation of airlines, railroads, and trucking eventually possible.

The only marketlike system of pollution control that is at all close to operational now is EPA's "bubble policy." Moving this policy from a concept to a program took years.[37] If the Supreme Court upholds the District of Columbia Court of Appeals' decision in *NRDC* v. *Gorsuch*, the ability to apply the bubble policy to nonattainment areas—and therefore to reap its greatest savings—will be blocked. Legislation may then be necessary, but the current political climate may make passage of such legislation extremely difficult. In this case, the implementation of an important regulatory reform concept will have been severely hampered by the regulatory relief approach taken by the Reagan administration.

Serious studies need to be undertaken to see how and where other marketlike mechanisms could be made operational and what the legal and political barriers to their implementation might be. Some studies were started under the Carter administration, but most were ended as a result of the Reagan budget cuts. Few if any follow-on efforts have been begun. Such "capital building" is sorely needed.

Legislation on the role that Congress should play in overseeing social regulation is also needed, but its proper form is uncertain as well. Until it was declared unconstitutional by the Supreme Court in *Immigration and Naturalization Service (INS)* v. *Chadha*,[38] Congress's favorite tool of regulatory control was the legislative veto. The reason for this is understandable. The veto permitted Congress to play both God and the traffic cop. In the former guise, Congress passed statutes declaring the nation's resolve to solve many social ills through regulation and granting broad delegations of authority to administrative agencies to permit them to carry out the statutory intent. In the latter guise, Congress presented itself as the nation's principal guardian against the excesses of overzealous regulatory bureaucrats.

In practice, however, the traffic cop was often "on the take." The legislative veto became a method by which narrow special interests sought to intimidate regulatory agencies into failing to regulate or to stop specific regulations that an agency insisted on issuing—all without forcing Congress to face up to the fact that the regulations generating the controversy usually had been developed in a good-faith attempt by the agency to comply with what Congress had demanded when acting in its "God" role. Regardless of its constitutionality, the legislative veto was bad public policy. The nation is well rid of it.

Congress does, however, have an important role to play in shaping U.S. regulatory priorities, and this role goes beyond merely passing enabling stat-utes, voting or withholding the funds with which to administer them, and holding occasional oversight hearings, often as much for the political drama they create as the substantive results they achieve. A number of techniques have been suggested that would put Congress into the process of regulatory priority setting—including the "regulatory budget" mentioned in chapter 5. None of these has as yet shown much promise. As Nordhaus and Litan argued persuasively in a recent book, the "regulatory budget" concept is fatally flawed.[39] Building on a suggestion of one of the authors of this report, Nordhaus and Litan have advanced the notion of a "legislated regulatory calendar" that would be much like a regulatory budget but without cost and benefit numbers.

We do not know what kind of process ultimately will prove to be de-sirable. But Congress's proper role in authorizing and overseeing regulation is a topic that demands considerable attention in developing any long-term agenda for regulatory reform.

Legislation addressing the statutory authorities of the social regulatory agencies, the role of Congress, and possibly even the operation of White House oversight is likely eventually to be needed. But in no case is the proper structure of this legislation now apparent. The legislative proposals that have been made are ones that either attack the perceived symbols of social regu-lation's excesses or institutionalize the current regulatory review process, possibly crippling it at the same time. They merely continue the long-running acrimonious debate over the legitimacy of social regulation. They do not significantly advance its reform.

Indeed, one of the great ironies of the Reagan regulatory relief program is that an administration committed to lifting the burden of social regulation was able to provide so little real, long-term relief. In the end, the carefully named ''regulatory relief'' campaign may have provided marginal reductions in some compliance costs and generated some short-run political capital. But it is likely to be seen by history as a costly, time-consuming, and ultimately unnecessary detour on the road to regulatory *reform*.

Notes

1. *America's New Beginning: A Program for Economic Recovery*, Executive Office of the White House, February 18, 1981.

2. David Stockman, "Avoiding a GOP Economic Dunkirk," mimeograph, December 1980, p. 15.

3. This term refers to regulation of such things as pollutant discharges, workplace health and safety levels, and levels of product safety. It is more fully defined at the end of this chapter.

4. Murray L. Weidenbaum, "Economic Policy for 1982," Address to the National Ocean Industries Association, March 8, 1982, pp. 1–2.

5. "Statement by the Vice President regarding actions taken by the President's Task Force on Regulatory Relief," March 25, 1981. The details of the savings are provided in "The First 100 Days of E.O. 12291, Federal Regulation," A Report to the Presidential Task Force on Regulatory Relief, prepared by the staff of the Office of Management and Budget, June 13, 1981, Table 3.

6. "President Reagan's Program For The U.S. Automobile Industry: Fact Sheet," April 6, 1981, p. 5.

7. Murray L. Weidenbaum, "Reforming Regulation: Moving From Talk to Action on the Reagan Economic Program," Address to the World Energy Conference, U.S. National Committee, April 16, 1981, p. 2.

8. Statement of James C. Miller III, in *Role of OMB in Regulation: Hearings Before the Subcommittee on Oversight and Investigations, Committee on Energy and Commerce, U.S. House of Representatives*, June 18, 1981, p. 48.

9. *Business Week*, January 24, 1983, p. 87. The question asked by the Harris pollsters was this: "Given the costs involved in cleaning up the environment, do you think that Congress should make the Clean Air and Clean Water acts stricter than they are now, keep them about the same, or ease them?" The results for the Clean Water Act were similar.

10. Tozzi's background and methods of operation during the Reagan administration were described in a story published after he had left the government. See John J. Fialka, "Reaganites Find Plans for Deregulation Stall after EPA Revelations," *Wall Street Journal*, June 6, 1983, p. 1.

11. Statement of Christopher DeMuth, administrator for information and regulatory affairs, Office of Management and Budget, before the Subcommittee on Administrative Law and Gov-

265

ernmental Relations of the House Committee on the Judiciary, on H.R. 2327, the Regulatory Reform Act of 1983, July 28, 1983, p. 1.

12. See Statement by Vice President Bush, Fact Sheet, and Reagan Administration Regulatory Achievements, August 11, 1983.

13. Murray L. Weidenbaum and Ronald J. Penover, *The Next Step in Regulatory Reform: Updating the Statutes* (St. Louis: Center for the Study of American Business, Washington University, 1983).

14. "Clean Water: Apocalypse Later," *Regulation*, July/August 1983, pp. 9–12, criticizes the failure of the administration's proposals to address these issues.

15. Murray L. Weidenbaum, "Regulatory Reform Under the Reagan Administration," in George C. Eads and Michael Fix, eds., *The Reagan Regulatory Strategy: An Assessment* (Washington, D.C.: The Urban Institute Press, in press).

16. See, for example, "Reagan at Mid-Term," *Regulatory Eye*, vol. 10, No. 11, January 1983, p. 1.

17. The General Accounting Office's assessments of the environmental enforcement efforts during the Carter administration include *Improvements Needed in Controlling Major Air Pollution Sources*, CED-78-165, January 2, 1979 (which contends that actual compliance by stationary sources with emissions standard or cleanup schedules is considerably less than the 92 percent claimed by EPA); *Better Enforcement of Car Emission Standards—A Way to Improve Air Quality*, CED-78-180, January 27, 1979 (which deplores the poor record of enforcement of auto emissions standards); *Air Quality: Do We Really Know What It Is?* CED-79-84, May 31, 1979 (which attacks EPA's air sampling and monitoring procedures); and *Costly Wastewater Plants Fail to Perform as Expected*, CED-81-9, November 14, 1980 (which reports that many wastewater treatment plants built with federal funds were not meeting performance standards and attacks EPA for not doing enough about the problem).

18. Presidential Task Force on Regulatory Relief, *Reagan Administration Regulatory Achievements*, August 21, 1983, p. 70: "These savings figures do not have to be readjusted downward on the grounds that benefits were eliminated along with the costs because the changes have not sacrificed any values protected by the relevant statutes."

19. On this point, see Bruce A. Ackermann and William T. Hassler, *Clean Coal/Dirty Air* (New Haven: Yale University Press, 1981), chapter 1.

NOTES TO CHAPTER 2

1. A. Freeman, "The Benefits of Air and Water Pollution Control: A Synthesis of Recent Evidence," report prepared for the U.S. Council on Environmental Quality (Washington, D.C., 1979), cited by Paul R. Portney in "The Macroeconomic Impacts of Federal Environmental Regulation," in Henry M. Peskin et al., eds., *Environmental Regulation and the U.S. Economy* (Baltimore: Johns Hopkins Press, 1982), p. 50.

2. On this point, see George Eads, "Chemicals As A Regulated Industry: Implications For Research and Product Development," in Christopher T. Hill, ed., *Federal Regulation and Chemical Innovation* (Washington, D.C.: American Chemical Society, 1979), pp. 1–19. See also Roger G. Noll and Bruce M. Owen, *The Political Economy of Deregulation* (Washington, D.C.: The American Enterprise Institute, 1982), chapter 2.

3. *Economic Report of the President* (Washington, D.C.: Government Printing Office, 1975), p. 159.

4. "White House Conference on Domestic Affairs and Inflation,: The President's Remarks at the Conference in Concord, New Hampshire," April 18, 1975, in *Weekly Compilation of Presidential Documents*, Monday, April 25, 1975, vol. 11, no. 17, p. 104. The President went on to say: "Even if the real costs are only a fraction of this amount, this is an intolerable burden on our pocketbooks."

5. Arnold C. Harberger, "Monopoly and Resource Allocation," *American Economic Review*, vol. 44 (May 1954), pp. 77–87.

6. Frederick M. Scherer, *Industrial Market Structure and Economic Performance* (Chicago: Rand McNally, 1970), p. 404.

7. The estimate appears at the end of a chapter titled "Government Regulation." The chapter is principally concerned with issues of economic regulation and antitrust policy; social regulation is mentioned only in the first section and there only tangentially.

8. Harvey Leibenstein, "Allocative Efficiency versus X-efficiency," *American Economic Review*, vol. 56 (June 1966), pp. 392–415.

9. That they might is suggested, among other places, in Harvey Arerch and L.L. Johnson, "Behavior of the Firm under Regulatory Constraint," *American Economic Review*, December 1962, pp. 1052–1069.

10. The monopolist might then be expected to reestimate his optimal price on the basis of the higher cost level (OB rather than OA). If true, the monopolist would charge a price higher than OB and produce an output less than OD. This result, however, would not be in the monopolist's interest since the total volume of profits (including those described as higher cost) would be thereby reduced.

11. Marvin H. Kosters, "Counting the Costs," *Regulation*, July/August 1979, pp. 17–25.

12. On this issue, see B. Peter Pashigian, *The Political Economy of the Clean Air Act: Regional Self-Interest in Environmental Legislation* (St. Louis: Center for the Study of American Business, Washington University, October 1982); Robert W. Crandall, *Controlling Industrial Pollution: The Economics and Politics of Clean Air* (Washington, D.C.: The Brookings Institution, 1983), especially chapter 7, and Robert A. Leone, ed., *Environmental Controls: The Impact on Industry* (Lexington: Heath Lexington Books, 1976), especially chapter 1.

13. Kosters, p. 23, emphasis in the original.

14. Ibid., p. 24.

15. Portney, "The Macroeconomic Impacts of Federal Environmental Regulation," in Peskin et al., *Environmental Regulation and the U.S. Economy*, pp. 52–54.

16. The OMB paper and GAO's critique of it are contained in "An Economic Evaluation of the OMB Paper on 'The Costs of Regulation and Restrictive Practices,' " Staff paper prepared for the Subcommittee on Oversight and Investigations of the Committee on Interstate and Foreign Commerce, House of Representatives, by the Office of Economic Analysis of the Office of Program Analysis, U.S. GAO, September 1975. The OMB paper directly addresses the question of *why* the estimate presented there differed so much from the estimate in the 1975 CEA report. OMB notes the distinction between deadweight losses, which it states are "of interest to economists," from the sort of numbers it presents (which, it claims, are a better measure of the burden on "consumers"). OMB then cites Leibenstein and Scherer as authorities for this "broader" concept of "regulatory burden." Ibid., pp. 23–24. As we have already seen, this argument carries weight *only* when dealing with private monopoly or monopoly that would not exist without the support of government. It does not apply to "social regulation."

17. Robert DeFina, *Public and Private Expenditures For Federal Regulation of Business*, Working Paper No. 27, Center for the Study of American Business, Washington University, St. Louis, November 1977 (mimeo).

18. Murray L. Weidenbaum and Robert DeFina, *The Cost of Federal Regulation of Economic Activity* (Washington, D.C.: The American Enterprise Institute, May 1978). Reprint no. 88.

19. Readers comparing table 1 of Weidenbaum and DeFina with a similar table in Weidenbaum's later article in *Regulation* will notice discrepancies in the industry-specific and paperwork numbers. As far as we have been able to determine, the estimates in *Regulation* are in error, since the figures in table 1 match the backup material for the estimates given in Weidenbaum and DeFina.

20. Murray Weidenbaum, "On Estimating Regulatory Costs," *Regulation*, May/June 1978, p. 17.

21. Op. cit., p. 17.

22. Probably the most ascerbic of the attacks was written by Mark Green and Michael Waldman, two of Ralph Nader's assistants. Green and Waldman's study, "Business' War on

the Law,'' attacked Weidenbaum's estimates, Weidenbaum himself personally, and Weidenbaum's Center for the Study of American Business.

23. Weidenbaum, op. cit., p. 17.

24. See, for example, the various issues of the *General Motors Public Interest Report.*

25. Portney, "The Macroeconomic Impacts of Federal Environmental Regulation," in Peskin et al., *Environmental Regulation and the U.S. Economy.*

26. A substantial revision of the BEA figures published in the June 1981 *Survey of Current Business* brought them into closer agreement with the McGraw-Hill numbers. Total estimated expenditures by manufacturing increased to $4.44 billion; durables, to $1.74 billion; nondurables, to $2.70 billion; and nonmanufacturing, to $3.14 billion. *Survey of Current Business,* June 1981, p. 20.

27. Portney, p. 37.

28. Weidenbaum and DeFina, p. 3.

29. Edward F. Denison. *Accounting for Slower Economic Growth* (Washington, D.C.: The Brookings Institution, 1979).

30. Ibid., p. 69.

31. Ibid., table 5-4, p. 71.

32. Gary L. Rutledge and Susan L. Trevathan, "Pollution Abatement and Control Expenditures, 1972-79," *Survey of Current Business,* March 1981, p. 22.

33. Robert H. Haveman and Gregory B. Christainsen, "Environmental Regulations and Productivity Growth," in Peskin et al., *Environmental Regulation and the U.S. Economy.*

34. William D. Nordhaus, "Policy Responses to the Productivity Slowdown," in *The Decline in Productivity Growth,* Proceedings of a Conference Sponsored by the Federal Reserve Bank of Boston, June 1980.

35. Denison, *Accounting for Slower Economic Growth,* chapter 9.

36. Ibid., p. 145.

37. Ibid., p. 129.

38. Alfred D. Chandler, *Strategy and Structure* (Cambridge: MIT Press, 1962), and Chandler, *The Visible Hand: The Managerial Revolution in American Business* (Cambridge: Harvard University Press, 1977).

39. Portney, pp. 39–46.

40. *The State of the Environment 1982: A Report From the Conservation Foundation* (Washington, D.C.: The Conservation Foundation, 1982), p. 35.

41. Kosters, op. cit., p. 23.

42. The rate on ten-year government bonds in December 1980 was 12.84 percent, up from 10.39 percent a year earlier. *Economic Report of the President, January 1981* (Washington, D.C.: GPO, 1981), p. 309, table B-65.

43. For example, between 1960 and 1964, when the increase in the GNP deflator (a broad-based measure of prices) averaged about 1.5 percent per year, 10-year government bonds yielded approximately 4 percent. For 1980, the GNP deflator increased by 9.0 percent. *Economic Report of the President, January 1981,* p. 239, table B-5, and p. 308, table B-65.

44. *Economic Report of the President, January 1981,* p. 49.

45. *Economic Report of the President, February 1982,* p. 59.

NOTES TO CHAPTER 3

1. For a sharp exchange of views on this point, see "Setting Regulations: A Question of Propriety," *Environmental Science and Technology,* May 1979, pp. 514–517. This article reports on hearings held in early 1979 by Senator Muskie.

2. This section draws heavily on an unpublished study by Katherine L. Bernick, "Executive Branch Coordination: The Quality of Life Review" (draft, September 30, 1977), prepared for the American Bar Association's Commission on Law and the Economy. This material is used with the permission of the author.

3. Ibid., Bernick, p. 4. In the fiscal 1972 budget, submitted in January 1971, budget authority for wastewater treatment works constructions grant is shown to rise from $800 million in 1970 to $8 billion in 1972 outlays are shown to rise from $175 million to $1 billion over the same period. *Budget of the United States Government Appendix, Fiscal 1972* (Washington, D.C.: Government Printing Office, 1971), p. 205.

4. Bernick, p. 5.

5. John D. Ehrlichman, Domestic Council Study Memorandum No. 15, June 16, 1971, as cited in ibid.

6. A *significant* rule was defined as any rule that would have a significant impact on the policies, programs, and procedures of other agencies; *or* impose significant costs on, or negative benefits to, nonfederal sectors; *or* increase the demand for federal funds for programs of federal agencies beyond the funding levels in the most recent budget requests submitted to the Congress. Schultz memo quoted in ibid., p. 11.

7. Ibid., p. 10.

8. Ibid., p. 18.

9. In a personal communication to the authors, Richard N.L. Andrews, Director of the Institute of Environmental Studies at the University of North Carolina, who was at OMB during the early 1970s, has written:

> . . . at about the same time Nixon set up the EPA and NOAA [National Oceanic and Atmospheric Administration] with great public fanfare, he more quietly established the so-called National Industrial Pollution Council in the Commerce Department, and it was this group that attracted the hostility toward the quality of life review process. [The Council] was made up exclusively of industrial leaders, who met in secret, refused access to both reporters and environmental groups, and was quite clearly an illegal inside track for business leaders to oppose regulations they did not like. It was not just that OMB let the Commerce Department review EPA's regulatory proposals, but that the industrial community itself was getting a direct and illegitimate bite at them before they were even announced as proposals so that other affected groups and individuals could comment.

Letter from Richard N.L. Andrews to George C. Eads, January 18, 1984, p. 2.

10. For an account of one such review, see John Quarles, *Cleaning Up America* (Boston, Mass.: Houghton Mifflin, 1976), chapter 7, "EPA and the White House." The review described here includes EPA's decision to remove lead from gasoline, an issue that the Reagan White House also became involved in. Ironically, the Department of Commerce representative in this review was Ray Peck, later to be Reagan's NHTSA administrator (see p. 125). Jim Tozzi also figures prominently in Quarles's account (pp. 138–39).

11. Quoted in ibid., p. 14.

12. Quarles, pp. 117–119.

13. For sharply contrasting views of some of the participants in the review process, ibid., pp. 18–28.

14. One concrete manifestation of this antagonism was a requirement inserted into the Clean Air Act Amendments of 1977—legislation that was passed long after the Quality of Life Review ceased to operate actively—that EPA place into the public rule-making record "all drafts of proposed rules submitted by the Administration to the Office of Management and Budget for any interagency review process prior to proposing such rule, all documents accompanying such drafts, and all written comments thereto by other agencies and all written responses to such written comments by the Administrator." A similar requirement was imposed for all final EPA rules. Title 42 U.S.C.A. 7907(d)(4)(B)(ii).

15. Executive Order 11801, November 27, 1974. The procedures developed by OMB were spelled out in OMB Circular A-107.

16. The Economic Stabilization Act of 1970, which gave the president authority to control wages and prices and which President Nixon had used in August 1971 to establish his wage and price control program, expired on April 30, 1974, and President Ford firmly resisted being given any such authority.

17. Public Law 93-387, Sec. 3(a)(7).

18. *A Review of the Regulatory Interventions of the Council on Wage and Price Stability, 1974–1980*, January 1981, appendix A.

19. Roger B. Porter, *Presidential Decision Making: The Economic Policy Board* (Cambridge: Cambridge University Press, 1980), pp. 94–95.

20. *The Challenge of Regulatory Reform: A Report to the President from the Domestic Council Review Group on Regulatory Reform*, January 1977, pp. 25 and 37.

21. Public Law 93-387, Sec. 3(a)(8).

22. The Brookings Institution published the lectures in a revised form under the title *The Public Use of Private Interest* (Washington, D.C.: The Brookings Institution, 1977); The American Enterprise Institute featured them prominently in the first issue of its new journal, *Regulation*; and an edited version also appeared in *Harper's Magazine*.

23. Bernick, p. 15.

24. The description that follows is taken from Charles Schultze's memo of August 1, 1977.

25. Memorandum from Douglas Costle to Charles Schultze, August 24, 1977.

26. Memorandum from Douglas Costle to Jimmy Carter, October 6, 1977.

27. Memorandum for the President from Charles Schultze, October 7, 1977. The president's approval and request for review after six months is indicated on the copy returned to Schultze and circulated to certain interested individuals.

28. Memorandum for the EPG Steering Committee from the Department of the Treasury, January 11, 1978.

29. Memorandum from Ray Marshall to President Carter, May 24, 1978.

30. *Washington Post*, June 7, 1978, p. 1.

31. Ibid., June 8, 1978, p. A-9.

32. Ibid., June 20, 1979, p. A-4.

33. Phillip Shabecoff, "Regulation by the U.S.: Its Costs vs. Its Benefits," *New York Times*, June 14, 1978, p. D-8.

34. "When Inflation and Safety Collide," *New York Times*, June 16, 1978, p. 26.

35. Christopher C. DeMuth, "The White House Review Programs," *Regulation*, January/February 1980, p. 20.

36. Quoted in ibid.

37. Ibid., pp. 20–21.

38. These suggestions are summarized in a memo from CEA staff member Robert Litan to RARG participants dated July 18, 1978.

39. See exchange of letters between Joan Davenport, assistant secretary of the interior, and William Nordhaus, member, President's Council of Economic Advisers, November 22, 1978, and December 6, 1978. See also Memorandum for Honorable Cecil D. Andrus, secretary of the interior, from Larry A. Hammond, acting assistant attorney general, Office of Legal Counsel, re: Consultation with Council of Economic Advisers Concerning Rulemaking under Surface Mining and Control Act, dated January 17, 1979.

40. *Natural Resources Defense Council et al.* v. *Charles Schultze, Chairman, Council of Economic Advisers et al.*, United States District Court for the District of Columbia, Civil Action No. 79-153, dismissed, January 16, 1979.

41. "Setting Regulations: A Question of Propriety," *Environmental Science and Technology*, May 1979, pp. 514–517.

42. Letter from Charles L. Schultze to Edmund S. Muskie, April 13, 1979, plus attachments. One of these attachments is a copy of the Justice Department memo to Secretary Andrus referred to earlier.

43. As noted earlier, Kahn wore two hats—as chairman of the Council on Wage and Price Stability and as Special Adviser to the President for Inflation. He also had two staffs—the CWPS staff and the staff that aided him in his White House position. Only the latter staff were involved in postcomment activities.

44. *Sierra Club* v. *Costle*, No. 79-1565, D.C. Court of Appeals, April 29, 1981.

45. Ibid., pp. 214–215 (footnote omitted).

46. Ibid., pp. 217–220 (footnotes omitted, emphasis in the original).

47. *American Petroleum Institute* v. *Costle*, 16 ERC 1435, *decided* September 3, 1981.
48. DeMuth, "The White House Review Programs," p. 23.
49. Timothy B. Clark, "Substance Over Process," *National Journal*, January 3, 1981, p. 28.
50. Information Collection Budget of the United States Government, Fiscal Year 1981.

NOTES TO CHAPTER 4

1. Christopher C. DeMuth, "The White House Review Programs," *Regulation*, January/February 1980, p. 23.
2. *Civil Aeronautics Board Practices and Procedures*, Report of the Subcommittee on Administrative Practices and Procedures, Senate Committee on the Judiciary, 1975. See especially Section III, pp. 77–176, for a description of the actions of Browne and Timm.
3. *Annual Report of the President's Council of Economic Advisers*, February 1975, p. 150.
4. Summaries of these studies dealing with the airline industry and several other industries were published by the American Enterprise Institute during 1977 under the general series title "Ford Administration Papers on Regulatory Reform." They are worth scholarly examination.
5. These moves by the CAB under Kahn are described in John R. Meyer et al., *Airline Deregulation: The Early Experience* (Boston: Auburn House, 1981), pp. 49–51.
6. For a chronology of regulatory liberalizations affecting financial institutions, see *Economic Report of the President*, January 1981, pp. 107–115.
7. The first two pieces of legislation substantially broadened EPA's responsibilities; the last gave FDA jurisdiction over devices "intended to support or sustain human life or to prevent the impairment of human health."
8. This account is taken from Peter Barton Hutt, "Investigations and Reports Respecting FDA Regulation of New Drugs, Parts I and II," *Clinical Pharmacology and Therapeutics*, vol. 33 (1983), pp. 537–548 and 674–687.
9. The best recent summary of this evidence is to be found in Henry G. Grabowski, and John M. Vernon, *The Regulation of Pharmaceuticals: Balancing the Benefits and Risks* (Washington, D.C.: The American Enterprise Institute, 1983).
10. Hutt, "Investigations and Reports Respecting FDA Regulation of New Drugs (Part II)," p. 677.
11. However, in a chapter of a book titled *Instead of Regulation*, David Weiner has proposed just that, suggesting instead relying upon the product liability system or a "no fault" system of post injury compensation modeled after the workman's compensation program. See David Weiner, "Safe—and Available—Drugs," in Robert W. Poole, *Instead of Regulation* (Lexington, Mass.: D.C. Heath, 1982), pp. 239–283.
12. American Enterprise Institute, *Regulation and Regulatory Reform: A Survey of Proposals of the 95th Congress* (Washington, D.C.: AEI, 1978), pp. 52–55.
13. The last item eventually became the Regulatory Flexibility Act.
14. Abraham Ribicoff, "For Effectiveness and Efficiency: S. 262," *Regulation*, May/June 1979, p. 17. This was only one of seven concerns listed in the article; the others were lack of opportunity for public participation, the close ties often existing between the regulated and those subject to regulation, wasteful paperwork burden, overlapping and duplication of responsibilities, undue delay, and economic problems created by restrictions on entry and competition.
15. Ibid.
16. Ibid., p. 18. A close examination of the text of S. 262 does not reveal specific language to this effect, however.
17. Under existing administrative law, reviewing courts are required to grant a "presumption of validity" to actions of regulatory agencies. Thus they consider *only* whether the proper administrative procedures were followed and whether the action had a rational basis, not the inherent wisdom of the action. The Bumpers Amendment would have removed this presumption of validity, putting courts into the business of reviewing both the procedure and the substance

of agency decisions. On the undesirability of this change, see David R. Woodward and Ronald M. Levin, "In Defense of Deference: Judicial Review of Agency Action," *Administrative Law Review*, vol. 31 (1979), p. 329.

18. For an account of these various controversies and analyses of the competing omnibus bills in both the House and the Senate during 1979 and 1980, see the American Enterprise Institute's publications *Major Regulatory Initiatives During 1979* (Washington, D.C.: AEI, 1980), pp. 38–39, and *Major Regulatory Initiatives During 1980* (Washington, D.C.: AEI, 1981), pp. 60–62.

Notes to Chapter 5

1. Environmental Protection Agency, "The Cost of Clean Air and Water," Report to Congress, August 1979, p. viii. These figures are in 1977 dollars. The data are what EPA terms "annual costs." Investment requirements are reported at $141 billion (p. vii).

2. Eugene Bardach and Robert A. Kagan, *Going by the Book: The Problem of Regulatory Unreasonableness* (Philadelphia: Temple University Press, 1982).

3. Eugene Bardach and Robert Kagan, *Social Regulation: Strategies for Reform* (San Francisco: Institute for Contemporary Studies, 1982), pp. 12–14.

4. A summary of several of these studies, including citations, is contained in Lester B. Lave, *The Strategy of Social Regulation* (Washington, D.C.: The Brookings Institution, 1981), pp. 101–102.

5. Sam Peltzman, *Regulation of Automobile Safety* (Washington, D.C.: The American Enterprise Institute, 1975).

6. The best recent survey of information on this issue is to be found in Robert W. Crandall, *Controlling Industrial Pollution: The Economics and Politics of Clean Air* (Washington, D.C.: The Brookings Institution, 1983), chapter 2, "The Effectiveness of Clean Air Policy."

7. Lester Lave and Gilbert Omenn, *Clearing the Air: Reforming the Clean Air Act* (Washington, D.C.: The Brookings Institution, 1981), p. 21.

8. See *Department of Transportation and Related Industries Appropriations for 1977*, Hearings Before a Subcommittee of the Committee on Appropriations, 94th Cong., 2nd Sess., March 1, 1976, Part 2, pp. 369–382.

9. See studies cited in To Breathe Clean Air: Report of the National Commission on Air Quality (Washington, D.C.: Government Printing Office, 1981), pp. 261–264. See also *Environmental Quality: Tenth Annual Report of the Council on Environmental Quality* (Washington, D.C.: Government Printing Office, 1979) p. 655.

10. See M.A. Peterson and G.L. Priest, *The Civil Jury: Trends in Trials and Verdicts, Cook County, Illinois, 1960–1979* (Santa Monica, CA: The Rand Corporation, Institute for Civil Justice, 1982).

11. National Commission on Product Safety, *Final Report* (Washington, D.C.: Government Printing Office, 1970), p. 7.

12. Lester B. Lave, *The Strategy of Social Regulation* (Washington, D.C.: The Brookings Institution, 1981), pp. 2–3.

13. Charles L. Schultze, *The Public Use of Private Interest* (Washington, D.C.: The Brookings Institution, 1977), p. 20.

14. *Economic Report of the President* (Washington, D.C.: Government Printing Office, February 1982), p. 42.

15. Charles Wolf, "A Theory of Non-Market Failure," *Journal of Law and Economics*, April 1979, p. 117.

16. For a description of these various incentives and their interactions, see George Eads and Peter Reuter, *Designing Safer Products: Corporate Responses to Product Liability and Product Safety Regulation* (Santa Monica, CA: The Rand Corporation, Institute for Civil Justice, 1984), especially chapters 2 and 6.

17. The nature of these incentives, as well as their quantitative significance, is explored in Richard B. Victor, *Workers' Compensation and Workplace Safety* (Santa Monica, CA: The Rand Corporation, Institute for Civil Justice, 1982).

18. Robert W. Poole, Jr., *Instead of Regulation* (Lexington, Mass: D.C. Heath, 1983), pp. ix–x.

19. The argument concerning the need for and inherent dangers in active, continuing presidential involvement in rule making is foreshadowed in Susan Tolchin, "Presidential Power and the Politics of RARG," *Regulation*, July/August 1979, pp. 44–49.

20. Lloyd N. Cutler and David R. Johnson, "Regulation and the Political Process," *Yale Law Journal*, vol. 84 (1975) 1395 (at 1414).

21. In 1983, in the case of *Immigration and Naturalization Service* v. *Chadha*, the Supreme Court declared the legislative veto to be unconstitutional. 51 U.S.L.W. 4907 (U.S. June 23, 1983).

22. Christopher DeMuth, "The White House Review Programs," *Regulation*, January/February 1980, pp. 13–26.

23. DeMuth's second article is an analysis of the benefits and costs, political and otherwise, of the regulatory budget. DeMuth, "The Regulatory Budget," *Regulation*, March/April 1980, pp. 29–46.

24. DeMuth, "The White House Review Programs," p. 26.

25. Robert M. Solow, "The Economist's Approach to Pollution and Control," *Science*, August 6, 1971, p. 498.

26. Ibid., p. 499.

27. The most comprehensive statement of this view, together with survey data on attitudes of congressional staff toward pollution charges, is contained in Steven Kelman, *What Price Incentives?* (Boston: Auburn House, 1981).

28. A good description of the history of the bubble policy and the problems in its implementation is contained in Michael H. Levin, "Getting There: Implementing the 'Bubble' Policy," in Eugene Bardach and Robert Kagan, eds., *Social Regulation: Strategies for Reform* (San Francisco: The Institute for Contemporary Studies, 1982), pp. 59–92. Levin argues that standard proposals for market-based approaches to controlling pollution attracted little or no support because economists had ignored the real world constraints within which pollution programs operate. This point is also made in Timothy H. Quinn, *A More General Theory of Environmental Policy with an Application to the Evolution of Groundwater Law in California* (unpublished Ph.D. dissertation, UCLA, 1983, especially chapters 3 and 4).

29. Adele Palmer et al., *Economic Implications of Regulating Chlorofluorocarbon Emissions from Nonaerosol Applications* (Santa Monica, CA: The Rand Corporation, 1980).

30. For a summary of some of the lessons learned from this study, see Robert W. Hahn and Roger G. Noll, "Barriers to Implementing Tradeable Air Pollution Permits: Problems of Regulatory Interactions," *Yale Journal of Regulation*, vol. 1, no. 1, 1983, pp. 63–91. This article contains citations to more extensive reports on the result of the California Air Resources Board Study.

NOTES TO CHAPTER 6

1. "Deregulation HQ," interview with Murray L. Weidenbaum and James C. Miller III, *Regulation*, March/April 1981, p. 21.

2. Major rules were defined as including any likely to result in (1) an annual effect on the economy of $100 million or more; (2) a major increase in costs or prices for consumers, individual industries, geographic regions, or federal, state, or local agencies; or (3) significant adverse effects on competition, employment, investment, productivity, innovation, or the ability of U.S.-based enterprises to compete with foreign-based enterprises in domestic or export markets. Categories (1) and (2) closely track the definition of major rules employed by the Carter administration; Category (3) was new to Executive Order 12291.

3. Just how the procedures prescribed by the executive order were to be made to square with the requirements of the Clean Air Act Amendments of 1977 specifying that EPA publish proposed rules *before* sending them to OMB was never addressed.

4. Executive Order 12291, Section (6)(a)(6).

5. M. Rosenberg, *Presidential Control of Agency Rulemaking: An Analysis of Constitutional Issues Which May Be Raised by Executive Order 12291*, Committee Print. 97-0, Committee on Energy and Commerce, U.S. House of Representatives, 1981, pp. 38 and 42. This report has subsequently appeared in a substantially revised form as a law review article.

6. Michael Sohn and Robert Litan, "Regulatory Oversight Wins in Court," *Regulation*, July/August 1981, pp. 17–24.

7. Ibid., p. 22.

8. Ibid.

9. Memo for Heads of Executive Departments and Agencies from David A. Stockman, Director, OMB, *re* Certain Communications Pursuant to Executive Order 12291, "Federal Regulation," June 13, 1981, p. 1.

10. See, for example, K.C. Davis, "Presidential Control of Rulemaking," *Tulane Law Review*, vol. 56, p. 856. See also Testimony of Douglas Parker, Director, Institute for Public Representation, Georgetown Law Center, in *The Role of OMB in Regulation*. Subcommittee on Oversight and Investigations of the Committee on Energy and Commerce, U.S. House of Representatives, 97th Cong., 1st Sess., June 18, 1981, pp. 8–30.

11. *Sierra Club*, V. Castle, pp. 207–208. (Emphasis in the original.)

12. David Stockman, "Avoiding a GOP Economic Dunkirk," December 1980 (mimeograph), p. 21.

13. As late as October 1983, Rep. Albert Gore, Jr. (D-Tenn.), was reported to state, "I think what they [officials at OMB] are doing is against the law." *Washington Post*, October 9, 1983, p. A-8.

14. Statement of Christopher DeMuth, Administrator for Information and Regulatory Affairs, Office of Management and Budget, before the Subcommittee on Administrative Law and Governmental Relations of the Committee on the Judiciary, U.S. House of Representatives, on H.R. 2327, The Regulatory Reform Act of 1983, July 28, 1983, p. 17.

15. "Statement by the Vice President Regarding Actions Taken by the President's Task Force on Regulatory Relief," March 25, 1981, and "Fact Sheet, President Reagan's Program for the U.S. Automobile Industry," April 6, 1981.

16. "Remarks of Vice President Bush at the Presidential Task Force on Regulatory Relief Briefing, Washington, D.C., August 12, 1981," p. 1.

17. "Statement of Vice President George Bush," February 4, 1982, and "Background Information on Paperwork and Regulatory Relief for Small Business," February 4, 1982.

18. Caroline E. Mayer, "Regulatory Cuts Save Billions, Officials Say," *Washington Post*, August 5, 1982, p. C-1. It may be that the value of such lists had by this time faded. Certainly the August list attracted far less favorable attention than had the earlier ones. (Recall the adverse comments of *The Regulatory Eye* quoted in chapter 1.)

19. General Accounting Office, *Improved Quality, Adequate Resources, and Consistent Oversight Needed If Regulatory Analysis Is to Help Control Costs of Regulations* (Washington, D.C.: Government Printing Office, November 2, 1982). Referred to hereafter as GAO Report.

20. Ibid., p. 50.

21. Ibid.

22. Ibid., pp. 36–37.

23. Ibid., pp. 51–52.

24. Ibid., p. 53.

25. Ibid., pp. 53–54.

26. Compare, for example, General Motors Corporation, *1980 Public Interest Report*, April 7, 1980, pp. 113–116, with Joan Claybrook (Carter's NHTSA Administrator), "Crying Wolf," *Regulation*, November/December 1978, pp. 14–16.

27. Kenneth W. Clarkson, Charles W. Kadlec, and Arthur B. Laffer, "Regulating Chrysler Out of Business?" *Regulation*, September/October 1979, pp. 44–49.

28. A version of this was later published by the Regulatory Council under the title *The Automobile Calendar: Recent and Pending Federal Activities Affecting Motor Vehicles* (Washington, D.C.: January, 1981).

29. The White House, "Automotive Policy, Talking Points," July 8, 1980, p. 1.

30. Fact Sheet, p. 3.

31. Ibid., pp. 3–4.

32. The auto industry asserts that the two-year delay that the EPA has granted will permit it to develop new paint formulas and processes that may limit pollution at less cost. The industry does not appear to have addressed the relative cost-effectiveness issue, nor would one expect it to. See Michael Wines, "Reagan Plan to Relieve Auto Industry of Regulatory Burden Gets Mixed Grades," *National Journal*, July 23, 1983, p. 1534.

33. President's Task Force on Regulatory Relief, "Reagan Administration Regulatory Achievements," August 11, 1983, pp. 56–58.

34. GAO Report, p. 53.

35. "OSHA's Unexpected Bite Has OMB Bristling," *Business Week*, March 21, 1983, p. 100-D. A subsequent article in the *Washington Post* suggested that the *Business Week* story was a "plant" designed to make Auchter appear "tougher" than EPA Administrator Burford, who at that time was at the height of her troubles.

36. Seth S. King, "Fight Grows Over Cotton Dust Rules," *New York Times*, May 11, 1983, p. B-6.

37. Joann S. Lublin, "OSHA Upholds Exposure Rules for Cotton Dust," *Wall Street Journal*, May 20, 1983, p. 4.

38. "OMB Seeks Change in EPA Lead-Gas Rule," *Washington Post*, August 16, 1982.

39. Ibid.

40. Mary Thornton and Martin Schram, "U.S. Holds the Ketchup in Schools," *Washington Post*, September 28, 1981, p. A-1.

41. Ibid.

42. William Warfield Ross, "New Rules for 'Major' Rule-Making: Living with Executive Order 12291," *National Law Journal*, April 27, 1981, p. 19.

43. Felicity Barringer, "Feud Tests OMB As Regulatory Watchdog," *Washington Post*, November 26, 1982, p. A-15.

NOTES TO CHAPTER 7

1. "Deregulation HQ," *Regulation*, March/April 1981, p. 23. The first quotation is from Weidenbaum; the second, which closely follows it in the interview, is from Miller. The emphasis in Miller's quotation is in the original.

2. Ibid., p. 22.

3. See *Appointments to the Regulatory Agencies*, Senate Commerce Committee, 97th Cong., 2d Session, April 1976, Committee Print; and G. C. MacKenzie, *The Politics of Presidential Appointments* (New York: The Free Press, 1981).

4. G. C. MacKenzie, quoted in "Team Players," *National Journal*, February 19, 1983, p. 385.

5. See Lawrence Lynn, *Managing the Public's Business* (New York: Basic Books, 1981), pp. 172–181.

6. Richard Nathan, *The Plot That Failed: Nixon and the Administrative Presidency* (New York: John Wiley & Sons, Inc., 1975), pp. 39–40, cited in Lynn, *Managing the Public's Business*, p. 54.

7. See *Appointments to the Regulatory Agencies*, p. 379.

8. The Surface Mining Control and Reclamation Act of 1977, 30 USC 1211. We should note that the administration's choice to head the Office of Surface Mining (OSM) was James

Harris, a former Indiana state senator who had chaired the state legislature's Standing Committee on Natural Resources, Environment, and Agriculture. Harris's legislative record earned him a 100 percent rating by the Indiana Izaak Walton League. Critics claim that he has not been a particularly forceful presence at OSM, however, because Secretary Watt initiated the major policy directives.

9. Scalia contrasts this group with what he characterizes as a "much older part of the Republican constituency" consisting of the "business interests large and small"—people who have given no systematic thought to regulation, but who know that in the past few years things have gotten out of hand. Antonin Scalia, "Regulation—The First Year," a symposium reported in *Regulation*, January/February 1982.

10. "Reagan at Mid-Term," *The Regulatory Eye*, November 1982, p. 2.

11. "Lavelle on Lavelle," *Fortune*, March 21, 1983, p. 44.

12. L. Mosher, "Distrust of Gorsuch May Stymie EPA Attempt to Integrate Pollution Laws," *National Journal*, February 12, 1983, p. 322.

13. See "Ruckelshaus' First Mark on EPA—Another $165.5 Million for Its Budget," *National Journal*, June 25, 1983, p. 1344.

14. Interview with James Cherry, assistant director for state affairs, Office of Intergovernmental Liaison, Environmental Protection Agency, December 28, 1982.

15. Moreover, for the FY 1980–1984 period, the Civil Rights Division of the Department of Justice would enjoy a 16 percent real increase in its budget, while the budget of the Office of Fair Housing and Equal Opportunity in the Department of Housing and Urban Development would increase by 33 percent.

16. "Ruckelshaus' First Mark on EPA," p. 1345.

17. The National Wildlife Federation, *Shredding the Environmental Safety Net: The Full Story Behind the EPA Budget Cuts* (Washington, D.C.: National Wildlife Foundation, February 1982).

18. Lynn, *Managing the Public's Business*, p. 85.

19. *Congressional Record*, September 21, 1981, S. 10165.

20. Letter from Rep. John Dingell, chairman of the Committee on Energy and Commerce, U.S. House of Representatives, to Rep. Neal Smith, chairman, Subcommittee on Commerce, Justice, State, and Judiciary, Committee on Appropriations, February 8, 1983.

21. Among OSM's responsibilities under the 1977 act (P.L. 95-87) are to protect streams from sedimentation and pollution, to protect downstream users of water from loss of water quality, to protect surface owners from damage caused by subsidence from underground mines, to ensure the stability of waste piles and embankments, to protect groundwater from contamination by toxic pollutants released from mining overburden, and to ensure that land is returned to its premining use and condition when mining operations are complete. See testimony of Robert Yuhnke before the Subcommittee on Civil Service, House Committee on Post Office and Civil Service, 97th Cong., 1st Sess., June 15, 1981, p. 106.

22. *Mandate for Leadership*, C. Heatherly, ed. (Washington, D.C.: The Heritage Foundation, 1981), p. 346.

23. Letter to James G. Watt, Secretary of the Interior, from Rep. Patricia Schroeder, Chair, Subcommittee on Post Office and Civil Service, U.S. House of Representatives, October 28, 1982.

24. Ibid.

25. Telephone conversation with Carolyn Johnson, Natural Resources Defense Council, March 5, 1983.

26. Statement of Joseph T. O'Connor, submitted to the House Interior and Insular Affairs Committee, U.S. House of Representatives, undated.

27. Testimony of David Shelton, director, Colorado Mine Land Reclamation Division; Bruce Hayden, administrator, Reclamation Division of Montana Department of State Lands; and Walter C. Ackerman, administrator, Land Quality Division, Wyoming Department of Environmental Quality, before the Subcommittee on Civil Service of the House Committee on Post

Office and Civil Service, U.S. House of Representatives, 97th Cong., 1st Sess., June 15, 1981, pp. 74–80.

28. Ibid., p. 78.

29. In one controversial case, the secretary of the Department of Health and Human Services sought the dismissal of three administrative law judges within the Social Security Administration. The judges' performance was found to be unacceptable when measured against administration-derived evaluation criteria: (1) the total number of cases scheduled, heard, and decided each month compared against a quota set by the agency's Office of Hearing Appeals; and (2) the ratio of cases decided in favor of claimants to cases decided against claimants. Former administrations also have sought greater productivity from these judges, but this is the first to attempt to force outcomes in the manner alleged in this case by the Association of Administrative Law Judges.

30. It has been reported that administration officials replaced more than fifty scientists on the various technical advisory boards serving the Environmental Protection Agency with more conservative scientists because conservative groups had attacked the incumbent advisers for their liberal environmental beliefs. See "EPA Removed More than 50 Scientists on Conservative 'Hit List'," *Washington Post*, March 2, 1983, p. A-2.

31. For example, the results of a recent poll of Federal Trade Commission staff revealed that three-quarters of the respondents believed that FTC Chairman James C. Miller is trying to end or reduce the FTC's effectiveness as a law enforcement agency. Sixty percent of the poll's respondents rated Miller's performance as "below average" or "poor." "Staff Poll Shows Heavy Majority Believe Miller Trying to Anesthetize Agency," *FTC Watch*, February 25, 1983, p. 4.

32. "Environmental Agency: Deep and Persisting Woes," *New York Times*, March 6, 1983, p. A-38.

NOTES TO CHAPTER 8

1. David Stockman, "Avoiding a GOP Economic Dunkirk," December, 1980.

2. *Reagan Administration Regulatory Achievements*, Presidential Task Force on Regulatory Relief, August 11, 1983.

3. *The Legal Times*, June 1983, p. 1.

4. Examples of this type of essentially negative action abound within the task force's March 1983 list of actions for which review had been completed and final actions taken. Within the auto safety area alone were the rescission of the passive-restraint standard as well as revocation of NHTSA's regulations governing fields of direct view, installation of theft protection devices, devices to warn motorists of low tire pressure, establishment of post-1985 fuel economy standards, use of uniform standards for grading tire quality, and standards for the use of multipiece rims. In each instance, agency actions involved the revocation or indefinite delay of a standard that was pending or in place when the Reagan administration took office. "Status of Review of Regulations and Paperwork Requirements Identified by Task Force on Regulatory Relief," March 9, 1983.

5. *State Farm Mutual* v. *Lewis*, U.S.C.A. D.C. No. 82-2220, June 1, 1982 at 26.

6. See 45 F.R. 24496, March 5, 1980.

7. 46 F.R. 62610, December 24, 1981.

8. See "Tylenol: Regulate in Haste," *Regulation*, March/April 1982, p. 12.

9. J. Scarbrough and M. Pfander, "New Merger Guidelines Not Always Less Restrictive," *Legal Times*, January 10, 1983, pp. 19–26.

10. Robert Crandall, "Has Reagan Dropped the Ball?" *Regulation*, September/October 1981, p. 15.

11. See, for example, H.R. 2867, 98th Cong., 1st Sess., introduced May 3, 1983.

12. See H.R. 2867, section 3001(d), May 3, 1983.

13. By spring 1983, the administration had backtracked so far on the revision of the Clean Water Act that the *Wall Street Journal* (April 22, 1983, p. 1) reported: "The steel and chemical industries push hard for easing on antipollution controls in the Clean Water Act. They could upset Reagan's hopes for a renewal with *little change.*" (Italics added.)

14. "Ruckelshaus Is Seen as His Own Man in Battle to Renew Clean Water Act," *National Journal*, July 16, 1983, p. 1499.

15. Ibid.

16. Statement of Christopher DeMuth before the Subcommittee on Administrative Law and Governmental Relations of the Committee on the Judiciary, U.S. House of Representatives, July 28, 1983.

17. 655 F.2d 1272 (1981).

18. 29 U.S.C. 794.

19. See "Providing Public Transportation to the Disabled, A Preliminary Report to the Pew Memorial Trust" (Washington, D.C.: The Urban Institute, May 1983).

20. The Federal Public Transportation Act of 1982, section 305(3), December 21, 1982.

21. "OSHA Upholds Exposure Rules for Cotton Dust," *Wall Street Journal*, May 20, 1983, p. 4.

22. See *State Farm Mutual* v. *Lewis*, U.S.C.A. D.C. No. 82-2220, June 1, 1982, pp. 24–25.

23. *Motor Vehicle Manufacturers Association* v. *State Farm Mutual*, U.S. S.Ct. No. 82-354, June 24, 1983.

24. 15 U.S.C. 1392(b).

25. Supra note 23 at 10.

26. Ibid. at 11.

27. Ibid. at 20 and 17.

28. Ibid. at 23.

29. *Center for Science in the Public Interest* v. *Treasury*, U.S.D.C. D.C. No. 82-610, Feb. 9, 1983, at 16.

30. The Clean Air Act established a comprehensive program to control pollution emission from new and existing sources. Congress charged EPA with developing air quality standards and charged the states with developing implementation plans for attaining federally designated ambient air standards. The Clean Air Act Amendments of 1977 mandated that permit programs be established for the construction or modification of new stationary sources of pollution in "nonattainment areas" (which require a net positive reduction in emissions). The amendments did not, however, explicitly define the term *stationary source*—a matter that has subsequently fallen to the courts and to EPA. Finally, regulations governing emissions in nonattainment areas are to be contrasted with the scheme set out for areas already in compliance with federal air quality standards. Areas already in compliance are controlled by rules implementing the Prevention of Significant Deterioration Program, which seeks to severely limit or hold constant preexisting emissions levels.

31. The court provided the following definition of the bubble concept: "Under this concept an entire plant and its emissions are viewed as if placed under one bubble. One then looks at any change proposed for the plant and decides whether the new effect of all the steps [taken in conjunction with the] change is to increase the emission of any air pollutant. Without the bubble concept, individual units of a plant affected by an operational change would be inspected to determine whether any of the units will consequently emit more of a pollutant."

32. The decisions were *Alabama Power Co.* v. *Costle*, 636 F.2d 323 (D.C. Cir. 1979), and *ASARCO, Inc.* v. *EPA*, 578 F.2d 319 (D.C. Cir. 1978).

33. *Building and Construction Trades Department AFL-CIO* v. *Donovan*, U.S.D.C. D.C. No. 82-1631, July 22, 1982 at 12.

34. *Building and Construction Trades Department, AFL-CIO* v. *Donovan*, U.S.C.A. D.C. No. 83-1157, July 5, 1983 at 9, 38.

35. 733 FCC 2d 457 (1979).

36. *United Church of Christ* v. *FCC*, U.S.C.A. D.C. No. 81-1032, May 10, 1983 at 8.

37. Ibid. at 37.
38. Ibid. at 57.

NOTES TO CHAPTER 9

1. Exceptions exist, of course. The Mine Safety and Health Act and the Surface Mining and Reclamation Act each designate a minimum number of annual inspections for regulated mines.

2. Eugene Bardach and Robert A. Kagan, *Going by the Book: The Problem of Regulatory Unreasonableness* (Philadelphia: Temple University Press, 1982), p. 123.

3. Ibid., pp. 207–208.

4. U.S. Department of Labor, Office of Compliance Programming, OSHA Instruction CPL 2.25C, "Scheduling System for Programmed Inspections," June 28, 1982.

5. OSHA defines its two basic types of inspections as *programmed* (inspections of establishments that have been selected on the basis of objective criteria) and *unprogrammed* (inspections in which alleged hazardous working conditions have been identified at a specific establishment).

6. U.S. Department of Labor, Office of Compliance Programming, OSHA Instruction CPL 2.25C, "Scheduling System for Programmed Inspections."

7. "Inside OSHA," *Washington Post*, March 18, 1983, p. A-17.

8. See U.S. Department of Labor, Office of Compliance Programming, OSHA Instruction CPL 2.50, "Enforcement of Section 5(a)(1) of Occupational Safety and Health Act, the General Duty Clause," March 17, 1982.

9. *Regulatory Eye*, vol. 4, no. 4, p. 10.

10. OSHA Instruction CPL 2.50, Section (H)(4).

11. See speech by John Fedders, director, SEC Enforcement Division, before the American Bar Association's Section of Corporation, Banking, and Business Law, reported in *Securities and Exchange Law Report*, vol. 14, November 26, 1982, p. 2057. In the course of his speech, Fedders cited the following Supreme Court language—*TSC Industries* v. *Northway, Inc.*, 426 U.S. 438 (1976)—defining "materiality":

An omitted fact is material if there is a substantial likelihood that reasonable shareholders would consider it important in deciding how to vote. . . . Put another way, there must be a substantial likelihood that the disclosure of the omitted fact would have been viewed by the reasonable investor as having significantly altered the "total mix" of information made available.

12. See Written Statement of John Shad, chairman, Securities and Exchange Commission, before Joint Hearings of the Subcommittee on Securities and the Subcommittee on International Finance and Monetary Policy of the Senate Committee on Banking, Housing, and Urban Affairs concerning S. 708, June 16, 1981.

13. Testimony of Anthony Roisman before the House Subcommittee on Oversight and Investigations, 97th Cong., 2d Sess., April 2, 1982, Series No. 97-123.

14. *The State of the Environment* (Washington, D.C.: The Conservation Foundation, 1982), p. 146.

15. This discussion draws on Angus Macbeth's thoughtful article, "Superfund: Impact on Environmental Litigation," *Environmental Law*, Winter 1982/83.

16. See Hazardous Waste Enforcement, Report of the Subcommittee on Oversight and Investigations, U.S. House of Representatives, 97th Cong., 2d Sess., Committee Print 97-NN, December 1982, p. 36.

17. "U.S. Is Moving Against Firms on Toxic Dump," *New York Times*, August 27, 1982, p. A-1.

18. "Superfund 'Fast Track' Mired in Procedure," *Washington Post*, February 14, 1983, p. A-1. Corporate critics of EPA's enforcement of Superfund have sued the agency, claiming that EPA's reliance on the theory of joint and several liability is unconstitutional. Under that theory, EPA can sue one or more parties that contributed waste to a site and seek all the remedies

and the entire cost of cleaning up the site only from the parties sued. See "Industry Confronts EPA Liability Standards," *Legal Times*, March 7, 1983, p. 4.

19. "EPA Asking a Voluntary Cleanup of Chemicals," *New York Times*, February 1, 1982, p. A-2.

20. Ibid., p. A35.

21. "Preliminary Antitrust Activity Raises Specter of More to Come," *Traffic World*, June 14, 1982, p. 31.

22. These figures do not include cases arising from the department's massive investigation into highway construction bid-rigging, which had been going on for several years. See "Reagan Appointees Produced Fewer Cases Than Their Predecessors at Justice, FTC," *Bureau of National Affairs Antitrust and Trade Regulation Report*, January 27, 1983, p. 200.

23. John E. Shockey, reported in "Bank Enforcement Actions Increase During Hard Times," *Legal Times*, March 14, 1983, p. 1.

24. U.S.D.C.D.C., No. 81-2134, September 30, 1982.

25. See Section 518 (h) of the Surface Mining Act [30 U.S.C. Sec. 1268].

26. Frank H. Easterbrook, "On Not Enforcing the Law," *Regulation*, January/February 1983, p. 15.

NOTES TO CHAPTER 10

1. *Economic Report of the President and the Annual Report of the Council of Economic Advisers* (Washington, D.C.: Government Printing Office, February 1982), p. 47.

2. Ibid., p. 147.

3. A recent publication of the Advisory Commission on Intergovernmental Relations described partial preemption programs as "[resting] upon the authority of the federal government to preempt certain state and local activities under the Supremacy clause and the Commerce power. . . . This is preemption with a twist, however. Unlike traditional preemption statutes, preemption in these cases is only partial. While federal laws establish basic policies, administrative responsibility may be delegated to the states or localities, provided that they meet certain nationally determined standards." See David Beam, "Washington's Regulation of States and Localities: Origins and Issues" (Intergovernmental Perspective, Advisory Commission on Intergovernmental Relations, Washington, D.C., Summer, 1981), p. 11. Examples of partial preemption statutes include the Clean Air Act Amendments of 1970, the Federal Water Pollution Control Act Amendments of 1972, the Occupational Safety and Health Act, the Resource Conservation and Recovery Act of 1976, and the Surface Mining Control and Reclamation Act of 1977.

4. This partial-preemption approach should be contrasted with instances where full federal preemption is invoked by the courts. Full preemption occurs when there is an outright conflict between the federal scheme and the state requirement. State authority is also barred when congressional action would be an implicit barrier, that is, when state regulation would unduly interfere with the accomplishment of congressional objectives.

5. The National Governors Association Committee on Energy and Environment, *The State of States: Management of Environmental Programs in the 1980s* (Washington, D.C., 1982).

6. The comments in this paragraph are drawn from remarks by Turner T. Smith, Jr., "Opening Address: Reflections on Federalism" (Airlie House, Conference on the Environment), reported in Articles and Notes, *Environmental Law Reporter*, vol. 12, p. 15067, December 1982.

7. T. Henderson, "Delegation of Environmental Programs to the States: Ohio's Experience" (Washington, D.C.: Environmental Law Institute, 1982).

8. Representative of the continued federal concern in the area of delegation of authority is the existence and work of the Advisory Commission on Intergovernmental Relations, an independent agency committed to examining issues bearing on the proper role of differing levels of government in the federal system. See, e.g., "Regulatory Federalism, Policy, Process, Impact and Reform" (Washington, D.C.: ACIR, December 1982).

9. See *NRDC* v. *Gorsuch*, 685 F.2d 718 (D.C. Cir.), which declared the netting of emissions in nonattainment areas under the Clean Air Act to be illegal. Plainly, the framers of EPA's emissions-trading guidelines did not anticipate that the guidelines' application would be constrained in this manner. See also *Scenic Hudson* v. *Marsh*, U.S.D.C. D.C. Civ. Act. No. 82-3632, *filed* December 22, 1982.

10. See Jerry L. Mashaw and Susan Rose-Ackerman, "Federalism and Regulation" in George Eads and Michael Fix, eds., *The Reagan Regulatory Strategy: An Assessment* (Washington, D.C.: The Urban Institute Press, in press).

11. The Supreme Court recently upheld state efforts in these fields in *Pacific Gas and Electric Company* v. *State Energy Resources Conservation and Development Commission*, 103 S.Ct. 1713 (1983). At one level, though, the goals of regulatory relief and the Reagan administration's delegation strategies to delegate authority are perfectly complementary. When state and local governments have been deputized to carry out the federal government's regulatory responsibilities and the federal rules governing the performance of those duties are made relatively flexible, the states, in their role as policemen, have been provided real relief.

12. The authors do not mean to imply that the administration's approach to the transfer of authority has been consciously designed. Rather, this typology is simply an attempt to categorize a set of ad hoc actions moving in a predetermined direction.

13. "On Delegation to the States," *The Environmental Forum*, January 1983, p. 9.

14. The three jurisdictions, the Virgin Islands, Hawaii, and Alaska, have relatively few hazardous manufacturing industries.

15. See Report to the Court, *AFL-CIO* v. *Marshall*, 570 F.2d 1030 (D.C. Cir. 1978), filed April 1980.

16. P.L. 97-257, 1982, states:

> Provided that none of the funds made available under this head for fiscal year 1982 may be obligated or expended to enforce or prescribe, as a condition for initial, continuing, or final approval of state plans under Section 18 of the Occupational Safety and Health Act of 1970, State administrative or enforcement staffing levels which are determined by the Secretary to be equivalent to Federal staffing levels.

17. See "Revision of Rules Regarding Final Approval of State Plans," 47 F.R. 50307, November 5, 1982.

18. Mississippi may represent a case in point. In 1982, the state accepted delegation of the prevention of significant deterioration, new source performance standards, and airborne hazardous pollutants programs despite pervasive fears at the state level that federal grant funds were likely to be severely cut. Moreover, fully 60 percent of that state's air program funds are provided by the federal government. Skeptical that future funds were actually going to be cut and eager to gain more autonomy in the administration of its air program, the state continued to pursue further delegations. As one official noted, "We've never liked to see EPA acting directly against Mississippi industry."

19. 47 F.R. 15076, April 7, 1982.

20. *Bubbles* allow existing sources to find alternative emissions reductions from other sources to meet a given legal requirement. The term *bubble* arises from the figurative notion that many emission points are aggregated under one umbrella, or bubble. Bubbles may exist within a plant or between plants.

Offsets relate to the requirement of the Clean Air Act Amendments of 1977 that new sources of emissions in nonattainment areas more than offset the emissions they will add.

Netting permits a plant in a nonattainment area to expand and to avoid new source review by reducing emissions at other parts of the plant to below certain threshold levels.

Banking describes those procedures that allow sources to store emissions-reduction credits in a legally protected manner for future use or sale.

See P. Domenici, "Emissions Trading: The Subtle Heresy," *Environmental Forum*, December 1982; and "Model Emissions Trading Rule: State Generic Bubble and Banking Provisions" (Washington, D.C.: Environmental Law Institute, August 1982).

21. Michael E. Levin, "Getting There: Implementing the 'Bubble' Policy," in Eugene Bardach and Robert A. Kagan, eds., *Social Regulation: Strategies for Reform* (San Francisco: Institute for Contemporary Studies, 1982), p. 59.

22. Memorandum: Emissions Trading—End of the Year Status Report, April 5, 1983, EPA. However, one recent study of Ohio's air program suggests that EPA's emissions-trading rules are likely to have a somewhat limited impact in that state. Ohio officials claimed that most of the trades likely to be proposed would involve particulate emissions and would call for complex, expensive technical analysis before they could be approved. Faced with uncertain future funding, state officials had determined that it would not be wise to commit the resources necessary to start and administer such a program. See Henderson, "Delegation of Environmental Programs to the States."

23. *NRDC* v. *Gorsuch*, 685 F.2d 718 (D.C. Cir. 1982), *cert. granted* by S.Ct., May 31, 1983 (No. 82-1591).

24. Levin, "Getting There."

25. The Corps' general permit rules differ somewhat from the generic rules developed with regard to emissions trading. One of the most obvious distinctions is that states must, in effect, volunteer for enhanced responsibilities under emissions-trading policy guidelines. Not only must they volunteer, they must adopt rules consistent with federally determined decision principles that are to guide program implementation. In the absence of those voluntary actions, state decisions remain subject to federal review. Under the Corps' nationwide general permit rules, the federal government in effect declared that it will no longer review a described set of actions, leaving the states to decide whether and how they will regulate those activities. Under the Corps' state general permit authority, federal deference is conditioned on the existence of an adequate state program. The standards a state program would have to meet were called into question by a memorandum from the Corps' deputy director to all division and district engineers directing them to implement "State Program General Permits" by May 28, 1982, whether or not the state program "measured up to Corps standards in all respects." (Memorandum cited in "Brief for the Plaintiff," *Scenic Hudson Inc.* v. *Marsh*, p. 59.)

26. 47 F.R. 31794, July 22, 1982.

27. See "First Round 404 'Regulatory Reforms' Reduce Federal Protection of Land, Non-tributary Wetlands—Other Changes to be Proposed This Fall," *National Journal*, March 6, 1982, p. 410.

28. Memorandum from John R. Pomponio to Paul Cahill, September 15, 1982, cited in "Brief for the Plaintiff," *Scenic Hudson Inc.* v. *Marsh*.

29. 46 F.R. 19009, March 27, 1981.

30. 46 F.R. 3919, January 16, 1981.

31. Ibid.

32. U.S. Department of Labor, Occupational Safety and Health Administration, Region V, "Evaluation Report of the Occupational Safety and Health Program of the State of Indiana for the Year Ending June 1982," (Chicago).

33. 48 F.R. 9199, March 3, 1983.

34. U.S. Department of the Interior, Office of Surface Mining, Lexington Field Office Quarterly Report, July 1, 1982—September 30, 1982.

35. Under Title I of The Clean Air Act the federal government is charged with issuing "national ambient air quality standards" (NAAQSs) for any widespread air pollutant that "may reasonably be anticipated to endanger public health or welfare." These standards may be primary (to protect public health) or secondary (to safeguard public welfare). Under the act states are required to submit implementation plans indicating how federal standards will be met. Those plans are "intended to be comprehensive bundles of strategies and commands, containing all the requirements necessary to attain the NAAQSs in that state." State implementation plans (SIPs) are specific to one of the six pollutants for which EPA has developed national standards. See William Pederson, Jr., "Why the Clean Air Act Works Badly," *Penn Law Review*, vol. 129 (1981), p. 1059.

36. 47 F.R. 27073, June 23, 1982.

37. In fact, a staffer termed efforts to eliminate the SIP backlog as "shoveling out all the garbage in order to get the system current"—scarcely indicating a systematic analysis of each SIP's merits.

38. 47 F.R. 27071, June 23, 1982.

39. Letter from David Doniger (NRDC) to John Hypola, Region VI, EPA, January 10, 1983, "Re: Alternative Emission Reduction Plan for Monsanto Chemical Intermediates Co."

40. "Preliminary Comments on Proposed Revisions to the Texas State Implementation Plan," 47 F.R. 27071, June 23, 1982, D. Doniger, S. Smith, NRDC, July 13, 1982, p. 9.

41. See California Air Resources Board, "Memorandum to All Air Pollution Control Officers; EPA Enforcement Program in Nonattainment Areas Concerning Stationary Source Not in Compliance as of December 31, 1982" (Sacramento, March 31, 1983).

42. Performance standards regulate according to general performance criteria, rather than by detailed specification of the means of compliance. They are often thought to permit more freedom of action for regulated concerns to reduce compliance costs, and to provide more freedom to discover new and more efficient compliance technologies. See U.S. Regulatory Council, *Regulating with Common Sense: A Progress Report on Innovative Regulatory Techniques* (Washington, D.C., October 1980).

43. "Regulatory Striptease—Watt Takes Aim at Surface Mining Regulations," *National Journal*, May 30, 1981, p. 971.

44. U.S. Department of the Interior, Office of Surface Mining, "Proposed Revisions to the Permanent Program Regulations Implementing Section 501(b) of the Surface Mining Control and Reclamation Act of 1977," Final Environmental Statement, vol. I, p. S-3, January 1983.

45. Ibid.

46. See Comments Submitted on Behalf of National Wildlife Federation, August 25, 1982, Ibid. vol. II, p. 292.

47. See chapter 7.

48. See, for example, letters from James Harris, director, Office of Surface Mining, to George Nigh, governor of Oklahoma, and John Carlin, governor of Kansas, March 11, 1982, regarding inadequacies of those states' programs.

49. See 47 F.R. 12092, March 19, 1982 and 48 F.R. 53280, November 25, 1982.

50. 48 F.R. 14844, April 5, 1983.

51. William Eichbaum, "State/Federal Relations in Environmental Protection: How Will They Evolve in the 1980's?" *Environmental Law*, Summer 1982, p. 1.

52. "House Votes to Restore EPA Funds to 1981 Level," *Washington Post*, June 3, 1983, p. A-1.

53. Edward Strohbehn, Jr., "The Bases for Federal/State Relationships in Environmental Law," 12 ELR 15094, December 1982.

54. An example is Minnesota's recently enacted state Superfund law, which, among other things, grants private citizens who have suffered health or property damage from wastes the right to sue parties responsible for their losses. The bill also provides for companies to be held strictly liable for damage and injuries resulting from hazardous waste dumping after January 1, 1973. Companies found to have engaged in "abnormally dangerous" dumping can be held liable as far back as 1960. See "At Last a Minnesota Superfund," *Minneapolis Star and Tribune*, May 10, 1983, p. 6-A.

55. "Chemical Industry Fears Pendulum's Swing Back to the 50 States," *National Journal*, November 13, 1982, p. 1927.

56. Telephone interview with Rick Jones, analyst, National Conference of State Legislators, May 15, 1983.

NOTES TO CHAPTER 11

1. See Stuart Auerbach, "Conservative Study Faults Reagan Deregulation Efforts," *Washington Post*, January 16, 1983, p. F-1. (This article reports on a Heritage Foundation study

critical of the Reagan administration's efforts.) See also Lindley H. Clark, "Is the Administration De-Regulating Transportation?" Wall Street Journal, July 27, 1982, p. 31.

2. "Statement by Vice President George Bush," August 11, 1983, p. 1.

3. Presidential Task Force on Regulatory Relief, Final Report, "Reagan Administration Regulatory Achievements" (Washington, D.C.: Government Printing Office, August 11, 1983), pp. 72–75.

4. Presidential Task Force on Regulatory Relief, "Fact Sheet" (Washington, D.C., August 11, 1983), p. 1.

5. Ibid., p. 2.

6. That chapter also distinguished between the expenditure of resources to correct a genuine market failure (which, technically speaking, costs the economy nothing and produces a dead-weight gain in social welfare) and regulations that are ineffective or inefficient (which may result in a net cost to the economy). This distinction is not generally recognized in the cost figures collected by government agencies and will not be pursued here, but the reader should keep its significance in mind.

7. Statement from Federal Home Loan Bank Board, August 9, 1983 (Issued in conjunction with release of August 11 task force report).

8. Another major deregulatory action that the administration has sought to claim credit for will lead to transfers in the opposite direction. The breakup of AT&T and the subsequent restructuring of the nation's telecommunications network will cause local telephone rates to rise. Economists believe that the decline in long-distance rates and in the cost of telecommunications equipment (plus other efficiencies) will more than offset this increase, reducing the total cost of telecommunications service to the economy. But by the logic that led the administration to credit its program with interest rate increases, opponents of the AT&T divestiture could charge the increase in local telephone rates as a "cost" of the regulatory relief program.

9. Arizona Governing Committee v. Norris 103 S. Ct. 3492 (1983).

10. "Weaker Bumpers on the Horizon?" Consumer Reports, August 1983, p. 396. In crash tests on otherwise identical Hondas, the loss payments due to the weaker bumpers were 30 percent higher. Based on these crash tests, one auto insurer, Allstate, increased insurance rates on 1983 Hondas.

11. Until the publication of the August 1983 task force report, the administration had been carrying the entire $300 million in claimed one-time savings on its list of savings attributable to the regulatory relief program. In the August 1983 report, the savings estimate due to this postponement was reduced to $75 million. The administration's reason for the change was that the rule had been postponed for only two years, and at a 10 percent real interest rate, the present value of the two-year savings would be $75 million.

12. In this case, the task force report does note that the Supreme Court's opinion may eventually lead to a change in "savings."

13. August 1983 Task Force Report, p. 71.

14. As pointed out in chapter 2, they generate a "deadweight gain" in social welfare.

15. Office of Management and Budget, "Executive Order 12291 on Federal Regulation: Progress During 1982" (Washington, D.C., April 1983), p. 5.

16. August 1982 Task Force Report, p. 70.

17. Ibid.

18. Recall that in the case of Denison's estimates reported in chapter 2, pollution control accounted for roughly twice the impact of expenditures to improve employee safety and health. It contributed slightly over half the total changes in the human and legal environment to which Denison attributed 12.5 percent of the observed slowdown in productivity growth in the period from 1973 to 1976.

19. Gary L. Rutledge and Susan Lease-Trevathan, "Pollution Abatement and Control Expenditures, 1972–1981," Survey of Current Business, February 1983, pp. 15–23.

20. Ibid., p. 18.

21. William J. Russo, Jr., and Gary L. Rutledge, "Plant and Equipment Expenditures by Business for Pollution Abatement, 1982 and Planned 1983," *Survey of Current Business*, June 1983, p. 25, table 2.

22. Gregory B. Christainsen and Robert H. Haveman, "Regulation, Productivity Growth, and 'Supply-Side' Economics," in George C. Eads and Michael Fix, eds., *The Reagan Regulatory Strategy: An Assessment* (Washington, D.C.: The Urban Institute Press, 1984).

23. "Statement by Vice President Bush," August 11, 1983, p. 2.

24. *Business Week*, May 30, 1983, pp. 74–75.

25. See, for example, "When States Talk Tougher Than the EPA," *Business Week*, May 30, 1983, pp. 33 and 37; Daniel W. Gottlieb, "Business Mobilizes as States Begin to Move into the Regulatory Vacuum," *National Journal*, August 31, 1982, pp. 1340–1343; and Martin Tolchin, "Industry Sees Dark Side of Deregulation," *New York Times*, May 1, 1983, p. E-5.

26. Michael Wines, "Reagan Plan to Relieve Auto Industry of Regulatory Burden Gets Mixed Grades," *National Journal*, July 23, 1983, p. 1532.

27. Ibid.

28. Robert A. Leone, "Ronald Reagan and the Automobile Industry," in Eads and Fix, eds., *op. cit.* (draft, June 1983).

29. Quoted in Phillip Shabecoff, "Ruckelshaus Says Administration Misread Mandate on Environment," *New York Times*, July 27, 1983, p. 1.

30. Christopher DeMuth, "A Strong Beginning . . .", *Regulation*, January/February 1982, p. 18.

31. "Statement by Vice President Bush," August 11, 1983, p. 2.

32. This final statute was passed during the Depression as a reaction to financial manipulations during the 1920s involving public utility holding companies. It apples to only about a dozen large public utility holding companies and requires these companies to obtain Securities and Exchange Commission approval of any plans for mergers, acquisitions, financing, and geographic expansion; they must comply with the act's reporting, accounting, and affiliate transactions requirements. If the act were repealed, the constituent operating companies would still be subject to regulation by the Federal Energy Regulatory Commission.

33. House Republican Research Committee, Task Force on Congressional and Regulatory Reform, "Regulatory Reform: The Quiet Revolution," January 18, 1983, p. ii.

34. Murray L. Weidenbaum and Ronald J. Penoyer, "The Next Step in Regulatory Reform: Updating the Statutes," (St. Louis: Center for the Study of American Business, Washington University, April 1983).

35. Although OSHA is prohibited from conducting "cost-benefit analyses" of its health-based regulations result in a "substantial reduction in risk." OSHA also considers that it is not barred from choosing the most cost-effective approach from among alternatives that are considered to be roughly of equal effectiveness in providing health benefits. As a result, OSHA can conduct the sort of "structured inquiry" into the costs and benefits of its proposed regulations that a formal cost-benefit analysis is intended to achieve.

36. On this point, see Steve Kelman, *What Price Incentives?* (Boston: Auburn House, 1982).

37. For an account of this effort, see Michael H. Levine, "Getting There: Implementing the 'Bubble Policy'," in *Social Regulation: Strategies for Reform*, ed. Eugene Bardach and Robert A. Kagan (San Francisco: Institute for Contemporary Studies, 1982), pp. 59–92.

38. Robert E. Litan and William D. Nordhaus, *Reforming Federal Regulation* (New Haven: Yale University Press, 1983), chapter 6.